[redacted]

[redacted]

To

GEA

. . . In the last century Western culture has developed in the direction of division and disjunction. The relationship, the mystical participation, of one thing with another is no longer experienced. We have instead learned to draw distinctions. The self is separated from the group. Self-consciousness is increased with natural consequences of individualization, autonomy, and self-awareness. But other less desirable consequences also follow: isolation, splintering, and disintegration.

Han Fortmann

Wat is er met de mens gebeurd? (1971)
(What is Happening to Man?)

Contents

Foreword to the English Edition

Illness, Body and Self

That illness involves the whole person and that for each person it is a unique experience is part of the conventional wisdom of almost all peoples and cultures. Healers have always striven to make the afflicted person "whole" again and restore the integrity of the body, mind and soul ruptured by illness. That is why Socrates tells the young Charmides, who seeks cure of his headache, "You must begin by curing the soul"[1]—something Socrates himself learned from the Thracian physician whom he quotes: "For this is the great error of our day in the treatment of the human body that physicians separate the soul from the body."[2]

This "holistic" conception of illness and therapy figured prominently in Western medicine, especially among those who were faithful to the tenets of Hippocratic medicine. Well into the nineteenth century, physicians still interpreted disease holistically as a disturbance of the whole body economy and directed their treatments to restoring the harmonious balance of the healthy body.[3] Only in the twentieth century did a reductionistic and fragmented view come to prevail among so many physicians.

The impetus for the reductionistic view derived from that concatenation of events that has culminated in today's scientific medicine. First was Descartes' notion of the body as a machine with parts that might malfunction; then came Sydenham's categorization of diseases as entities each with its own natural history, followed by the powerful idea of disease localization in organs (Morgagni), in tissues (Bichat), and cells (Virchow) and now, in subcellular and molecular entities.

These vectors pointing towards reductionistic medicine were power-

1. Plato *Charmides*, 156.
2. Plato, ibid., 157.
3. Charles E. Rosenberg, Medicine, Meaning and Social Change in Nineteenth Century America. in *The Therapeutic Revolution,* Morris J. Vogel and Charles E. Rosenberg, ed., Univ. of Pennsylvania Press, 1979, 3-25.

fully reenforced by the discovery that causation of specific diseases could be assigned to microorganisms, toxins, genetic defects, or deficiencies of vitamins or hormones. When specific cures fitted to these specific causes became commonplace the attractions of reductionism became all but irresistible.[4] The medical sciences now promise the synthesis of biological molecules designed to counteract specific diseases at their sub-cellular loci. There is considerable warrant for hoping that all disease might thus be amenable to its radical cure of its radical cause.

And, indeed, available specific and radical cures do make it possible to treat many diseases and to ignore Socrates' advice to cure both body and soul with relative impunity. Pneumococcal pneumonia, meningococcal meningitis, pulmonary tuberculosis, Addison's disease, pernicious anemia, cretinism—the list grows daily—all are subject to radical cure by specific chemical agents. One need not necessarily attend to cure of both body and soul to cure these diseases—although admittedly many features of illness might be neglected by reductionist therapies. So compelling are the dramatic results of radical therapeutics that many physicians identify medicine itself only with its high technology. The care of the "whole patient"—the psychosocial and personal dimensions—is relegated to others: nurses, social workers, psychologists.

Its successes notwithstanding, reductionistic medicine is coming under increasing challenge from a host of critics who are dissatisfied with cure without care. Those critics comprise a variegated company—dissatisfied patients, psychiatrists and behavioral scientists, consumer advocates, and a congeries of proponents of "holistic" medicine. These latter embrace everything from organotherapy, naturopathy, Eastern archaic medical systems, acupuncture and spirit surgery, to more moderate and sophisticated approaches like family and psychosomatic and the new behavioral medicine, based in cogent biosocial, psychosocial and psycho-biological theories of disease and medicine.

Impassioned debates increasingly separate those who would cure disease and those who would cure patients. The conventional wisdom that illness affects the whole person is rarely denied outright. Rather, its meaning, therapeutic implications and relevance to the physicians role are at issue. Even the ardent reductionists will pay lip service to the importance of the "whole patient."

When the din of ideological battles subsides a clearer idea about what

4. Edmund D. Pellegrino, The Socio-Cultural Impact of Twentieth Century Therapeutics in *The Therapeutic Revolution,* Morris J. Vogel and Charles E. Rosenberg, ed., Univ. of Pennsylvania Press,1979, pp. 245-266.

medicine *is*, what illness *means*, what healing *entails* and what is the best partitioning of the tasks of healing among health professionals may emerge. At issue is nothing less than the nature of medicine and of healing, and consequently of the moral obligations that bind those who profess to heal.

What is abundantly clear is that we are far from comprehending what we mean by the conventional wisdom that illness is an assault on the whole person. In modern times, numerous partial explanatory modes have been advanced to deepen our understanding of the conventional wisdom. Psychosomaticists have demonstrated how emotions and mental states can produce symptoms, and even pathophysiological changes in the body. Behavioral scientists have shown how the response to illness is psychosocially and culturally determined. Theologians have focused attention on the spiritual dimensions of healing as have the proponents of the more exotic systems of non-Western medicine. Social workers, rehabilitationists, and family physicians have turned attention to the importance of managing the family and immediate life milieu of the sick person.

Each of these approaches illustrates some important facet of the multi-faceted experience of illness; each amplifies some conception of what illness means as a human experience and what reductionistic diagnosis and treatments ignore. But none is wholly satisfying, and none, as yet, can serve as a satisfactory generalizable theory of medicine or healing. Whether any such theory can ever be fashioned is problematic but new avenues of inquiry should help us approach such a theory at least asymptotically.

In this book Professor Jurrit Bergsma opens some newer avenues of understanding of the still-vague concept of treating the whole person. Bergsma carefully examines the neglected side of the body-psyche equation. Instead of psychosomatics, he speaks of psychological medicine—of the effects of the fact of illness on the psyche, on the way illness alters the emotional life of the patient, his concept of self and the balance he has struck with the world of his own existence. Bergsma's study explores the lesser known aspects of the uniqueness of the personal experience of being sick.

The sick person he shows is an altered person in a state of existential challenge, required to make new adjustments in his social, cultural and family relationships. The sick person, too, is a vulnerable person forced to enter a relationship with the physician and other healers in a state of impaired humanity. In the decision to take a particular healing action there is always some intersection of values between what the physician and society think to be good and what the patient thinks to be good *for him*. The moral management of these value intersections is a crucial requirement in modern medicine where technical capabilities enlarge the choices for both patient and physician.

Calling on the methodology of psychology, Bergsma explores the way illness alters the self image of the sick person, and the way the experience changes the person who is ill. He takes us through the psychological impacts of the first clinical moment when the patient realizes he is in the altered state of illness as well as the subsequent effects of pain, hospitalization, being bed-ridden, fatigued or disabled.

Bergsma is particularly acute in his analysis of the way illness creates alienation and mistrust of the body and loss of bodily identity. He draws heavily on Merleau-Ponty's concept of embodiment in his linkage of the psychological and phenomenological conceptions of bodily image and self concept. Like many psychologists, Bergsma favors nonmedical models of disease and healing, or at least a conjunction of medical and extra-medical models, like the integral health care ofOuerido or Tubesing. (See page 58).

The intersections and conflicts of value systems occasioned by the assault of illness on the selfhood of the sick person are tentatively explored. Bergsma offers an interesting analytic matrix worked out with Professor Ray Duff of Yale of the several levels of value adjustments that must be made by the patient—the macro, meso, and personal. He shows how the triadic structures of the patients' values come into contact, and potential conflict, with the corresponding three-tiered structures of the physicians' values.

Bergsma's closing chapter opens up the new but highly important question of the moral implication of the psychological transformations induced by illness. The philosophical psychology of disease and illness will need far more precise and profound analysis but Bergsma's first attempts at the articulation of phenomenological philosophy and psychology are commendable.

Thomasma's translation and associate authorship of Bergsma's book comes at a moment propitious for such an articulation. Interest is growing, as his citations of recent (American) literature show, in the way the experience of illness alters the existence of individuals. Sally Gadow, in a recent essay, offers a philosophical analysis of the way the ontological unity of body and self may be disrupted by illness.[5] Engel offers a practical and theoretical formulation for assessing the full range of factors that may induce illness and influence care.[6] Cassell has clearly outlined the clinical dimensions and personal dilemmas of being a

5. Sally Gadow, Body and Self: A Dialectic, *Journal of Medicine and Philosophy,* Vol. 5:3, September 1980, pp. 172-185.

6. George Engel, The Clinical Application of the Biopsychosocial Model, *The American Journal of Psychiatry,* 137:5, May 1980, pp. 535-544.

patient.[7] I have tried to derive a philosophical basis for medical morality rooted in the nature of illness, *The Fact of Profession and the Act of Medicine.*[8]

Bergsma's book is a valuable bridge that could link some of the philosophical explorations of the meaning of illness with its psychological and the biological manifestations. The fragmenting tendencies of studies of human illness perceived through different disciplines is disturbing but understandable. Each discipline has the capacity to enlarge our knowledge of some feature of the complex being we call man. Bergsma's book, though predominantly psychological in method, offers some interesting linkages to philosophy, and to biological medicine. For this reason, the book should prove valuable, not only for psychologists and physicians but to all the healing professions and those philosophers with a deepening interest in the phenomenology of health and illness.

If we are to reconcile the reductionistic with the holistic views of medicine, somatopsychological observations like those of Bergsma must be taken into account. It is not too much to say that some resolution of the debates between holism and reductionism must be sought in the years immediately ahead. Is it likely that one physician can synthesize and encompass them in his practice? Or is the inherent tension between these two theories of medicine so irreconcilable that two kinds of physicians must eventuate—one who is primarily a technician and reductionist and one who cares for the person—the generalist? Bergsma's work is not definitive in this respect, but it advances our thinking about what is perhaps the most serious fundamental issue facing physicians and philosophers of medicine in the next decade.

During his sojourn at Yale, I had the privilege and the pleasure of many hours of discussion with Professor Bergsma, particularly about the philosophical implications of his work. Having his book in translation will afford many other Americans some of the insights and challenges I appreciated so much in our dialogues.

EDMUND D. PELLEGRINO, M.D.
President: The Catholic University of America

7. Eric Cassell, *The Healer's Art*, N. Y., Lippincott, 1976. pp. 47-83.
8. Edmund D. Pellegrino, Reconstruction of Medical Morality, *Journal of Medicine and Philosophy*, 4:1, March 1979, pp. 32-56.

Translator's Preface

I am very pleased to have had the opportunity to help Professor Jurrit Bergsma prepare this English edition of *Somatopsychologie.* This edition represents some changes from the original Dutch. Among the changes are a completely revised introduction and final chapter, additional material throughout each chapter, suggestions on the interaction of psychology and medical ethics, and, as might be expected, citations from works in English related to the topic.

Readers will find a new perspective of psychology in this work about the trials of patients and physicians in coping with disease. The new perspective is a viewpoint seldom found in psychology, namely, a clinical psychology that shares with medicine an appreciation of the clinical imperative. In the main, psychology is confined to assessments of status, counseling, and referrals to psychiatry. As Professor Bergsma makes clear in his introduction, however, the usual employment of psychology is altered in this volume: instead of a focus on scientific categories of disease, on psychosomatic disorders, the discipline of psychology is now turned on the disturbances caused by disease in the patient's "body-image" and consequent self-concept. The inescapable conclusion of his work is that if medicine neglects these aspects of "being-sick," it fails to heal.

In accepting the offer to translate the book and assist in the English edition, I anticipated its having a significant impact on at least four audiences: health professionals, psychologists, medical ethicists, and patients themselves.

Physicians and other health-care professionals will discover considered and balanced material about aspects of healing that often go unattended. The suggestion that a disturbed body-image may lie at the heart of many diseases is well worth considering. As health professionals know, though often only instinctively, recovery may not mean the same as being healed. Yet "healing" seems to be such a broad and all-encompassing category, involving as it does so many features of human life, that medicine shies from considering it a valid object of its craft. The distinctions drawn by Professor Bergsma will assist those health professionals who do wish to consider their obligation to heal, for the distinctions can clarify what can and cannot be accomplished by medicine, what is caused by society and culture and what is not.

Psychologists and psychiatrists will also find this volume helpful. In it, the structure of clinical psychology, or somatopsychology, is laid out as a discipline, a convenient summary of current research in clinical psychology is presented, and original insights about "dis-ease" categories, pain, disablement, and other topics are dealt with in a clear and orderly fashion. A new form of clinical psychology will germinate from the approach taken in this book because of its attention to the clinical imperative. Too often psychology and the other behavioral sciences are avoided by the other specialties in medicine, because the former do not understand the pressure to make decisions in the clinical context. Their methodology impedes recommending a course of treatment without a battery of tests (often impractical in the clinical setting) and counseling sessions. However, using the themes in this book, practitioners of the behavioral sciences could, in fact, make recommendations about patients who do not suffer from the usual psychosomatic disorders.

A third audience for the book is composed of those writing on and researching medical ethics. Some translation of ethical principles and humanities insights is required by the clinical imperative stressed to this point. Too frequently, medical ethics confines itself to broad applications of ethical principles, rather than offering helpful commentaries on patient's problems and the quandries of health professionals. In other words, in order to be effective, medical ethics must pay attention to the realities of psychological and sociological aspects of disease and its treatment, categories of which are found in this work. Finding the proper, realistic basis of ethical reflection in a grid of descriptive analysis of human behavior, medical ethics can also make recommendations about the problems of patient management.

Finally, by reading this book patients can gain a profound understanding of their illness. It will pay them more to consult this volume than a more scientific book about their disease. For Professor Bergsma's book can help patients perceive the real processes of illness as it runs its course in their bodies, what happens to them emotionally in the hospital and at home during their recovery, and how society, through its culture and values, molds their self-concept during this period.

The arts have often portrayed the human drama involved in becoming sick. One can read this book as an analysis of that drama.

David C. Thomasma

Preface to the Dutch Edition

Health Care: Its Psychosocial Dimensions originated as a set of notes for university psychology students during the years 1973 to 1975. Material for the notes was culled from observations of and interviews with physically ill patients in diverse services of health-care institutions. Further discussion with the students led to clarification of problems and crystallization of ideas, both of which necessitated and made possible a reworked text. Before reworking, I shared the material with practicing physicians for their comments, which are incorporated in the text. Their contributions were very important and I would like to thank them wholeheartedly: C. Cornellisse, internal medicine; H. Gerritse, family practice; J. Harms, psychiatry; P. Van Velthoven, surgery; and A. Verkuyl, rehabilitation medicine. With respect to psychology, the comments of Doctorandus J. de Vries were especially helpful.

I have relied on Grada Rullmann and my wife, Gea, for help in researching relevant literature—their contribution should definitely be acknowledged. Similarly, Jeanne van Oosterhout and Els Koks offered stimulating observations during the long hours of typing.

During many conversations about the ideas contained in this volume I have derived valuable insights and inspiration from Professor Raymond Duff and Doctorandus Jan van de Koppel. For these I thank them. For critical review of the final text I thank Grada Rullmann, Doctorandus Jan van de Koppel, and Doctorandus Rik Seur.

Finally, I must express my admiration for Ben Bergmans, who managed under difficult circumstances to take photographs illustrating the text that often captured in one picture the ideas of half a chapter.

JURRIT BERGSMA

Preface to the English Edition

During the summer of 1977, I arrived at Yale University in New Haven, Connecticut, to begin my six month period of study as a Fulbright Fellow. At that time, Edmund D. Pellegrino, M.D., was Professor of Medicine and President and Chairman of the Board of the Yale–New Haven Medical Center. Studying with him on a post-doctoral fellowship from the Institute on Human Values in Medicine was Professor David Thomasma, then Director of the Program on Human Values and Ethics at the University of Tennessee Center for the Health Sciences.

These new friends as well as other physicians, philosophers, theologians and ethicists were inspiring and stimulating. Surprisingly I discovered that few clinical psychologists have found their way into the medical field. In fact, I still do not understand why the Behavioral Sciences do not have more of an impact on medicine than they seem to enjoy at the present.

For this reason I was encouraged to find that my contribution—the original Dutch edition of this book—and the insights stemming therefrom, were judged to be worthwhile by outstanding professionals such as Dr. Pellegrino, Dr. Thomasma, and Raymond Duff, M.D., medical director of the Newborn Center at Yale. I was very pleased that Dave Thomasma was willing to translate and to criticize my book. In the many communications we had before and during the translation process, Dave provided many ideas for improvement. Many changes and additional passages, including an entirely re-written ninth chapter, can be directly ascribed to his helpful comments and suggestions. Because we anticipated such interchange prior to the translation, I insisted that Dave be listed as a collaborating author for this edition.

I was also profoundly encouraged by Dr. Pellegrino's support. As a physician and philosopher his perception of the importance of such psychological research for the improvement of clinical medicine meant a great deal to me. He has made me very happy by agreeing to write the Foreword to this edition, now titled *Health Care: Its Psychosocial Dimensions.*

Hopefully the reader will enjoy this volume and find in it many useful insights. In this way, the pleasure we had in preparing this volume with the help of our editors, John Dowds and Hilary Horton, can be shared by the reader.

JURRIT BERGSMA

Introduction

Why look into "the other side" of medicine? Because an exploration is needed in the realms of illness not covered by the strictly clinical situation. Clinical signs are the object of technology, but the whole person is the object of medicine, and the psychosocial aspects of medicine, inherently part of the healing process, deserve fleshing out. Obviously, not all such aspects can be covered, since many remain unknown. Hence the reader should not expect a comprehensive study of all such aspects. But he or she can expect the posing of important questions about aspects of disease not normally covered in medical textbooks, an exploration of these questions, and suggestions for further research.

During our explorations a method has been followed that permits elucidation of the personal situation of patients and the relevant literature. Rather than the social structure, the focus is on the individual patient and his or her situation. Thus, the problematic is addressed from the standpoint of clinical psychology. Philosophical insights are also included.

Even though we have emphasized the exploratory nature of this work, we would be less than candid were we to deny any thesis. Our thesis is that persons are in a dialectical relationship with their environment such that they both shape and are shaped by it. Although persons may be distinguished by different aspects, they should not be divided into parts paralleling these aspects. The distinction between "distinguishing" and "dividing" is important: To distinguish is to clarify an aspect of a person or environment for the purpose of reintegration; as the Scholastics used to say, "Distinguo ut unitur." To divide is to contribute to disintegration. With respect to medicine, distinguishing aids the process of healing the whole person; dividing dehumanizes.

Unfortunately, medicine, science, and technology all rest upon a method of dividing persons into parts, making the body and its organs into the appropriate object of medicine. This objectification neglects the many ways in which our bodies organize our environment, affect one another, and suffer such impacts. In order to bring about healing of the whole person, medicine and its use of science and technology must re-establish the integrity of persons with their environments, by attending to the additional aspects of illness described in this book.

Medicine should contribute to healing the whole person. Ironically, however, it creates conditions that in curing clinical indications displace or disenfranchise the person, which impedes healing. Thus, medicine's twofold obligation, to cure disease and to heal persons, requires the removal of the very conditions that traditionally have permitted the curing of disease. Medicine must "implace," or re-enfranchise, persons in order to heal them. Failure to achieve this means that while curing disease, medicine quite simply creates patients! The starting point of our study, then, is a rather theoretical look at the body, in which distinctive terminology is defined for use throughout the book. In the first chapter we introduce the concept of "body-image." Following this, we explore various modes of "dis-ease" that alter the body-image for individual patients (chapter two). Workups with respect to this altered body-image are discussed in chapter four. The importance of the doctor-patient relationship in setting clinical determinations (by which we mean more than the usual clinical orders in the chart) is addressed in chapter three.

The initial impression left by a standard workup is that it considers only three outcomes of illness: complete recovery, recovery with a permanent handicap, or death. However, a more detailed prognosis reveals other possible outcomes. Among these are pain (chapter five), fatigue and communication problems (chapter six), and permanent handicaps without recovery (chapter seven). The ramifications of total recovery are not treated, as they lie outside the scope of this book. The last chapter (nine) is offered as a practical summary of the previous chapters. It includes, however, some new materials. Four primary characteristics of disease are discussed. We also present four cultural models of the health care-patient relation, the final one being that for the future of medicine. Our thesis is, in that chapter, that technology cannot replace, but must be applied within the context of, the healing relationship. It takes persons to heal.

A final note should be made about the last point. This book is characterized as an exploration, although each page is not sprinkled with new ideas. We present a gradual deepening of insights about the material covered. During this presentation familiar ideas might surface, or points of critique of these familiar ideas. In the final analysis, communication between the authors and the reader results if the ideas expressed resonate with experience. As any further research in this field will result from reactions to the book, responses are invited.

Cases are presented in parts of the text. The cases were developed from notes and fragments of interviews with patients, some of whom are still alive. Every effort was made to protect confidentiality. Should some cases resemble actual situations of patients, even of those we do not know, we beg these patients' indulgence, for our intent is to explore the common problems of the sick.

Methodological Considerations

Clinical psychology, as employed in this book, is directed at the physical and social implications of medical disorders. It has been called somatopsychology, to distinguish it from psychology aimed at mental disorders. Generally speaking, somatopsychology is a new application of the discipline of psychology that has not yet been organized to any significant degree. Hence, when we refer to "patients" in the text, we will always mean those with physical rather than mental disorders, unless otherwise noted. Thus, in the pages to follow we will be exploring the psychic and social implications of physical illness and disease processes. We will not treat psychosomatic factors contributing to physical disorders, as this field belongs properly to psychosomatic medicine. We will refer to the latter only when it might shed some light on a particular discussion.

There are four factors that have led to this new application of psychology. We will discuss each of them in turn.

1) The medical model dominates our thinking about illness and disease processes. Such a dominance has resulted from deterministic ideas about causality, which have influenced both etiology and nosology; that is, that illness is caused by a cadre of physical and biological factors. Thus, within such a limited arena of factors, interpreted materialistically or mechanistically, there is no room for psychic and social factors that are not materially determined. This holds true both for the explanation of the genesis of disease and for its therapy.

During the relatively brief history of psychosomatic medicine, however, it has already become clear that one cannot fully explain processes of illness by appealing only to a mechanistic model of disease (C.P. Kimball, 1970). Certainly in the forefront of the growing realization of the inadequacy of mechanistic models have been the anthropological studies by Margaret Mead. These studies reveal that socio-cultural and socio-economic determinants have an important role to play in both the disease process and in its explanation or presentation.

Further insight into the role of nonmaterialistic determinants in the genesis of disease was provided in 1945 (1948) by H.B. Richardson who required that attention be paid to social and psychic factors in managing patients. This requirement was reformulated by A. Querido in 1955 in his concept of *integral* medicine. From what was once an exclusively physical view of the processes of illness has gradually developed the current interest in a more inclusive view. This view places specific physical processes in a broader framework. The framework includes factors of physical components of disease originating in a nonmaterialistic environment within both the genesis of disease and its therapy. As a consequence, the disease and the patient are viewed as more than a sum of physical symptoms: they are regarded as a totality with a history originating in the environment. This is holistic health care.

2) A second complex factor contributing to this new application of psychology to physical illness and the patient has been the institutionalization of health care in advanced nations. For a long time, the hospital was regarded as a place for only the very ill and the dying. However, in our day the social structure of hospitals has changed; the economic and scientific situation has become such that most patients must be treated in specialized institutions. But once the social judgment was made that patients receive better care in a technologically advanced institution, the medical expert in such an institution was faced with a number of nonspecific medical problems having to do with the patient, his living environment, and his family relations. The first to pay some attention to the psychic and social factors patients brought with them into modern hospitals were the chaplains and nursing staff, since they had the most frequent and intense conversations with patients.

Out of these concerns came revelations about what it means to be sick. At first, the concerns took the form of individual confrontations with the problem. However, the concerns are now well enough developed that one can speak of them in a systematized language. Instead of the former isolated observations, one may now use this language to contribute to diagnosing the patient's problem, the strategies for treatment, and the foundations of these strategies in the life of the patient.

3) A third reason behind the rise of somatopsychology can be found in the movement called patient-centered care. This movement rests upon empirical credentials; research by nurses and medical sociologists has been the main contribution to the movement (for an overview, see Bergsma and G. R. Rullmann, 1975). The empirical tone of the movement stems from its direction at effects to be measured, effects that are

the results of total care, as compared with standard therapy. Comparisons are made between current patient-management techniques and a more holistic care, wherein patients take an active role.

How well this research is conducted and can sometimes hold up to methodological critique is still open to question. However, initial results indicate that total care not only is a positive contribution to the well-being of patients, but also has a beneficial effect on the physical processes of disease themselves.

4) A fourth and final factor stems from the overwhelming number of persons over sixty-five who receive medical care. In the United States more than twenty-five percent of the expenditure for health care originates in the population of those over sixty-five years of age, even though they constitute only ten percent of the population. No one can stop the ravages of time and environment on the health of these patients, but the degree of medical sophistication needed to care for some of this population is matched only by the degree of psychological and social concerns heaped upon dieticians, nursing-home personnel, and medical professionals, especially those in geriatrics. The movement toward a geriatric specialty is not unlike that which fostered family medicine, originating from a desire for a more holistic approach to the care of patients. Thus this movement joins the others from within medicine itself to repudiate a purely mechanistic explanation of disease and a purely technological plan for its treatment (see Society for Health and Human Values, 1978).

In conclusion, we note that in addition to a causal model of disease—the current medical model—new ideas about the origins of disease leave room for questions about a more integrated approach to the explanation of disease process and the care of patients. These developments have their roots in social changes, economic changes, and, indeed, in the success of modern technological medicine. Currently, however, the new developments are employed in somewhat spotty fashion, and as a consequence, are not very widely accepted. Hence, the purpose of this book is to map out the territory in which the new developments are given order and a systematic presentation.

As already noted, the terrain of somatopsychology is largely uncharted. Of course, we will not attempt to fill in all the blanks. Instead, efforts will be made to map out and clarify a few of the more important areas. Of special importance is the question of the methodology that will guide the endeavor.

Most of the material in the book will be presented descriptively: after a number of observations we will offer qualitative discussion of our findings. This approach has the merit of allowing a larger number of possibilities to emerge from a field of observation than would a statistical approach. It is consonant with the methodological urgings of L. Festinger and D. Katz (1953)—for the necessity of field exploration—and S. Andreski, a formidably critical thinker. Andreski has called for more works in the field which are to be based on careful and protracted observation but which depict the social realities which often escape questionnaires and statistics (1974).

A number of our findings and conclusions have, therefore, the character of hypotheses that are capable of being quantitatively or objectively measured in research projects. It is our intention, however, first to arrange the field as a whole by contributing initial qualitative observations. This arrangement allows for the birth of a new discipline.

Consequently, as we work out this new territory, we offer concrete qualitative discussion following a large number of observations and conversations with patients. This is then followed by a brief discussion of literature that handles points raised in the text from a more empirical point of view. However, it has not always been possible to maintain this pattern, as much of the material in the literature does not exactly fit with the patient orientation of the book, the latter being still quite new and not yet the focus of empirical research.

Each Chapter begins with a different consideration of the impact of disease on patients, descriptively presented, in which some phenomenological insights are incorporated. Important literature is examined thereafter for confirmation or illumination of points of conflict. From these discrepancies, research projects are suggested. The problem we faced in assembling the literature was that it represents collections of a wide variety of research methods and studies, some of which were difficult to apply to our observations, and others totally inapplicable. For example, it proved impossible to compare our case-studies approach with many more general empirical research studies.

As a consequence, in order to handle the literature so that its ramifications could be somewhat expanded, we divide it into the following three categories:

1) *Observations:* literature in which descriptions of phenomena or groups of phenomena are guided by the subjective interpretations of the author.

1) *Descriptions:* explorations of disease, disease processes, and projects related to illnesses, on the basis of quantitative givens where possible.

3) *Experimental research:* the results of research on the basis of comparison or experimental procedures utilizing accepted methodologies.

1. The Body and the Self

Can there be any doubt that Western culture thinks of the body as an object? We extend it into the environment through our tools, we pamper it as an object of almost narcissistic attention, we feel guilty about its feelings and urges, and we exalt it as the peak of our materialistic rituals. In short, we feel ambiguous about the body. This tendency to view our bodies as objects of love or scorn lies in the cultural movements that have occurred since the seventeenth century. Since that time it has become exceedingly difficult to consider a person as a unified whole of body and soul. In fact, the language of those whom we will cite attempting to re-establish this unity becomes contorted and difficult to follow. Partially this is owing to the fact that they are stating the obvious, and partially because they are stating a neglected insight clothed in the obvious language of daily speech. We often talk about bodies and selves, but do we really see the relationship between them? What happened to make this topic so difficult?

At the beginning of the seventeenth century Descartes put an end to speaking of body and soul as distinctions in an otherwise unified individual. His contribution, the distinction between "thought" and "extension," could no longer be ignored. By reason of this distinction it became possible to objectify the body and to conduct scientific research that had previously been unthinkable. The seeds of this development were present in art (Michelangelo) and in science (Vesalius). But the seeds needed Descartes's language and thought to provide the mulch. The mystique surrounding the human body could now be cleared away forever.

Descartes's distinction, coupled with the scientific and cultural tone of the age, made it possible for an interested observer not only to study the body, but also to manipulate it to obtain additional information. Less than a hundred years after Descartes, for example, La Mettrie attempted to describe the body in totally mechanistic terms, terms such as *watchworks, pistons,* and *pumps.* This view of the body was certainly based on Descartes's materialistic and mechanistic thinking.

Although we no longer subscribe to such simplistic explanations, there is no doubt, as we have already observed, that mechanistic determinism has been the ruling theory guiding research and therapy of disease. History demonstrates that it was as of the time of Descartes, that the medical sciences of anatomy and physiology grew enormously. Harvey's discovery of the circulation of the blood, also occurring at the beginning of the seventeenth century, was the start of remarkable advances in medicine. While this discovery influenced medicine itself, it also had broader implications for other sciences and for a new vision of man. Flourens noted these implications in 1854 in his study, "De la découverte de la circulation du sang date la physiologie moderne" (Cf. J. H. van den Berg 1962). These medical and cultural implications belong to our study, for Descartes's distinction broke the mystique of a body-soul-spirit unity in man. As one might suspect from its advances, science regarded the distinction as definitive.

From 1940 to 1945 Maurice Merleau-Ponty, acting on a string of previous attempts by such thinkers as Henri Bergson and Edmund Husserl, tried to restore a measure of unity to man through his concept of "body-subject." However, developments in science and medicine had pursued a materialistic course to such an extent that a reversal to a more unified approach to man seemed an unrealistic possibility. After all, anatomy and physiology, along with the germ theory of disease, had obtained advances precisely by regarding the body as an almost "dead" object of study, upon which external factors acted to produce disease. It was virtually unthinkable that a reverse in this trend could take place.

But Merleau-Ponty's view should not be given such short shrift. In fact, it has influenced both philosophy and psychology, and in this respect it is very valuable. He describes the body as an ambiguous whole of body and subject. Thus it is viewed as a single entity, which is simultaneously matter and spirit. It is one reality, a gestalt, in which each part relates to the whole and to the environment. As such, it is a single center of consciousness. As Merleau-Ponty describes it, the body is subjective. By this he means that it stands in a dialectical relationship with the objects of its environment, and in this way forms its own world or field of consciousness.

Since our study will require a model of body and self, it is worthwhile to pursue this dialectical relationship in more detail. F. J. Buytendijk (1948) proposed that the gestalt "body" and the gestalt "external world" (*Umwelt*) are congruent; there is no causal relation between the two. That is to say—as Merleau-Ponty did in his first work, *The Structure of Behavior*—the subjectivity of the body transcended any causal relationships. The body and its environment act upon each other to such an extent that it is impossible to stop this circular process at any one point and draw out a linear causal chain without doing violence to reality. T. Von Uexkull (1970) also denied any causal chain. Of course, this denial does not cover our ability to draw a distinction between the body and the world of objects, but rather it supports the view that a continuum exists between the body and the environment such that one cannot be conceived without the other.

Sometimes Merleau-Ponty speaks ambiguously about the body, as when he says that the body helps one to be open to the world, but can also close off the world. Clearly he cannot mean that the continuum is somehow shut off; this interpretation would do violence to his own statements elsewhere. Instead, he must mean that the body as a "unity of the self" is oriented more or less to the external world, either open or closed. Consequently, he argues that the body undertakes a dialogue with the world, in which movement is an important aspect of the circular process classically described by Buytendijk (1948).

The theory of the body-subject as a unity of self is far more helpful for modern medical practice and theory than Descartes's distinction between thought and extension. For example, even the germ theory of disease has been refined to demonstrate that infectious diseases are responses of the body to the presence of certain viruses, such that the body itself "creates" the disease: the body is not an object of attack by the viruses, but rather a partner, as it were, in the disease process.

Our study, as mentioned above, requires a theory that can pose concepts relating the fact that we have bodies with our conception of ourselves. In this regard, E. Erikson's thinking can supply us with a missing link in the discussion so far.

As one of a number of "selves" Erikson distinguishes (1968), he formulated a concept of the "body-self." The body-self is an aspect of human identity. It is therefore capable of being distinguished from other aspects. In the same vein, we will also draw a distinction between the body-self (the body as representing the identity of a person) and the body-object, the objective aspects of the body that appear when the body no longer functions as a subject. The integration of the body-self, a person's identity and unity, can disintegrate. That is to say, when the body-self, as the aspect of human identity, is no longer treated as such, the body becomes dissolved from the self as the body-object.

The process whereby the identity of persons is destroyed through an artificial splitting of the self and the body we shall call dissolution. In this process the integrated "subparts" of the body-self are split off from one another and are, as it were, uncoupled. In some cases, as we shall see, persons can subsequently become repelled by their bodies.

The above discussion should be considered no more than an attempt to construct a working model for the problems to be addressed in this study. In order to refine this model, it is necessary to turn to a discussion of "body-image," as it is known in the literature.

A. BODY AND BODY-IMAGE

Developmental psychology has been the discipline most responsible for creating and fostering the concepts of "body-experience" and "body-image." We have only to think of J. Piaget (1971), whose study of the development of the concept of space demonstrated a direct correlation with a corresponding body-image. This theme was further advanced by M. Laurendeau and A. Pinard (1970), and has been treated philosophically by S. Spicker (1975). If the demonstration is correct, it means that what Kant thought was a category of the mind is actually an experience of the body in creating its own image.

S. Fisher (1970) continued this interest in embodiment by conducting a great number of studies. In addition to these studies he further served the development of the concept by assembling a bibliography devoted to the concept from a variety of disciplines.

If we were to trace the development of the concept of body-image, we would have to start with B. J. Cratty, who described it as "A global concept encompassing all the movement capacities as well as the sensory impressions created by these movements" (1970, p. 131). Yet, as Cratty himself observes, this is a vague and unwieldy description, one that is difficult to put into operation. As a consequence, he offered another description, distinguishing measurable from less measurable factors. However, although the new description facilitates further investigation, it is also less suitable as a description of body-image.

Fisher also dealt with a distinction within the concept, seeing clearly, however, that distinctions of aspects of a thing do not necessarily contribute to a real understanding of its essence. His description is as follows: "The experienced body is a world within a world. It is a complexly shaped and yet bilaterally symmetrical simplified object which has spatial and geographical features second to none in their diversity" (1970, p. 567). And further: "For example the body possesses an interior, which, though hidden from others and therefore socially invisible, continues to be evident to oneself with vivid intensity. One knows one's body from the inside, although the insides of other opaque objects are almost never perceivable. This 'transparency' exemplifies but one of its numerous special qualities" (1970, p. 567).

These difficult and sometimes contorted expressions demonstrate how hard it is to lay bare the roots of the concept. Fisher himself has written a few hundred (!) publications on the "complexly shaped object" in an effort to bring this root to light.

At this point it is perhaps worthwhile to return to the observations of Merleau-Ponty that the body is a kind of gestalt, a whole wherein all relates to all, a center of consciousness. In our view, this perception of the body as the center of consciousness is a way to link up the treatments of body-image by Cratty, Fisher, and Merleau-Ponty. The concept is used to designate the manifold complexity of the body, paying specific attention to the fact that while having subjective and developing experiences leading to a full adult human life, the body also can be considered as an object of subjective experience. Put another way, the growth toward personal integration requires a high degree of coherence between "body-concept" and "self-concept" (R. Wylie 1967).

In the main, we will understand by "body-image" what is contained in Cratty's first observation: that it is a "global concept," a universally understood view of a unique body, which is largely determined by motoric functions. But in addition to the sensory aspects, which in any case are regarded as belonging to the sphere of automatic functions, we will place primary emphasis on the body's *possibilities* and *limitations.* These possibilities and limitations are not always automatic.

The sensory and motor functions are determined primarily by factual, perhaps "objective" possibilities of the body. By contrast, the body also involves subjective valuations of its own possibilities and limitations. One could therefore propose that the more the relation between objective possibilities and subjective valuations is clarified, the greater the development of an integrated body-image.

Although we have now gained some clarification of the concept of body-image, it is still essential to see if there are any nuances left to be explored. One such is provided by J. Gerstmann, who says:

> By body-image or body-scheme, is understood the inner-picture or model which one forms in one's mind, of one's body or one's physical self in the course of life; and which one carries with one unwittingly, that is outside of central consciousness. It is a kind of inner mental diagram representing one's body as a whole as well as its single parts and territories according to their location, shape, size, structural and functional differentiation and spatial intercorrelation (1958, p. 500).

and further:

> It also represents the cardinal directions of the body: right and left, anterior and posterior, up and down. The body scheme can thus be conceived of as a complex of intimately correlated and integrated individual schemes; some of them seem to predominate over the rest (p. 501).

For these refinements of the concept, Gerstmann attributes ideas to P. Schilder (1923), whom he perceives as having played an important role in the growth of the concept, above all in its relation to neuropsychology and psychopathology. The treatment by Gerstmann, however, is far more subtle and detailed. It stresses primarily the character of "wholeness," and in that way relates to Cratty's and Merleau-Ponty's accounts.

J. A. M. Fredericks can also be read as contributing to the discussion on body-image. In 1961 he disapproves of the use of the concept body-scheme. As he suggests, it is no 'scheme' but the lateral awareness of a varying idea or spatial image of a unique body. Mostly from pathology, Fredericks then offers a number of other ways to understand the concept of body-scheme: he distinguishes 1) corporeal aesthetic impulses; 2) the optical picture of one's own body, 3) vestibular impulses, and 4) psychological aspects and other linguistic factors.

Most interesting for our purposes is the observation Fredericks makes that the body-image is not homogeneous, by which he means that certain aspects of this body in individual experience have greater importance than others, on the basis of sensory motoric psychology and linguistic determinants. He surmises therefrom that one must draw a distinction between plastic aspects (H. Head's "plastic model") and static aspects of the body-image. By static aspects is meant the bundle of experiences provided by sensor-motor activities, while the plastic aspect is malleable and changeable on the basis of "actual impulses." In other words, new stimuli create growth and change in one's image, while previous stimuli serve as a more stable ground for the newer stimuli.

However much of Fredericks's polemic against the term *body-scheme* one might choose to accept, the arguments against it can be overcome by adopting the term *body-image.* In our opinion, this is a far better term. Fredericks does not deal any further with the concept body-scheme, except to say that it is a very complicated aspect of our psycho-physical reality, and cannot lead to any further clarity (1961, p. 21).

We are strongly inclined toward the term *body-image* as representative of what Gerstmann has so excellently described. In addition, current research offers the opportunity for familiarity with the term. Many experiments in psychology and allied disciplines employ the "Draw a Person" test (Wachs et al. 1960 as cited by Fredericks), which can portray an objective sense of a person's own body-image. Finally, the concept itself is, quite simply, best expressed by *body-image,* rather than *body-scheme,* for the reason cited by Fredericks.

Gerstmann's description of body-image is clearly the most developed and clearheaded, while retaining a greater sense of the totality to be described than do other formulations. Hence we will adopt this description for our concept of the body-image in the pages to follow. Nonetheless, the distinction between plastic and static body-image is also worthwhile (Head in Fredericks 1961), and will be employed when necessary.

A last note is required to close this section. The body-image is very vaguely present in our own consciousness, as both Fredericks (lateral awareness) and Gerstmann (outside of central consciousness) have noted. In other words, it is passively present. In addition, it is a form of directed attention by consciousness to a portion of the body or to the body as a whole. To describe this aspect of body-image, we shall employ the terms *body-consciousness* and *body-experience* to represent either an active "directedness" of central consciousness to one's own body or an attentiveness to a part or functional aspect of the body.

B. BODY-IMAGE AND SELF-CONCEPT

It is not sufficient for our presentation simply to use the concepts of body-image and body-consciousness. As we mentioned in earlier pages, it is necessary to describe their relation to the concept of self.

We must, therefore, turn our attention to what R. Wylie calls the "self-concept" (1967). As she has done a superb job of rationally defining the concept, it is not necessary to follow her arguments step by step. Her approach was prompted by the vagueness of existing theoretical formulations. Previous endeavors had floundered, because empirical research required an operational description that, simultaneously, could be related to theoretically important variables. As she asserts, "This is probably due in part to the vagueness of the theoretical formulations concerning such constructs as 'organization,' 'configuration,' 'differentiations,' and 'consistency.' It is not even easy to draw sharp lines around the problem of a concept of self, since so many other factors enter in to this concept" (1967, pp. 317 ff).

Wylie continues, "Part of the explanation lies in the scientific shortcomings of all those personality theories which emphasize constructs concerning the self." In another analysis, she arrives at this conclusion: ". . . constructs such as self acceptance or self-esteem, especially when referring to specified attributes, have yielded more manageable and fruitful research procedures" (1967, p. 318).

It is not germane at this point to retrace Wylie's thorough analysis of the entanglements associated with the concept of self; with respect to the purpose of this section, which remains somewhat theoretical, her analysis offers too many possibilities for pursuit. Instead, we will emphasize the term *self-acceptance.* We ask the reader to bear in mind Wylie's discussion of this concept as well as the suggestions offered by the term *self-regarding attitudes* in the discussion that follows. By *self-acceptance,* we understand self-valuation in the sense of one's acknowledgment of self-value, the term *valuation* thus acquiring a positive tinge.

Wylie notes that the relationship between body-image, embodiment, and self-acceptance (body-image and self-image) was underscored by S. M. Jourard and P. F. Secord, (1954), who found positive correlations between self-concept and the size of one's body, as well as the size of certain parts of the body: "Significant correlations between Body-Cathexis and Self-Cathexis" were discovered (Wylie 1967, p. 319). She adds to these considerations the research done by P. H. Mussen and M. C. Jones (1957), who could prove a relation by negative means ("significant differences"), by studying negative self-acceptance and a retarded physical development.

Smith and Lebo (1956) are also cited by Wylie. They used a modified Vineland Maturity Scale to prove correlations between physical development and a sense of personal worth (self-regard and self-concept). Throughout her discussion Wylie remains very critical, yet she comes to this conclusion: "The total pattern of findings is congruent with the assumption that deviations of body-characteristics from someone's ideal may lead to lowered self regard" (1967, p. 320).

The importance of this conclusion is not that it is easy to accept, established by a wealth of judgmental experience, but that it stems from a very critical study from which the conclusion can rightly be drawn. As Wylie once states, the conclusion originally had a more hypothetical character. But now it rests upon a stronger and more responsible foundation, namely, the authoritative study she conducted.

In conclusion, we must make one more terminological observation. In addition to the concept of self-regard that we will consider the same as self-acceptance, we shall from time to time employ the term *self-concept.* Whenever the reader confronts this term, he or she will know that by it we mean what C. Rogers suggests.

Rogers holds that the self-concept or self-structure might be thought of as an organized configuration of perceptions regarding the self. These perceptions are admissible to awareness. Such a self-concept would be composed of the following kinds of information: one's perceptions about abilities and characteristics; the concepts of self in relation to others and to one's environment; the kinds of values one ascribes to things, events, and to life itself, as well as one's own experience; and the ideals, ends and goals one has carved out for oneself, especially as these might be negatively or positively valued (Rogers, 1961). The notion of value within the self-concept is a very important point often missed if one conceives of the concept in more substantive or essentialist terms. Values are at risk when a person becomes a patient, and therefore, the self-concept is also at risk.

As mentioned earlier about the self-image, the self-concept, too, remains in the background of consciousness. It rarely reaches the focus of our active awareness, as Wylie points out in her discussion of the concept. Both concepts, however, can come to the foreground whenever there is a confrontation with the self or the environment. It is as if the self-image and the body-image rested behind the "translucent screen" of our consciousness. They rest until they are evoked by some event or challenge in which they are actualized. Once actualized, they can become part of our conscious thinking process.

In fact, in such confrontations the person's body-image, body-consciousness, self-acceptance, and self-image all come tumbling out as more than just the content of consciousness about which one can speak—it is more than just bringing the concepts out into daily speech. The sick person, for example, finds himself in such a position of suffering that these images are brought into a more intense kind of consciousness, a kind of direct confrontation with one's own being and environment. A "radical" experience is thus created.

Even though we have now reached a point in our discussion at which theoretical constructs have been clarified, it is still necessary to relate these constructs to aspects of human development. The theoretical concepts of self-image and body-image as discussed by Head, Schilder, Fredericks, and Gerstmann were all related by them to a base within human development and experience. But none of these authors accents the experience of self-development, though they often refer to "development" and "growth" in the treatment of their topics. In some writings, the accent lies on dialogue or dialectic (the phenomenologists M. Merleau-Ponty and G. Gusdorf), or cognitive processes (Piaget, J. M. van Meel, W. J. Bladergroen), or sensor-motor functions (Fisher, Fredericks), or even linguistic experiences of the self (A. J. de Witte, cited by Fredericks). We will not try to combine all of these concepts in a comprehensive plan of comparison. Instead, we offer a sketch of how one can understand human development with respect to the body-image by tracing certain major steps. Thus, we will divide the development of a child's perception of the self into four steps.

1. Discovery

The development of a body-image and a self-image begins at the very moment that a child discovers something about his or her own body, however primitive and unstructured this first discovery might be. Actually, this first discovery is nothing more than a repeated recognition of an image of the self (a hand, a foot) within the context of a field of sight (Bladergroen 1971). With repetition a connection is drawn from a *familiar image* to an *encounter with resistance* to an *awareness* (usually through pain), all of which then create a sense of belonging-to. Initial discovery is thus not a fleeting experience, but rather a constantly developing process.

In adults this process is seldom repeated in its most essential form. For example, the "discovery" of an amputation after an accident belongs to a different order and is accompanied by totally different processes. We have perceived this childhood process of discovery in only a number of patients with serious skull injuries who awaken after a long coma. In this phase, the patients are not yet responsive, nor are they in a present or retrospective state of self-observation. Attention to one's body, which characterizes this state, has also been seen after temporary amnesia when the degree of restored cognition is not yet known, or in situations of terrible, nightmarish trauma, such as that experienced in death camps (T. Des Pres 1978). Only in situations such as these can one observe adults in the phase of childhood discovery.

The process of discovery in the child is protracted over years. The changes brought about by holding and learning to sit and stand bring new boundaries of possibility to consciousness. These new boundaries become meaningful through a combination of visual perception and sensor-motor skills. Simultaneously, a similar growth in cognitive and linguistic skills occurs.

It is striking how the circle of tentative discovery at first remains largely external: the hands, feet and knees, navel, sexual organs, and the surfaces of arms and legs, even a portion of the back. But once the child can stand and the body becomes optimally visualized, there is a place for "the inside," accompanying the discovery of the functions of that very body. What is noticed is the surprising fact that food is ingested and related to urine and feces; coming thus from the body, it is obscurely manifested "after," so that at first it is barely recognized or assumed into the body-image. Only after consciousness is directed to the internal functions, and relationship between "input" and "output" is discovered and located within the body, are the functions integrated into the body-image. Fisher conducted an interesting study of the back in his *Body Experience in Fantasy and Behavior* (1970). Because of its inaccessibility, the back is the most obscure portion of our bodies with respect to our own experience, and consequently it is the weakest component of our body-image.

The child is highly susceptible to what happens in and around the body. It takes some time before differentiation between inner and outer functions can occur. During that time the body is the most nearly total object for the child.

As noted, the discovery phase in childhood continues for some time, until a new element intrudes into the growth process, namely, experimentation.

2. Experimentation

An essential component in the development of the body-image is "trying-out," or experimentation. It is distinguished from discovery by elements of clearly directed and (supposedly) more conscious activity. Whereas discovery is a passive encounter with the self interlarded with casual occurrences, experimentation involves activity of a more goal directed character.

Of course, the child does have something to do in discovery, beginning with investigation of the feet, and moving on to the head and hands. During discovery the possibilities of one's body are probed, to judge from appearances, for two reasons. First, the child seeks an effective measure of the possibilities of its own body, in tests of imaginary and real potential. Second, and simultaneously, the child seeks to learn the functional purpose of motor possibilities, which will allow the body to respond to demands in the environment.

During experimentation, a new element is pursued. What in discovery is a very introverted, self-oriented activity becomes, in experimentation, activity oriented toward the external world and its conditions. Thus, experimentation occurs in the relation between one's own body and the external world, in a motor-technical, an affective, and a cognitive sense.

In the technical, instrumental sense there is a direct coupling between embodiment and the objective surroundings (jumping on a cushion or stool, trying to fly, manipulating obstacles), in which the development of a spatial sense plays an essential role (Piaget 1971). In the affective sense, there is a relation between experimentation and the rules of surroundings (learning cleanliness, playing with one's sexual organs, pursuing objectives, learning by resistance the properties of physical objects, spatial and normative constraints). Finally, in the cognitive sense, one learns to recognize the possibilities and limitations appearing both in one's body and in the surroundings. In fact, body-image depends a great deal on the difficulty these present for the child. A child reared in a state of "free nature" will develop an entirely different body-image from a baby raised in a tiny apartment.

3. Subjection

The subjection of the body appears to be an initial completion of the phase of growth. To it belongs motor-function commands within a bundle of challenges presented by a specific situation. The body-image has now sufficiently developed such than an explicit cognition of what one's body can and cannot do is possible. In this way one's perception of possible and impossible can be more or less realistically appraised against the demands of a situation. Among other things, such an appraisal requires a developed spatial sense: knowledge of spatial relationships and the orientation within these of one's body. When such an appraisal is achieved it means that through body-consciousness the "global concept," or body-image, has been well developed. Once again, it is important to realize that subjection, like the preceding phase, occurs within the situation's challenges and accompanying possibilities.

4. INTEGRATION

In our opinion, the last stage of growth moves one step further than subjection. Integration is this last step, and it occurs in the relation between body-image and self-acceptance (Wylie 1967). As discussed earlier, there is a strong bond of dependence between these two concepts. The dependency of one on the other means that they appear beyond the commands (subjection) of one's body to the challenges of situations. When one is faced with an entirely new set of challenges, one will not disintegrate in a sudden setback.

Thus, we are here describing the *permanent* power to exploit possibilities of the body and surroundings. Without this power, identity can be shattered and dissolution is the only outcome. This power can be observed in crises, such as when an administrative official must work in a coal mine during a strike; a young man is sent to the front, a person is in a building that has suddenly caught fire.

In crisis situations one cannot speak solely of the potential of the body or even of the self. Rather, the construction of one's identity is due, in large measure, to the experiences that have engaged the self. New experiences can be recognized by the body only when there has also been a cognitive and emotional perception of the situation. Situational challenges and body possibilities can be related only when the self recognizes enduring potential, so that it can take realistic appraisal of the situation and its strangeness. Only when the self and body can "tap" wells of deep experience adequately to appraise and face a challenge can we speak of a real identity. Only then is there a fulfillment of identity in Erikson's sense, when the body-self and the self are an integrated whole.

C. FUNCTIONS OF THE BODY

Following the brief sketch, given above, of the development of embodiment, we now turn to some essential observations for thinking about the psychology of patient care. These observations entail distinguishing embodiment as a whole from a number of its functions. These functions are not addressed as specifically physiological, but rather as ends of corporeal behavior that can be recognized and realized. We draw eight such distinctions:

1. The Machine Function

The machine function can be seen as the basic one. Obviously, if the machine does not work, one cannot speak of other functions. By this function we mean the relation between the "product" as a form of energy and the intake and use of "fuel" by physiological functions of an anatomic whole. Thus, the body can be seen as a self-regulating physiological system that, receiving its energy requirements, can continue its existence.

2. The Maintenance Function

The body is distinct from pure "input-dependent" machines by reason of its biological maintenance function. This is revealed in its search for input, which, in the form of usable energy, can be sought when the body needs it, and in the body's avoidance of offers that are gross or unfit. This function can also be recognized in the search for ways optimally to guarantee the input against external deceptions. Actually, the maintenance function is a sort of instinctual activity, and not *conscious* directed activity, which can have its own goals. The latter is on a different order.

3. The Instrumental Function

The instrumental function is a consequence of both foregoing functions. The body utilizes its highly differentiated instrumentarium to pursue its maintenance function. The machine employs mechanical functions that move principles of maintenance into reality. Teeth, hands, arms and legs, including the necessary muscles, as well as the body as a whole (pushing, pulling) belong to this instrumentarium. Thus, one can observe that respective possibilities of different parts of the instrumentarium represent a scale from the coarsest to the most refined utilization. Various parts of the body can be summoned for the most delicate operation or the most demanding. The same holds true for the entire body acting as a whole.

4. The Propagating Function

Theoretically, at least, machines can be designed to imitate the first three functions. But self-propagation, the fourth function of the body, is the first function definitively to demarcate bodies from machines.

Every body contains within itself the potential to bring about new bodies, more or less modeled on itself. Each body has the ability to reproduce and multiply, that is, to create new independently maintained body machines.

With this independence of the newly created body to maintain itself yet another demarcation from machines suggests itself. When the propagating function is fully realized it leads to the independence of its creations, something machines cannot do. Obviously, propagation requires a direct contact in the physiological sense of one body with another; it is the first function of those considered that is not confined to the single body alone, but demands a reach beyond the body toward the external world—i.e., another body—in order to be realized.

5. The Signaling Function

Signaling goes in two directions. The first is toward the body itself. Disturbances and threatening events within the body system are uniquely signaled. Disruptions of function are signaled or localized so that the body can impose its own regulatory adjustments on the disturbance to rebalance its functions. The results of hunger and thirst belong in this category, as does pain. However, there are also any number of adjustments made by the body in response to its signals that are never raised to the status of consciousness; many response mechanisms of the body, initiated by signals in the physiological system, never reach our perception. They are hidden and automatic.

The second direction of signaling is outward. Because this system is oriented toward the external world, its receptors constantly signal that which has a definite significance for the system. Thus, the signals from outside the body, received and monitored by the body, allow the body to respond to their significance for its other functions. Clearly, the significance of a signal depends on the environment from which it was sent and received, as well as the meaning it has within that environment.

The element of relation to the external world, new in this function, can now be developed further.

6. The Expressive Function

The expressive function of the body is a breakthrough in orientation, notwithstanding the relation of propagation and signaling to the external world. Not merely a "hull" of a self-dependent system, the corporeal exterior is also a "mirror" for interior occurrences. The body does not only signal; it also transmits its signals outward. The body "expresses" its interior events through its exterior.

Thus, an observer attentive to these expressions can surmise what is going on within the body, even though all the signals transmitted cannot be exactly interpreted. Indeed, one can argue that medical specification of disease requires correctly interpreting the signals of a body, with technical assistance if necessary.

From the behaviors of a body, one can extrapolate goal; from the movement of limbs, body, and musculature, one can "read" physical feelings and emotions. All of this is independent of the question of proper interpretation or how the signals will be judged. What is seen occurs, and not only that, but also what is smelled, felt, heard. Expression employs all possibilities of the body: movement, odor, sound. By means of its expressive function, the body can be considered an interpretative system.

7. The Communication Function

If one still considers the body somewhat passive in its expressive function, such an interpretation is laid to rest by the body's ability to communicate. Communication involves reception and transmission of signals created by the interface between body and surroundings: reception of signals and notice of such reception, and, of course, a response. The body is a means by which signals are processed and returned. Consequently, it is the instrument by which the relation with surroundings is continually upheld.

8. The Mediating Function

The body's function as mediator follows directly from communication, but is of a different order. First, it can mediate signals in the sense that some are received from one sector of the environment, perceived as such, and then sent back into another sector. Corporiety, thus, has a greater object than simple reception and transmission. In addition, it serves as a means, an intermediary, for sending signals from sector to sector. The ballet dancer moving through a piece of choreography, the actor in a scene, even the mother who translates to her child adult conversation, are all examples of mediatorship.

The second aspect of mediatorship, signal-processing, is actually involved in all eight functions and is the bedrock from which higher functions are mined. By signal-processing is meant the ability of the body to interpret the world and itself logically prior to conceptual understanding. To discuss this aspect further would divert us from our theme; suffice it to say that the notion of preconceptual perception and interpretation has occupied thinkers such as Merleau-Ponty, Husserl, Bergson, and Heidegger, and commentators such as J. Wild and J. Edie (*see* D. Thomasma, 1972).

REMARKS

We have distinguished eight functions of the body. We have not considered such specific aspects as learning, consciousness, and creativity as bodily functions—although they are largely linked to corporeity—because it is our intent to demonstrate by these eight functions the utter vacuity of La Mettrie's attempt completely to mechanize the body and simultaneously to discredit the overly positivistic approach to the human body as a dead object. In this respect we should note that learning belongs to an integrative function through recognition of signals, relation of signals to others, and handling symbols adequately. Learning is of paramount importance for the body's use as instrument (motor learning) and as a communication support system.

Self-consciousness and consciousness are further removed from simple functions of the body, as we have tried to show in the earlier pages of the chapter. They should be treated in a discussion of personal or social desires and norms, or perhaps in a discussion of self-understanding or processes of personal growth. What we have established is that body-image and body-consciousness are essential to an image of the self.

Creativity, too, while based on the expressive function and necessary for communication and mediatorship, will not be further discussed here. However, we are of the opinion that the special skills of interpreting the signals undergirding the arts of drama, poetry, painting, ballet, music belong to the most refined levels of the mediating function, since they are all forms of processing and expressing signals. Finally, we do not touch on instinctive behavior, which is outside the scope of our interests.

What we should emphasize is that we do not view the different functions as independent entities, but rather as definite, interrelated, hierarchically organized functions of the body as a whole, a whole in which the distinction between interior and exterior is nothing more than two aspects of the selfsame unity. This distinction can cause confusion precisely because it does have a place in the experience of the body. But it is incorrectly applied when it leads to distinctions such as "form" and "content" as representations of reality, for these are not in reality so separated. Certainly in the conception of body-subject form and content are fully transcended. In some descriptions to follow, therefore, the term *body-boundary* will be used as a more accurate and useful representation of what is implied by *body-form.*

Our object in this chapter has been to trace the relation of the body to the self both in theory and in genesis, and to describe functions of the body that transcend its interpretation as a machine or an object. Included in this has been our intention to establish a basic language about the body and the self for the chapters to follow.

CONCLUSION

The body is an apparatus of movement. But it also perceives the significance of this movement. The relation between the two functions has not been explored to the extent it should be. "When we consider the biological antiquity of communication through the body, it seems surprising that so little is known about it," say J. P. Spiegel and P. Machotka (1974, p. 1) in the opening sentence of their study, a study aimed at the body in its capacity as messenger of meaningful signals by physical movement. Kinesiology has appeared only in the past few years. A. F. Scheflen's interest in body language (1972) led him to observe that very little is known about it, and more fundamental knowledge in this area emerges only sporadically and is fragmentary.

Even though Scheflen discusses kinetic dependency upon certain higher forms of developmental determinants, he concludes, as do Spiegel and Machotka, that cultural values play a special role. Scheflen judges that developmental determinants and cultural influences occur in every case, strengthening and modifying each other. He is correct in his observation that the modification resulting from cultural influences causes the difficulties encountered in studying body languages. J. P. Spiegel and P. Machotka propose a system of codification that would make it possible systematically to organize observations about kinetic deportment. Although no judgment is made about the appropriateness and consistency of this method, it appears that kinesiology can offer important contributions to the study of the effects of physical handicaps on personality development.

"Kinesic frames of interaction," of direct importance in territorial behavior, and kinetic accompaniments to language (Scheflen's system) are, by their absence, significant for the handicapped person. This is especially important when one considers the usual reduction of kinetic behavior to *nonverbal communication.* The intrinsic significance of human physical activity is far more comprehensive, chiefly for the patient himself, than is allowed by the more restrictive sense of *nonverbal communication.*

The inability to move, for example, in a quadriplegic certainly has a greater effect than the inability to communicate nonverbally. In this case it is probable that the inability kinetically to express territoriality is a serious hindrance to the growth and maintenance of the personality. All we can do is suggest that the same problem in a child, or any disability of the motor function or its parts, has a negative effect on cognitive and emotional growth. It is good to see, therefore, that kinesiology has taken initial steps and that some researchers are leaving behind the highly anecdotal character of earlier probes in this area. For the sake of the many physically handicapped, a scientific intensification of kinetic studies is most desirable.

2. Dis-ease

Disturbances in body-image and experience of our bodies occur during sickness or as a result of accidents. But sickness and accident are not the only causes of such disturbances. Changes in social norms can also cause them. Consideration of such disturbances can shed light on how they are artificially created by external conditions. Hence a number of distinctions regarding forms of disturbance are possible.

Our focus is, however, on types of disturbances experienced by patients. Throughout this chapter we will refer to such disturbances as dis-ease, in an effort to underline their importance in considering illness and disease. *Dis-ease* is considered a fundamental experience of the patient, while *disease* should be taken as the scientific category of illness reached after a period of diagnosis. Patients do not initially experience disease, but rather experience a disturbance in their self- and body-images. We can draw distinctions between four categories of dis-ease, after which they will be described in greater detail.

A. Mechanical Dis-ease

By mechanical dis-ease we mean the disturbances directly or indirectly resulting from an accident. In such cases the cause is less important than the "confrontation" between body and environment resulting in primary *structural* damage to bodily experience. Mechanical dis-ease is therefore a structural disturbance caused by an external event over which the patient had little or no control.

B. Biological Dis-ease

In contrast to mechanical dis-ease, biological dis-ease includes first and foremost all the forms of sickness that both have a biological cause and govern the functioning of the body. Secondarily, the biological processes that are inherent in the human life span are also included.

For example, puberty might be ranked among biological disturbances (whether or not it should will be examined only very briefly as we restrict our study to the process of maturation and later decline).

C. Normative Dis-ease

To the category of normative dis-ease we would assign those disturbances resulting from socially given norms that have a contradictory impact on the personal body-image or body-experience. These norms are almost always linked to a culture or subculture.

D. Artificial Dis-ease

Artificial dis-ease includes all the necessary disruptions of the body caused by medical technology as it is employed to heal the person. Thus, the category includes on the one hand mutilating operations designed to minimize a more serious condition and, on the other hand, reconstructive operations designed to improve the patient's behavior condition and restore it to normal function.

With these introductions it is now possible to examine dis-ease in more detail. Our emphasis will be on patients' accounts of the disruptions caused by dis-ease, with the obvious implication that care for the whole person requires attention to this factor of illness as well as to the usual scientific indicators.

A. MECHANICAL DIS-EASE

Four characteristics are almost always present in mechanical dis-ease: 1) the acute character of the event, 2) the occurrence of pain either immediately or subsequently, 3) structural damage to the body (dis-ease), and 4) a localized cause outside the body. Each of these will be discussed in turn.

1. The Acute Character

Almost every accident entails a more or less acute character. The event happens suddenly, without warning; one can barely grasp what has actually happened. Even when one is forewarned, a relatively acute impact occurs, especially if there is little time to prepare for it. Because accidents are events generally described as occurring without much chance to anticipate them, when we can speak of preparation for an accident we usually mean a conscious reckoning of the kinds of risks involved in certain situations: entering traffic; climbing a stepladder to wash a window; going onto the field to play a game. Usually these situations barely suggest anticipating an accident because they are so commonplace, or because their character summons from us all of our conscious attention. Obviously of a different character are those situations wherein a preoccupation with special risks occurs at the expense of full attention to the situation itself, for example, driving in the Indianapolis Five Hundred. In these cases the chances are reviewed explicitly and the risks are related to the question of possible bad luck.

The acute character of mechanical dis-ease has a perplexing effect on those who survive accidents. They are dazed. No ready answers are at hand to describe what happened, because they cannot grasp the whole situation at once. The usual perspective within which human beings function, that of acting toward some goal, however minuscule, has suddenly been broken. The clock stands still, as it were. These perplexing effects are the result of disruption in the normal expected order of events. The present and its immediate past have become structureless, fleeting, without an anchor in normal experience. Victims lose themselves; they are lost, so to speak, in the event for a short time or even a longer period. The situation is unknown, lacking any recognizable landmark.

After an accident one must turn inward upon oneself; that is, create order in the resultant chaos, restructure the situation and oneself. Because amnesia of some sort almost always occurs, it must be linked to the sudden loss of self: one is so involved with the event that the usual boundary between the ego and the environment is overstepped, the ego-structure is temporarily dissolved. Without doubt, this situation is due to a number of factors, factors such as the context and seriousness of the accident, personality variables, and the degree of anticipation. These factors determine to what extent amnesia will present itself.

In fact, many variations in response can occur, ranging from complete shock (in which the victim can wander for hours, in danger of becoming a victim again) to a very quick perception of the situation (in which the victim can summon up adequate reactions and protect against further mistakes). From discussion with patients and investigators we have reached the conclusion that the degree of the victim's opportunity to assess the risks of certain situations has an important role in the manner in which the event is undergone.

Nevertheless, disorganization almost always occurs after accidents. This should be borne in mind when helping victims, who often react inadequately at the scene of the accident or later in the hospital. It is not unusual for victims to feel no pain, or to speak of their pain in an oddly objective manner, or to localize it in a wrong part of the body. Neither is it unusual for a victim with modest wounds to react with extreme apathy or for a seriously wounded victim to display a high degree of euphoria. Thus it is important to remember that diagnosing the results of an accident requires almost total disregard of the usually significant reactions of patients.

Case I

On a foggy evening a car with four occupants crashed head-on with a truck. The crash was not particularly serious, yet three persons in the car were badly wounded. An older woman had a bleeding head wound and was comatose; the driver, also older, was crumpled behind the wheel with an obvious broken leg. A young man sitting in the back seat had been thrown against the bank of the road and had difficulty breathing. Only the young woman, also a rear passenger, seemed unharmed. She ran from the car and called for an ambulance from a nearby house. The ambulance arrived quickly. The young woman helped the attendants in a professional manner. When the three victims—her parents and husband—were ready, she accompanied them to the hospital on a jump seat in the ambulance. When they arrived at the emergency room, she helped get the victims in, lavishing care on her relatives. At the moment that the three were properly attended to, the woman went limp. Subsequent examination showed that she had sustained an ugly break in her left lower arm during the accident.

Immediately to conduct an extensive medical examination on the young woman, given her performance after the accident, seems uncalled for. Clearly, her behavior does not indicate that she has suffered injury during the accident. This case suggests that the complete disorientation of the victim after an accident—perhaps disintegration would be a better term—leads to a destroyed self-image, the ego-experience of the victim. But in diagnosing, it is also impossible to rely upon the global body-image of the patient; it, too, has been altered. The case shows that the normal body's basic orientation to the world has been seriously destroyed. This orientation and its destruction directly depend on the seriousness of the accident in objective terms.

This case does not indicate that one should neglect obvious bodily causes of inadequate behavior. A serious head injury, for example, may lead to bizarre behavior. A car crash might thus lead to amnesia in the victim. What the case does demonstrate is that bizarre behavior may also stem from shock. Here what is perceived as normal behavior is actually bizarre: the young woman's assisting the accident victims even though she had a broken arm. What we wish to emphasize is the high probability that after a serious accident the victim will experience acute disorientation, whatever the form. This disorientation is usually related to the sudden character of the event experienced, and it is not always revealed in the behavior of the victim. Thus, one must pay particular attention to the "meaning" of the accident victim's behavior. This person's dis-ease may manifest itself either through obviously bizarre behavior or through behavior perceived as normal.

2. Pain

No matter how detailed a discussion of pain might be, it nevertheless remains objective. But because pain is a phenomenon of experience it is clearly understood by all of us. Its objective discussion is difficult and ultimately leads to silence. Objectively described pain is but a hollow shell surrounding the almost inexpressible experience of dis-ease. Since we will discuss pain in chapter five, we will only mention it here as an important component of mechanical dis-ease.

For this reason, the phenomenon of pain is difficult to place within the scope of medical care. No one has ever questioned the role of objectively described physiological pain in the medical model, but the phenomenon *pain* has never received a definite place in this model. Obviously, a discussion of pain should accompany any discussion of accidents. But the noteworthy experience of accident victims is that pain is seldom felt at first; the experience of pain usually comes later. The cause of this anomaly lies either in the "stupor" at first experienced by the accident victim or in the disorientation between the self, body, and situation. At any rate, as in the case that follows, the absence of immediate pain is remarkable.

Case II

This is a conversation between a surgeon and a young man, nineteen years old, after the latter's foot amputation:

—When you were lying there with a metal beam on your foot did you have pain?

—I did not feel anything at all. I didn't know what happened.

—But later, when you arrived here at the hospital, you really did have pain?

—Yes, when you said that you were going to operate I suddenly felt an overwhelming pain in my foot.

In this case, one could argue that the pain was present at the outset, but owing to the dazed condition of the patient and his consequent disorientation, he did not feel the pain. Also, one might argue that in this case there seems to be a high degree of trust between the patient and the surgeon, such that the leading questions might have been answered out of rapport rather than fact. Most probably, however, a sudden and delayed experience of pain contributed to disorientation such that the self could no longer exist: the self is completely overwhelmed by the pain. In this case, one can speak of "pain shock." Such overwhelming pain represents a dissolution between the self and body, in which the boundary of the self is lost. Even though the experience of pain was missing in the early stages of the accident, the level of dis-ease demonstrated by the objective destruction of the foot should indicate to physicians that some dissolution has occurred. In some cases, the sudden experience of delayed pain can lead to a permanent loss of consciousness.

As we have seen, therefore, pain can contribute to a dissolution of the self. However, it can also have the opposite effect, namely, the turning of the self back in on itself. Awareness of pain can actually be the first step in reorientation of a damaged self. Orientation toward one's own body through a profound experience of pain can be a stage of reorganizing perceptions of the environment. It can heal. Egocentricity, "inward"-directed experience, helps to some extent replace the self-image that has been lost in a disintegration of the boundary between the self and the external world. Pain therefore remains, in its clinical presentations, a symptom with a rich variety of consequences. Clinicians can pay the strictest attention to pain, but it is a confusing and often unreliable indicator of the seriousness of dis-ease in patients.

3. Structural Dis-ease

The experience of an enormous power overwhelming a person and the subsequent dazed state of the accident victim do not easily vanish. This power exerts its effect after the accident, and can be reinforced by the alterations it has wrought in the structure of the body. The body appears unfamiliar to the patient: it no longer seems the trusted body through which we act in daily life. The contiguity between one's self and one's body is disrupted.

The body becomes unrecognizable because suddenly it no longer matches one's concept of it. Instead, it is associated with things we judge to be destructible. The form of one's body no longer offers the usual comforting image, and it even conflicts with the image of human bodies in general; some patients pay dearly for this alienation from a broken body, not even recognizing themselves as human beings. After an accident, clothing no longer appears what it was. Limbs are skewed in relation to the rest of the body; they cannot be used, or have taken on strange forms (broken bones). Blood seems to clothe the body in a disorienting way (what was within the body is suddenly outside it). All these experiences create an extremely threatening situation.

Along with the destruction of the boundaries of the normal body, the actual functioning of the body is altered in significant ways. Thus, in his altered capabilities, as well, the victim no longer recognizes himself. The relationship between possibilities and impossibilities, intrinsically part of the body-concept, are suddenly invalidated, and the very self-concept has been seriously threatened. A victim of an industrial accident in which the arm has been torn out of its socket experiences a feeling afterwards of the arm's actually falling off the body. He cannot work, cannot mow his lawn, cannot sleep on his stomach as he always did, cannot hug his wife, cannot lift his child. He must begin relying on neighbors and friends to do even the most menial tasks around the house. Not only has his body-image suffered, but his definition of himself has been overturned. Long after the arm heals, he will suffer from this disruption of the self.

It is important to note that what we have discussed occurs in patients who have not lost consciousness. Such distress occurs only when a certain amount of consciousness remains after an accident, or is recovered soon after the accident. Unconsciousness or the appearance of a loss of consciousness do not always have a structural cause. Naturally, a skull trauma can induce unconsciousness—we could not raise this point in situations in which there is a direct link between unconsciousness and a cerebral accident—but loss of consciousness can also be a reaction to pain, a sort of defensive mechanism of the body. It can also be caused by an experience of total disorientation and stupor. Thus, in events in which there is no demonstrated incidence of skull injury, the loss of consciousness is either a reaction to complete disorientation or, simultaneously, a defensive mechanism permitting the patient to escape from the immediate shock of the situation. In diagnosing an accident victim, one must be very cautious in the interpretation of unconsciousness as a symptom.

4. Causal Location

Accidents are distinct from illnesses largely because a concrete cause external to the victim is responsible for the dis-ease. External causes play an important role in the personal assimilation of the event. For the victim, the direct relationship between the external cause and the accident is very important, because there has been a confrontation between the body and that which is exterior as a causal factor. The "object" is present as "other" to the victim. It follows that the external cause accents the defenselessness of the victim: the patient has been a victim in the true sense of the word. Some power outside himself has been responsible for his downfall. Experiencing externally caused accidents is experiencing dependence and almost total subjection. In a manner of speaking, the victim is doubly dependent. First, he is dependent upon a situation in which he has been damaged and lost his power to "speak" of himself in whole or in part; second, he is also dependent upon the externalized aspect of the event. He did not request this confrontation. The "other" was stronger than he.

Thus, in this situation, not only the body is compromised. The self is, as well. Self-consciousness must now deal with the "something" external and stronger in the accident. This externalized power is what causes the astonishment always found in accident victims. Not only is there astonishment over what has happened; there is also astonishment about the suddenly revealed power that has pounced on the victim. This suddenness means that the instinct of self-preservation had no chance of being put into action. Total helplessness results, so much so that it has an amazingly negative effect on the victim's self-concept. This fundamental experience of powerlessness with respect to being or not-being can damage the self-concept and endure beyond the normal period of recovery. Note its presence in the following case.

Case III

A recently married twenty-five-year-old coach had a serious motorbike accident. His right leg had to be amputated. Although he had suffered no serious skull fracture, he was comatose. After he had lain in a coma for a week in the intensive-care unit, his consciousness began to return and one could talk with him. A few days later, he seemed completely oriented to time and place, and could even remember all events, including those that had occurred while he was in the intensive-care unit. However, whenever the conversation turned to the accident itself or his current status, he seemed to fall back into his "coma" and could not speak. This situation lasted almost six weeks.

Feelings of apathy and concomitant depression caused by the experience of an overwhelming power beyond one's control can appear very rapidly. The ability to perceive things and place them in perspective has usually been so strenuously tested that its normal realization is abruptly severed. It can even be permanently damaged.

When an accident occurs through no fault of their own, victims also appear to be noticeably passive, manifesting a despondent meekness out of character with the concrete dependencies of the moment. This passivity is due to the externalized force continuously present in the self's attempt to assimilate it. In the first phases of recovery, the patient cannot impose a structure on the force, much less verbalize it. Without a doubt, the suffering induced by this experience adds an extra dimension to the instinct or temptation toward dissolutionment of the self. The external cause of an accident, therefore, creates dis-ease in the body, the self, and the environment far out of proportion to its actual power when seen in a normal setting. Thus, traffic on side streets entering your lane is not considered a threat to you; but the victim of a traffic accident may still flinch, years later, when he sees such cars out of the side of his vision.

B. BIOLOGICAL DIS-EASE

Inasmuch as biological dis-ease will be discussed in one section, we must make a distinction between 1) dis-ease within the disease processes and 2) dis-ease consequent upon biological changes in the body. Under the first category ("Disease Processes"), we will discuss the features most often related to:

a. the slow progression of the disease process ("The Process')
b. the generalized feeling of illness (sometimes resulting in pain) ("Globalization")
c. the causality of the disease—even if not clearly direct—that most often is localized within the body ("Causality")
d. the presence of disruption in bodily function ("Functional Disorders")
e. gradually altered relationships with the environment ("Altered Relation to the Environment")

Under the second category ("Dis-ease Caused by Biological Process"), we will discuss:

a. the biological process related to dis-ease ("The Course")
b. the generalized feeling of "aging" ("Globalization")
c. the unclear causality that is always located within the body ("Localization")
d. the gradual manifestation of disruptions in bodily function ("Functional Disorders")
e. the very gradual alterations in relation to the environment ("Altered Relation to the Environment")

1. Disease Processes

(a) *The Process*—Illness is a process we experience within its own gradual tempo. Only in unusual circumstances does one feel well one moment and in the next recognize that "I am sick." Unusual circumstances include a stroke or heart attack, which are not preceded by a period of dis-ease.

In most cases, it is normal to begin feeling unwell for several hours before recognizing that one is sick. A period of days, and even weeks in some cases, is not unusual. The meaning of this gradual development is that at the onset of illness the patient barely realizes he is becoming sick, but later he can recognize that a dis-ease is creeping up on him. One can then anticipate further developments in the disease process. It is the ability to anticipate and prepare, to marshal defenses, that distinguishes biological dis-ease from mechanical, illness from accidents.

One has a number of responses at hand for the onset of biological dis-ease, whereas the lack of such responses in an accident contributes to its disastrousness. There is a place for "being sick" in one's experience of life—sometimes people even put out the welcome mat for a cold! Welcome or unwelcome, an illness seldom is so overwhelming that an unraveling of the person occurs. Perhaps some disorganization in one routine takes place, but anticipating the normal course of the illness offers at least the possibility of a structure, in space as well as time. With this spatiotemporal structure one can manage during the altered situation created by an illness. Thus, dis-ease in the normal course of an illness from which we expect to recover occurs during its onset and is then replaced by the spatiotemporal structure of a diagnosed and treatable disease.

(b) *Globalization*—The structure and process of a disease rarely is confined to one organ or part of the body. Even if the disease, such as an infection, is in fact objectively localized, the patient's experience of the disease is of the whole body. One has a generalized feeling of dis-ease, a global sense of "being different than usual." This strangeness is not of an unrecognizable character, just of a different perception from the usual. The perception of something being amiss, not normal, can create anxiety, but it does not completely estrange the self from the self-concept. There is an impact on the self, but not a dissolution.

Instead, a gradual distancing of the self from the disease occurs. In this distancing it becomes possible to observe the body with some degree of objectivity. Thus, patients, as E. Cassell observed, refer to their disease as "it," an object separate from themselves. With a sophisticated consciousness the patient watches indicators, such as temperature, pulse, and coloring. An inner Argus eye checks on whether there is pain, if the pain can be localized or otherwise identified, and whether one can reach a tentative diagnosis: a not unwelcome grasp of the seriousness of the condition.

Nevertheless, the whole body is to some extent invaded, both externally and, in a manner of speaking, internally, in its inner surfaces.

Case IV

"I didn't feel well for a couple of days . . . especially on Friday . . . I was warm, slept a lot, and had to go to the bathroom a

> lot . . . On Saturday the doctor came and said I had a case of diarrhea . . . Even as he said this I started to feel better . . . I'll pull through . . . so I thought, feeling better, I had to go back to work on Monday, because we had a big job and I didn't want to leave the boys sitting around . . . Good, I felt better on Sunday and figured I'd go back to work Monday . . . But it was tough . . . I went but had to keep going to the bathroom . . . and that's not easy to do when you work outdoors like me . . . I never felt so rotten . . . The boys saw something was wrong and urged me to go home . . . at last I did . . . I had to drag myself along and just got there by the seat of my pants. I hardly got home before my wife called the doctor, because I was doubled over with pain . . . man, it was something . . . He said he could come in a bit, but my wife, you know, said that's impossible . . . 'Come now!' There was no way to get away from the bathroom . . . The doctor got in right away . . . Man, it wasn't five minutes before he called the hospital and an hour later I was on the operating table . . . No, I wasn't afraid. I didn't care anymore, I wasn't a man anymore, I didn't care if I lived or died . . . I was so miserable . . . I'd like to die . . . you really don't care anymore."

Attempts to objectify one's body by "measuring and comparing" never prevents illness from overcoming the whole person. Man is taken over by his illness—the process "belongs" to the person. Man is no longer the sole ruler of his body. He has to share this rule with something as yet undefinable. This is dis-ease in its rawest form.

In his *Psychology of the Sickbed,* J. H. van den Berg suggests that "the healthy person may identify himself with his body. Of this assessment he makes eager use: he is his body. But the sick person loses this assimilation. The body becomes a stranger, and a strange ruler invades his quarters and makes them uninhabitable. An evil reigns over this body and weaves its way into its tissues, organs, with sores and swellings. The body becomes a betrayal" (1963, p. 45).

This sharing of rule over the body with some undefinable thing is precisely what leads to our searching for a more particular diagnosis. By concretizing this "co-ruler," one can detect whether it is a friend or foe of the body: one can fix the disease and determine its course. Dis-ease becomes disease. This determination relieves some of the anxiety of the patient, which is partly the reason for seeking medical help. The ability to diagnose is, in itself, a first step toward healing the dis-ease experienced by the patient.

(c) *Causality*—Experiencing the onset of a disease and the process of determining the nature of the disease are colored by an increased focus on the self. Causality is experienced as an internally localizable event. Even if the cause can be placed outside the body (a virus, for example), the primary experience comes to the sick person from within. Two reasons exist for this inner experience. First, biological illness, even if caused by an external agent, is really the result of a reaction by the body to the agent. One does not experience a virus, one experiences the viral infection.

Second, a person taken ill begins to focus on the sources of suffering in the body ("my head hurts"). An illness makes us introverts overnight. If the sick person cannot pinpoint a source of suffering in the body early in the course of the disease, anxiety increases. Such failure of an early prediagnosis can have an important impact on the outcome of recovery. If the patient does not seek help right away because of this failure, the disease may progress further than it might have if treatment were immediately sought. Or if the patient's anxiety about the illness increases because he cannot identify a cause in the body, the anxiety itself contributes to the degree of dis-ease he suffers.

(d) *Functional Disorders*—As opposed to an accident, in which disruption of bodily functions immediately occurs, illness only gradually manifests a decay in function. At some point, of course, a moment occurs which tilts the person toward recognizing the disorder. But prior to that moment standing, sitting, and general posture already have been affected by dis-ease. One copes before recognition by altering one's usual habits. Intestinal disorder? Stay close to toilets. Trouble breathing? Take off the heavy jacket. In other words, sick persons become vaguely aware of the fact that they have a body before they actually identify a functional disorder.

The gradual deterioration of function that is disease, combined with the corresponding anticipation of further deterioration that is being watched, makes it improbable that too great a disjunction between self-image and body-image will occur from moment to moment. However, this situation can change. When one of a number of functions is so destroyed that it can no longer be included in a revised picture of the whole body, then self- and body-image are definitely affected. Nevertheless, at the onset of the disease this situation rarely presents itself.

(e) *Altered Relation to the Environment*—As the course of the disease manifests itself, changes occur in the body's relation to the environment and to the objects therein. The environment undergoes a gradual alteration in significance, in the sense that it now has meaning in relation to the disease itself. The process of introversion, already discussed, creates a different perception of the environment. New things are noticed and old ones neglected in the altered situation of the patient. This, too, is a kind of dis-ease. The place of work, school, relaxation, gradually carry less significance and drift, as it were, further from the "I"; the protective boundaries of the house or bedroom receive a whole new significance in relation to the experience of illness. Even dimensions such as "far" and "nearby" acquire new meanings for the confined person, demonstrating how dimensions themselves depend on one's relation to and function in the environment. The stairs near the bedroom, which before guaranteed privacy, now can become a barrier to communication, impeding access and requests for help from others. The living room is "far"; "near" is only what one can reach at hand.

The bedroom becomes an isolation ward or sickbay. The concept and content of the room are now adapted to the wishes of the sick, altered to accommodate recovery or an anticipated longer course of illness (only last night's paper or a staple of library books to relieve the boredom). The picture offered by the sickroom is a good indicator of how a patient suffers—or chooses to suffer—an illness and perceives recovery.

It also discloses what role an altered time dimension may have for a patient. In keeping with the patient's recognition of fundamental events in the time perspective he had previously developed, he will be more or less prepared to arrange the given of his current situation. Whenever daily events are threatening in themselves, time might be seen as an ally that can contrast its wealth of experiences to the threatening reality.

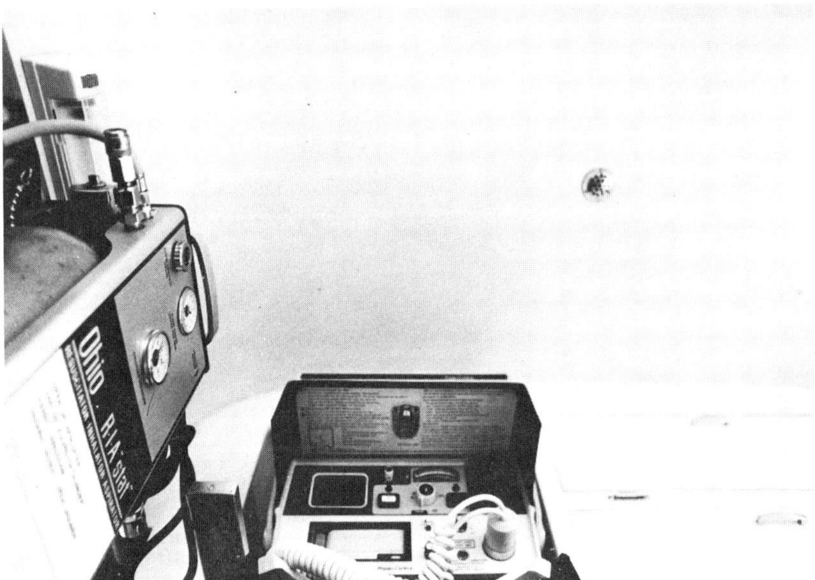

In the ambulance

Entering the emergency room

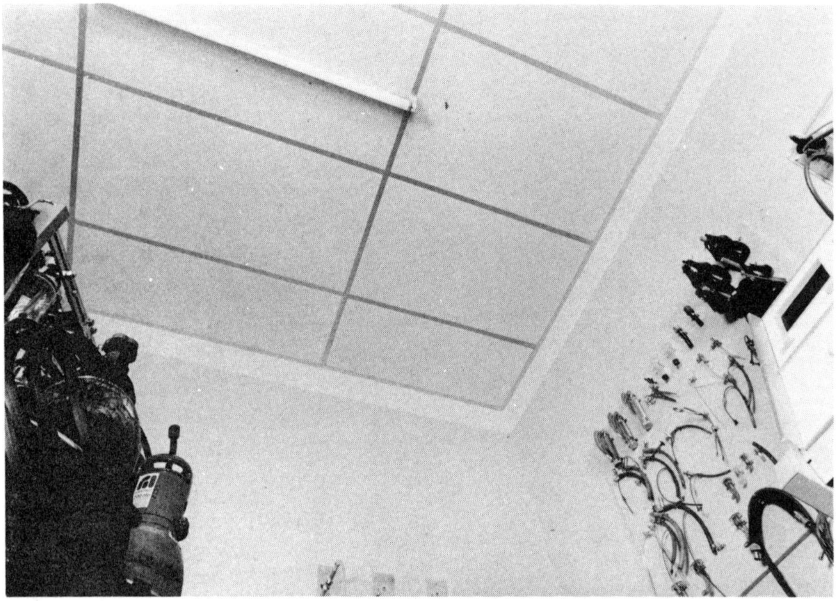

First glance results in the emergency room

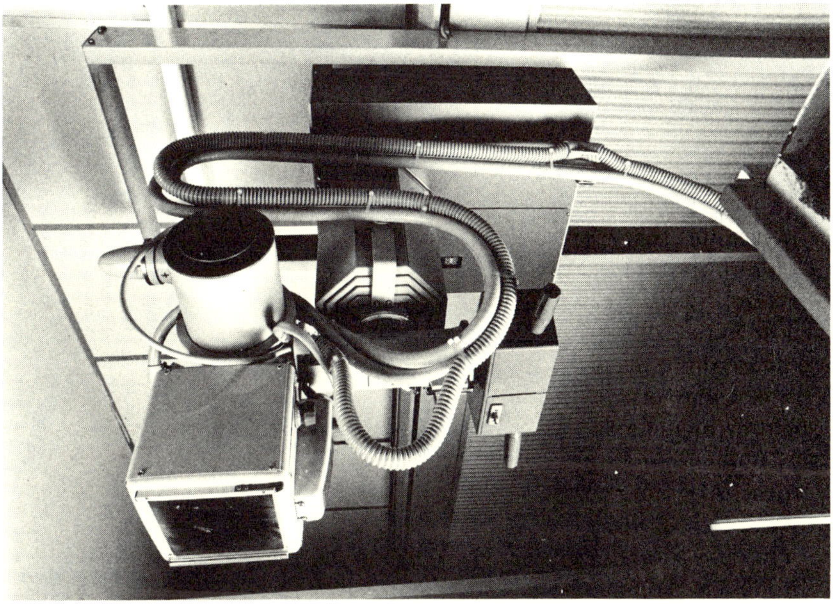

Under the X-ray machine

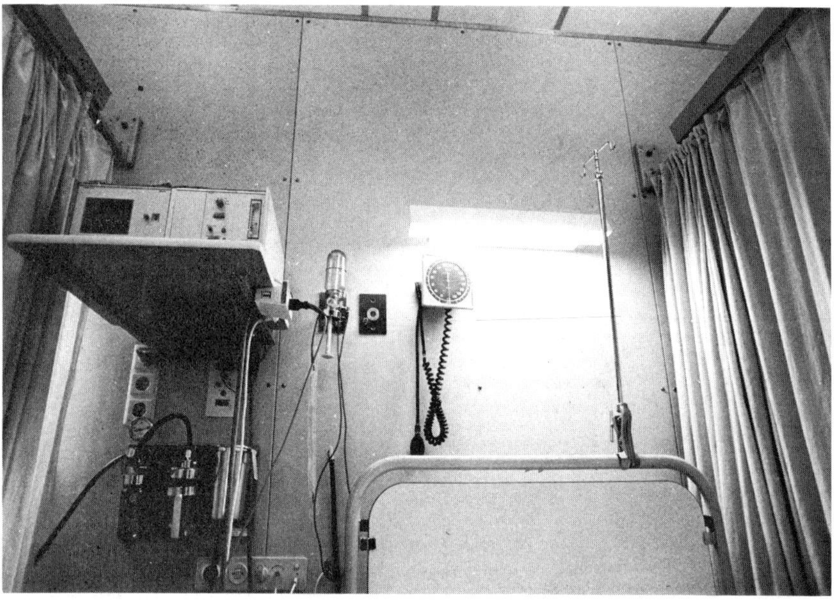

Entering the cardiac-resuscitation unit

2. Dis-ease Caused by Biological Process

(a) *The Course*—The process of aging has a very imperceptible course, stretched as it is over many years. It can barely be located at any one time. One can refer to statistical means and averages, but these cannot be applied to an individual. No *terminus a quo* can be identified. The commonplace "A day older and a day wiser" is too far removed from the biological processes that could describe the apogee between growth and decline. The reason it is so difficult to speak of such an important watershed is that, in the life of an individual, one seldom finds any awareness of the potential problems the body may signal now and then. Both the biological processes and the accompanying decline are so minute from day to day that only much later, usually during comparison, are they revealed. Hence, during the normal course of aging there is little chance of an abrupt dissolution of the self.

We should, perhaps, make an exception to this rule. Under certain conditions, menopause in women (and, as D. Levinson et al. show [1978], sometimes in men) is accompanied by such changes in bodily function that it can produce certain substantial dissolutions (menopausal depression). But in all probability, the experience of menopause is dependent in large measure on cultural determinants.

(b) *Globalization*—Normally, the course in aging as well as illness is a global course. Humans experience themselves altered in their totality, not piece by piece. Even though the process is anchored by individuals in certain noticeable changes—white hair in sideburns—the experience of these changes is a total one. I, as a whole, grow older, not just my legs, my head. This totality course of aging prevents dissolution. The body-concept slowly alters, such that conflicts with the self-concept in the form of discongruities seldom surface. Adaptation to the continuous process of aging goes on at all times, without any direct difficulties. In the most literal sense, this adaptation occurs in the context of continued change. (Social norms in regard to aging, important for self-image, are to be discussed on page 46).

(c) *Localization*—Although the process of aging is identifiable, it cannot be externally localized, like the cause of an accident. Aging is primarily an internal process, in which one cannot lay the blame on others. Over the long haul this fact is of real importance: it is one's body, one's self, that ages.

(d) *Functional Disorders*—Excepting the impact of sudden functional disorders such as apoplexy, functional dis-ease from biological changes appears gradually in an almost invisible daily tempo. It is clear that for the aging person these gradual functional changes and/or disorders are signals that slowly alert one to the process taking place. Consider this case:

Case V

"Yesterday my grandchildren came to visit. That is always fun. They played real well outside, and we naturally like to spoil them. My son didn't get spoiled by us, but we just naturally do it to our grandchildren, just as much as he does not do it to his own children. At noon I took them for a walk in the woods. I wanted to stroll around, but they wanted to run around, of course. I couldn't get out of it. I had to play football with them. What do you do? You do what you can. Well, not ten minutes later I was really out of breath! So I stopped and watched them until we later walked calmly back to the house. But, you know, I was happy to get back home! Naturally you know that you're getting older and can't do everything you used to, but this outing was a real eye opener for me. You can't play football anymore at all! That was certainly brought home to me."

Changes in function that are not so dramatic as this can also produce alterations in body-image. Functional changes are, so to speak, the key points whereby a measured change in body-image is sustained.

In the course of the aging process it is especially important to observe that functional changes do not all occur at the same tempo. This means that over the course of time dis-ease can occur when one or another function is impaired, especially if that function was identified for the individual with youthfulness or vigor. Thus, signs of aging—slower walking, reduced eyesight, difficult urination—can, depending on their importance to the person, be essential signs of reduced function. For each aging person the problems of aging are distinct and sometimes unique.

(e) *Altered Relation to the Environment*—Alterations or dis-ease produced by impairments in different functions of the body normally correspond to equivalent alterations in body-image, as we have seen. The same dis-ease can also, through this changed body-image, make an indirect modification on the person's relation to the environment. The meanings of objects in the surroundings alter, just as in the case of illness. Perception of distance changes, because it now takes more effort to overcome distances; self-extension becomes smaller, because extra effort is now needed to overcome obstacles. The boundaries of one's life-world are diminished, owing to obstacles newly defined in terms of reduced energy or function. A tiny obstacle, once so easy to set right, becomes a major hindrance. A small table is a welcome point of support. Thus, the object-world is redefined in terms of an altered and diminished body-image.

In the normal course of events, however, the dis-ease produced by biological deterioration is gradually encompassed and absorbed by equally gradual changes in body-image and self-concept. Sudden changes, on the one hand, and social norms, on the other, can contribute to a lack of recovery from this dis-ease. Nonetheless, they normally do not create so profound a disturbance that the self is permanently damaged.

C. NORMATIVE DIS-EASE

Dis-ease in body-image caused by social norms is of an entirely different order from the two types of disturbance so far discussed. In this situation there is no direct internal or external causality. Rather, an indirect dis-ease is produced by comparison between reality and socially established norms. From the perspective of the body—that is, its appearance and function—society "measures" it by comparing it with more or less explicit norms. These are in some form assimilated by the body and self. It might be better to call these norms of judgment social guides or values. Sometimes these social values are brought out in direct personal contact, as experienced by the hero of Balzac's *Lost Illusions,* or the hero of Dreiser's, *An American Tragedy.* But most often social values exert a judgment force on the body and self through advertising and fashions in clothing, and they are most singularly revealed in the work ethic and sports.

Broadly speaking, there are two types of norms, each with their own subsets. Both can exercise differentiated effects on body and self. The two types are aesthetic norms and achievement norms. We now turn to a discussion of both.

1. Aesthetic Norms

Every social value in this category passes judgment on the body and clothing in terms of beauty and ugliness. What is considered beautiful in one culture is out of place or ugly in another. What complicates this picture is that social values and norms within certain societies shift rather rapidly, although this is not true of every culture.

In Western culture, we are to an extraordinary degree under the influence of advertising and the world of fashion (see pages 41-45). The power of norms over an individual's life means that every person must continually adjust to prevailing values; some persons are forced to confront the ruling norms of the moment. Shifts in values require constant confrontation and comparison which are important for individuals, their experience, and their body-image. Of primary importance is how individuals deal with shifting values. If poorly, a negative experience results: ultimately the discovery that one has "misjudged" prevailing norms—by dropping a style too quickly or waiting too long to drop it—can have a damaging effect on body-image, and dis-ease occurs. If positively, increased personal stability and responsibility result.

Examples abound. In the 1960's, for example, stout women had a lot of trouble with superslinky clothes dictated by the styles in that period, especially by the short skirts and high, platform shoes. Here social values created styles which might even have been injurious to posture and feet. Thus the implied narcissism of fashion may not only have had deliterious effects on body-image but also on the body itself. The current fad of "natural foods" is built, by contrast, on a theory of a healthy body in tune with its environment. But it, too, can lead to negative self-images in those who choose to eat without following the fad. They are greeted by natural food proponents with derisive smiles as they down their hamburger and shake.

As a result of rapid changes in fashion, accelerated by TV advertisements and magazines, cultural and social displacement are especially severe. Sometimes there is a tendency to block off these influences and to develop defense mechanisms against a "buy now" culture that constantly goes out of date. But usually one finds that developing such defenses is inadequate. The negative influences seem all-pervasive. One has only created a negative stance toward one's surroundings and even oneself. When this defense is not valued by society, feelings of singularity and oddity are strengthened. These feelings can easily contribute to a negative perception of one's body and consequent destruction of self-worth.

The category to which these norms belong functions as a measure against which one might judge one's standing. Whenever one sets out to defeat conformity and is defeated by it, the disappointment is that much greater at losing. Negative feelings are enhanced, especially with respect to one's body and one's self. The same is true of those who exert themselves and are at first successful but later cannot sustain the effort against their culture's values, particularly when these are so contrary to one's fundamental attitudes.

Not all aesthetic norms have to do with fashion-conscious social values. There are some that relate to more deeply anchored cultural values. Norms establishing beauty and ugliness are coupled with concepts such as attractive-unattractive, sexual and sexually deviant, which are often more subtle. The same norms also imply racial and religious prejudices. As a consequence, these norms often relate more to innate prejudices than to external style, and are less subject to change. One cannot easily change the structure of one's face; one's height cannot be altered as easily as one's girth. As L. Fiedler points out (1978), failure to conform to society's expectations of average

Case VI: Shifting fashions, 1969, '70, '75, '81

ANZEIGE

Immer weniger ist das Geburtsdatum ausschlaggebend für die Jugendlichkeit moderner Frauen.

Wie alt würden Sie diese Frauen schätzen?

Ein Bericht über Frauen, die um viele Jahre jünger aussehen, als sie sind. Wir sagen Ihnen, wie sie arbeiten, wie sie leben, und was sie tun, um so jung zu bleiben.

Marieluise Nelz: Mit Oil of Olaz fühlt sich meine Haut weich und glatt an. Und sie hat alles, was sie braucht.

Marieluise Nelz ist blond, sportlich, unternehmungslustig. Eine von den Frauen, die immer sieben, acht, zehn Jahre jünger geschätzt werden, als sie sind. „Das ist mir nicht immer so gegangen", sagt sie. „Wissen Sie, erst so um die 30 habe ich gelernt, meine Vorzüge und meine Mängel zu sehen und mit beidem zu leben." Heute ist sie 42 und wird häufig jünger geschätzt. Was tut sie für ihre Schönheit? Die Antwort: Oil of Olaz. Sie benutzt es regelmäßig morgens und abends, seit sieben Jahren. „Wenn ich einmal mit etwas zufrieden bin, dann bleibe ich auch dabei. Und ohne Oil of Olaz spannt meine Haut. Deshalb nehme ich es für Gesicht und Hals. Es dringt schnell ein und fettet nicht. Und macht die Haut so elastisch. Warum sollte ich da ständig was Neues ausprobieren?"

Sie ist glücklich verheiratet. Seit 19 Jahren. Und ihr macht vieles Spaß: ihr Halbtagsjob, Sporttreiben (Schwimmen, Skilaufen), Kochen. „Überhaupt bin ich ein positiver Mensch. Das ist wohl der Hauptgrund, weshalb ich so jung aussehe", meint Frau Brandt. Und sie ist 38 Jahre.

Marie-Luise Brandt: Oil of Olaz dringt sofort ein, und vor allem: es fettet nicht.

Ihre Schönheitspflege besteht im wesentlichen aus Oil of Olaz und Schlaf. „Morgens und abends nehme ich Oil of Olaz für mein Gesicht – das erfrischt und macht die Haut richtig schön glatt. Wenn ich abends dusche oder bade, trage ich es gewöhnlich etwas dicker auf. Anschließend schlafe ich, wenn's geht, neun Stunden. Etwas Besseres kann ich, glaube ich, nicht für mich tun."
Ihr Äußeres gibt ihr recht. Meinen Sie nicht auch?

Sie ist 36, eine attraktive Frau und Komplimente gewöhnt. Das größte Kompliment ist freilich, daß man sie und ihre achtzehnjährige Tochter Sabine für Geschwister hält. Dabei ist sie Mutter von drei Kindern, schwimmt gern und viel, beschäftigt sich mit Mode und hilft auch noch ihrem Mann im Büro.

Hannelore Primus: Ich reinige morgens und abends Gesicht und Hals, verteile Oil of Olaz darauf, und danach ist meine Haut entspannt und zart.

physiognomy can create what we have called dis-ease, a personal sense of being a "freak."

Nonetheless, there is no culture that does not permit some degree of flexibility in comparing oneself with the average. This "average" varies from the simple little nose of the child to the cosmetically pampered nose of a fashion model. That the average varies is of little importance. What is problematic for a person is some pathological physical deviation that both complicates his or her life and clearly afflicts the person in relation to others. For example, being bald falls within the norms: one can either be proud of it, pay little or no attention to it, or, if it causes some dis-ease, get a wig or hair transplant. But being a dwarf does not fall within the norm. It is considered a pathological affliction.

2. Achievement Norms

It seems as if aesthetic norms are forced most upon women, while achievement norms are most often applied to men. The background for these applications lies in the traditional male-female role relationship in Western culture. Nevertheless, achievement norms can illustrate the role such values play in cultural life. Work and sports are goal-oriented activities. As such they are predominately the measure by which achievement is judged.

Prestige clearly reveals the extent to which a norm is bound to cultural expectations. It is true that every culture has its norms of achievement, but the content of these norms varies widely. Western culture is infused with achievement norms and goal-oriented comparisons, and success is positively rewarded in this culture: the more and better, the greater the money, status, power. Every executive, every team, every company, every country wants to be "number one."

The establishment of these norms in our consciousness is so integrated with our view of the world, that we pass judgment on other cultures according to these norms. We judge others by what is familiar to us—what is familiar is "normal." Our awareness of the arbitrary nature of these norms is so puny that it is revealed only in a clash between authentic achievement and achievement as measured by the norms of pacesetters. The Nixon era was a good example. The pacesetters and superachievers interpreted the norm as being strong,

◀ *Supposed freedom from norms in contemporary society*

Norms presented as if related to bodily proportions ▶

Slanker lijken

Jonger lijken

Zoekt en gij zult vinden. En hier zijn ze dan. Drie modieuze japonnen voor dames met een grote maat. Modellen die prachtig afkleden. Geen vervelende, ouwelijke hobbezakken, maar vlotte, elegante japonnen die slanke, jonge vrouwen ook graag zouden willen dragen. Wie van de drie?

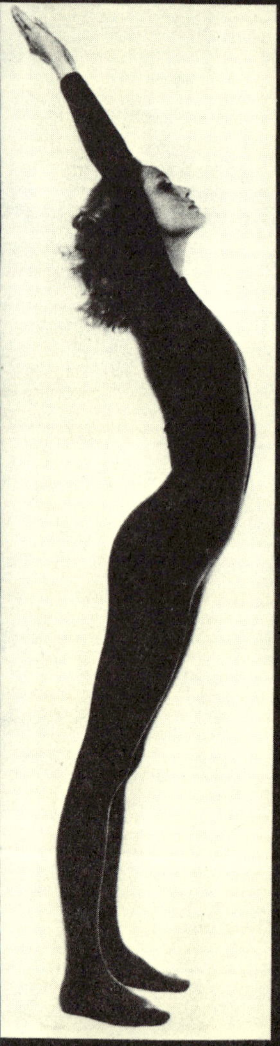

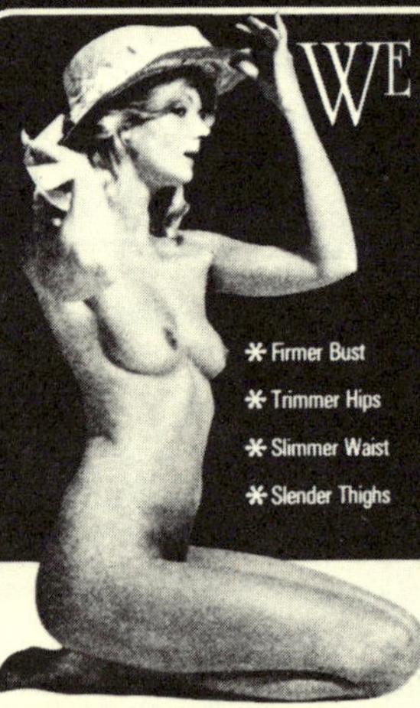

WE CARE ABOUT THE SHAPE YOU'RE IN...DON'T YOU?

* Firmer Bust
* Trimmer Hips
* Slimmer Waist
* Slender Thighs

At last a highly sophisticated Slimming and Beauty Centre has opened in Kensington to help you achieve your ideal figure.
The Morlé Slimming and Beauty Centre Method uses new and exclusive products and techniques from France. Only at the Centre can these passive and active exercise treatments, combining our medically approved eating plan, be experienced.
Within the luxurious and relaxed atmosphere of the Centre your personally supervised figure programme will start to take shape by pulling in the bulges, trimming your hips and thighs and improving your total shape and posture.
These exclusive techniques, used only at the Morlé Centre, are safe, passive and most relaxing.

The Morlé Slimming & Beauty Centre

The most luxurious Slimming Centre in Europe

Call in or phone for your free figure analysis

937 9501/3

Open 9.30 a.m.–9.00 p.m. Monday to Friday and 9.30 a.m.–2.00 p.m. Saturday
176 Kensington High St. London, W8.

schlank und schön mit fugoa

ohne Hunger ohne Mühe

Befreien Sie sich rechtzeitig von lästigen Pfunden, denn Sie wissen ja, Schlanksein bringt so viele Vorteile: Sie wirken attraktiver, fühlen sich gesund, können jede Mode mitmachen. Kurz: Sie haben mehr Erfolg.

Machen Sie deshalb eine Schlankheitskur mit FUGOA.
Jeden Morgen ein Dragée – das nimmt den Hunger für den ganzen Tag, entwässert und entschlackt zugleich und befreit Sie ohne Mühe von lästigen Pfunden.
Denken Sie daran:
FUGOA – denn die Zukunft gehört den Schlanken!

Wir suchen die fröhliche Dicke!

Wer weiß denn heute, daß die üppige Frau die sinnlichste Haut hat, seidenweich und rosig, weil sie viel Feuchtigkeit enthält, frisch bis ins Alter? Wer kennt ihre unvergleichlich runde, weiche Schulter, den glatten Rücken ohne abstehende Schulterblätter und knochige Wirbel? Wer kennt ihr warmes heiteres Temperament, ihre liebe Art mit einem Schuß Selbstironie?

Eine Frau, die es nicht schafft, sich selbst zu disziplinieren, ist auch nachsichtig und tolerant. Und wer das Glück hat, eine solche Frau zu lieben, der wird mit vielem belohnt.

Wo ist sie, diese Frau, knackig natürlich, frisch wie ein Pfirsich, die es schafft, so genommen zu werden, wie sie ist – und die es schafft, sich selbst zu bejahen, obwohl die Modewelt kein Auge für sie hat. Wir suchen die Frau, die es uns beweist: es ist schön, üppig zu sein.

Triumph. Schönheit, die man einfach anzieht.

unyielding, "tough," while the real achievements of the era seem now to lie in compromise and peacemaking. The clash occurs for individuals at the moment when power wanes, the tempo changes; most of all, it occurs when an individual is recovering from an illness, during periods of recreation and rest, and over the span of a lifetime.

If the achievement norms relate from time to time to aesthetic norms, the former result in even greater effects on personal worth and honor. Diminution of power, a decrease in energy, have direct consequences in most cases on the material rewards of the affected person.

When a decrease in achievement, due to aging or an invisible handicap, has a direct effect on an individual's body-image and consequent self-concept, the increase in self-deprecation is heightened by the consequent restriction on material rewards. Work harder; get more, Work less; get less. A decrease in rewards carries with it a double significance through its twofold effect: decreased rewards restrict personal circumstances and also give rise to feelings of less acceptance by the community. One feels divorced from society. For some the challenges are lost. How can they exist without jousting with some social or economic obstacles? The threat to the self-concept in these cases is particularly severe. Further attempts to bridge the discrepancy between achievement and norms become very difficult, and discouragement is correspondingly greater. The classic case of a forty-nine-year-old engineer, a successful father and citizen, who is fired to make way for a less expensive junior partner illustrates the tragic dimensions of this problem.

Sports represent a special case in Western culture. Sports have norms which are somewhat distinct from the work ethic. In other cultures, achievement norms have evolved in close conjunction with athletic prowess; in some they are identical. Thus, the hunt is hardly necessary for survival in the West. It becomes a ritualized sport. But in other cultures the hunt is, in fact, the locus of achievement and survival.

Athletic norms differ from those of health and aesthetic norms in another way. Deviations from the latter can be observed rather easily. An observer can usually spot an illness, an accidental injury, or a person out of touch with fashion. But an observer cannot as easily tell if someone is not living up to an athletic norm, unless that person has a record as an athlete. When a failure is spotted, its cause can be misperceived. A clumsy child can be labeled lazy, unsociable, uncooperative, to the detriment of his self-image. Judgments are made in any case that separate a person from his environment, his neighborhood, his colleagues, at his expense. Likewise, the person concerned is substantially familiar with the level of the cause and can marshal some excuse. In this way he can sometimes ward off unfavorable effects on his self-concept stemming from the negative judgments passed on him by his society. Furthermore, he is himself a part of the culture that established the achievement norm. It is an integral part of his own existence. This implies that by his inability to meet socially established norms, he may not be able to meet a personally established one, either.

These considerations reveal the impact on self-concept that achievement and athletic norms can have: a threat to the self-concept arises on the basis of a clearly variable range of guilt feelings about oneself and one's social context. To a large extent the dis-ease produced is both expected and surprising. It is expected because a gradual biological decline can prepare one gradually to drop out of the social picture of achievement and work. It is surprising because the effects of negative judgments about value to society can hurt one personally. One finds that the social norms are also one's own. No clearer example can be given than that of the retiree. At sixty-five years of age, this person may enjoy the fruits of many years of labor, his contribution to society: leisure. But it is a leisure that others, though openly envying, secretly disvalue, because of achievement norms. And the retiree feels left out of the mainstream, cut off from coworkers. This mandatory retirement appears to be a personal affront by society to the person's dignity and self-worth. Dis-ease results if the retiree has not prepared for this eventuality and the resultant guilt feelings.

Finally we should emphasize that achievement norms, just like aesthetic ones, vary a great deal from culture to culture, and within any society. They are clearly related to vocation, class, and age. Over the course of time the norms also shift within these social subgroupings. However, the shifts are not as capricious and irresponsible as those appearing in fashion and style (M. Fabre, 1967).

D. ARTIFICIAL DIS-EASE

The fourth and final category of dis-ease stems from a number of artificial interventions that accidentally contribute to the destruction of the body-image. In some cases this destruction is the result of an existing condition, caused by an accident or illness, that has required further "destruction" to eliminate it (amputation of a leg). In others, it involves "destroying" a birth defect through surgical intervention. The discussion thus now turns to some forms of "destruction" that are not always essentially negative, but rather are purgative, artificial alterations of an existing condition. Nevertheless, dis-ease in body-image can result. We will discuss in turn: 1) requested destruction or reconstruction, 2) medically induced ("Artificial Dis-ease") destruction, and 3) socially/medically induced destruction ("Social/Medical Indications for Dis-ease").

1. Requested Destruction or Reconstruction

When patients request some destruction of their body, in order to achieve alterations in body-image, they usually do so voluntarily, out of subjective and emotional considerations. Plastic surgeons meet this case often. When clients request alterations or reconstructions, the surgeon must deal with both the technical and the human questions. However, the motivation behind the request contains many problems. Surely some motives are rooted in a clash between the person's physical features and social norms. A second category of motives stems from identity crises. Some patients present both kinds of problems, others primarily one or the other.

As already noted on page 39, aesthetic norms can affect cultural values and individuals such that an unfavorable impact on body-image, and therefore on self-concept, results. Among the opportunities available through medical advances is the chance to make changes in body structure through surgical intervention in order to "measure up" to some socially posited norm. Most cases in this category arise from impediments to social intercourse presented by a feature of the body that is considered abnormal. Hence, plastic surgery is most frequently requested on parts of the body that play an important role in social contact. One can consider a woman with extremely large breasts who is the butt of jokes and finds herself more and more isolated, a facial deformity that impedes speech, deformities in the skin in and near erogenous zones that impede sexual enjoyment. All of these can present motives for requesting plastic surgery, as in this case:

Case VII

A twenty-nine-year-old patient had, at age fourteen, an indeterminate intestinal infection after a stay in the tropics. It was resolved to operate on her to remove a number of comparatively small growths from her large bowl. After suture, she experienced a localized infection in the surgical wound, which left a particularly ugly scar. Later the patient was distressed by this ugly scar on her abdomen and would not wear a bikini. She was married when she was twenty-seven. Her husband rapidly developed an aversion to the scar, no doubt in sympathy with the aversion to it held by the young woman. After a while sexual relations deteriorated and the man seemed to become impotent. In order to save her marriage after two years of this, the woman sought help from a plastic surgeon to remove the scar.

Such help has a manifold effect on those children who are born with a malformed upper lip and cleft palate (so-called harelips). The situation of these children is such that they cannot even say their name, much less speak clearly. A number of operations by a plastic surgeon, assisted by an oral surgeon, can produce an almost normal-looking face, while the repair of the upper jaw and palate can assist in developing normal speech. Without such repair, the child is condemned to a permanent social and personal dis-ease, which would be extremely difficult to overcome.

With respect to identity problems, it is obvious how surgical intervention in physical deformities can help, particularly among adolescents, who are normally much afflicted by identity problems. (The identity problems are different in the parents of children with a defect such as a harelip; they frequently labor under severe guilt feelings, often stemming from uncertainty about their identity in terms of heredity factors).

Questions regarding their identity in both adolescents and adults with deformities are most often related to their external features, such that the problem arises more in the experience of their world than in a real clash with social norms. Often psycho-traumatic experiences condition the identity problem. The experiences are so private, so subjective, so bound up with the individual person, that an observer has difficulty understanding and empathizing with them, unlike evident confrontations with social norms. Some people can suffer obsessively from thoughts that their nose is too big, while objectively speaking the nose may be nearly comparable to the average. A more extreme example is that of a transsexual who feels himself essentially a woman but unfortunately has all the objective characteristics of a male.

When the form of the body, or an aspect of it, functions as an impediment to a wholesome self-identity it is important first to consult with a psychologist or psychiatrist regarding the advisability of an operation before undergoing the surgery. Necessity for this is grounded in the fact that a person's observation about his or her body often is only a symptom of a more extensive personality problem. In this case, if one attends only to the isolated physical problem, in all probability the deeper problem will not be addressed, and will surface later in a new form. We find examples of this in cases when a "functional" complaint disguises a psychic disorder "appearing" as a physical one (a subject not examined in this book). In general, we propose that plastic-surgical intervention in cases involving a problem of social norms needs less strict regulation than intervention that is based on problems of identity, as the former involves fewer secondary psychological risks and threats of dis-ease than the latter.

2. Medically Induced Artificial Dis-ease

A number of physical disruptions are necessitated by medical techniques; most surgery is based on the principle of sacrificing parts for the good of the whole. Our current discussion, as in the above consideration, could not possibly cover the entire field, but we will focus on a category of artificial dis-ease in contradistinction to that requested by patients, namely, artificial dis-ease that is required, in order to save the life of the patient, sometimes immediately and sometimes in the long run. Within this category we will consider two possibilities, acute intervention and an operation performed after a period of consideration. Following these distinctions we will also distinguish between operations that effect a directly perceived improvement and those that remain invisible to the naked eye.

The essence of an acute intervention in the body of a patient lies in the fact that there is usually little time for consideration and consultation. The patient is presented in a deplorable physical state, usually a life-threatening condition. An operation is imperative to impede the effects of the condition. Sometimes the patient is comatose, so that discussion about voluntary participation in the operation is precluded, although one must, when possible, involve the family in the difficult discussion about the course of treatment. If patients are alert it is often possible to engage them in (restricted) conversations about their condition. Moreover, such cases usually appear in the emergency room, where it might be impossible to contact the family physician for health details and history, and the managing physician may not be able to find out what actually happened. For example, a patient may have a chronic hidden bowel inflammation with much bleeding, which may turn out not to be too serious, but which does call for the exchange of a great deal of information. Serious amputation accidents and physical dismemberment are not so frequent as less critical conditions, but nonetheless, if the patient is alert an information exchange should be attempted.

Many situations in which the patient is comatose call for decisions by the operating team. Ethicists describe these cases as possibly exhibiting medical paternalism: acting for the benefit of others without their knowledge or even, sometimes, their consent. What is of uppermost importance to remember in such cases is that neither the family nor the patient has had much chance to anticipate the dis-ease. When the patient later wakes up, he is confronted not only with the direct results of an accident or sudden illness, but also with the indirect results of the medical intervention, including amputations and scars. Thus, the patient not only can identify external agents of his accident and localize them, but he also can concretely identify those who have "completed" the accident or condition. The patient might be hostile toward those who caused the accident, and will sooner or later also direct anger toward those "accomplices"—the medical team—who were responsible for the amputation, or other "completion" of the accident. Every patient will eventually question whether the doctor made a good decision, whether he might have been too hasty, irrespective of the physician's ethical and professional stance. An amputation creates a special problem, because it results in a severe disruption, or dis-ease, in one's experience of the body; at the moment that doubt appears concerning the necessity of the operation, the full force of the aggression and depression resulting from the accident (discussed under A) and of the dis-ease in body-image is directed against those who made the decision. This may also include the family if they were involved in the decision to amputate.

Indeed, an amputation done by medical intervention after an accident produces more intense feelings in the patient than does an amputation resulting directly from the accident. This is probably because the agent of the "second part" of the accident is close at hand; his or her decision was made with little or no patient input, and the patient must, willy-nilly, depend on this person for recovery, even if he has never met the doctor before. The result is a very complicated, ambivalent reaction to the surgeon, who doubtless does not always understand what is transpiring in the interpersonal relationship with the patient. This problem hits many surgeons and orthopedic specialists the hardest, because patients in this category are at greater risk of complications during recovery than are other patients, and because a greater chance exists for the patient to experience the famous syndrome of phantom-limb pain.

Case VIII

The patient was thirty-seven years old when he was admitted, three years ago, after the automobile accident that caused him to have his leg amputated. Since then his complaints have been wholly concentrated on severe pains in the foot of his amputated left leg, even though the amputation was at the upper leg. Although the complaint has been treated repeatedly with operations by the neurosurgeon, all were without success. Before the accident the man had been a drummer in a famous dance orchestra, and had traveled extensively. He had a tendency to drink heavily, and even more so after a performance. On the night of the accident, after the close of one performance, troubles and alcohol combined to make him lose control of the steering wheel on a lonely stretch of highway and run into a large tree. A fellow passenger, a colleague, lost his life. The patient was forced to lie twisted in the wreck for more than an hour, suffering from a severe concussion, and with his left leg smashed. After he was discovered and dragged out of the wreck, on admission to the emergency room, no hope was given for saving the leg. Despite the patient's occupation, which demanded his use of his leg, all consultants advised its immediate amputation. Recovery was very slow. The patient was depressed and seemed to have suicidal tendencies. Two factors contributed most to this depression: his guilt feelings about the death of his companion and the knowledge that he could no longer work at his profession. The first complaints about the serious pain in his foot began two months after the accident. Since then the pain has been reported as continuous.

A different kind of situation occurs when the doctor and patient can thoroughly discuss an impending operation, which is much preferable to the situation cited above. First of all, a relationship is established between the doctor and the patient, however short its duration. In the second place, the patient can gain insight into the seriousness of his or her condition; whenever the patient can grasp the extent of the complication—for example, what may result from an accident if the patient is not treated—the better the patient can perceive the physician as the rescuer from a life-threatening situation.

Case IX

A farmer, thirty-two years old, had an accident with his tractor, which smashed part of his right foot. The surgeon tried to save the foot and at first seemed to succeed, thanks to an effort lasting many hours. Though the recovery at first proceeded without incident, it soon became clear that the wounds would not heal. Infection set in and proved to be resistant to all forms of treatment. By now the condition of the foot was so bad that no other course but amputation remained. The patient was aware of a continuous throbbing in his foot and could perceive its lack of response to therapy. He himself asked if the efforts made so far were worth it. As a result, he was able to agree completely with the recommendation of amputation. After the operation he recovered quickly and was soon fitted with a prosthetic device. He never experienced phantom-limb pain.

The same point—that the patient does better when prepared and consenting—can be observed with respect to surgery necessitated by disease: amputation of a leg in bad condition because of a degenerative disorder in the blood vessels or a breast-tumor operation requiring total mastectomy.

In general one can assert that the better the relationship between doctor and patient and the greater the patient's insight into the seriousness of the condition, the better the patient can manage recovery from a destructive, invasive operation affecting his body-image. Doubts in the patient about the parameters of the decision are less apt to arise. More time for assimilation occurs. The doctor is perceived as a helping hand rather than as an extension of the causal mechanisms present in the accident. These psychological verities are certainly a component in the long-standing movement of medicine toward respect for patients and informed consent.

Experience also demonstrates that in properly managed situations, less risk of complication occurs, including the risk of pantom-limb pain. We have postulated that whenever medical necessity requires destructive intervention in order to save a life, it is absolutely essential to distinguish visible and invisible destruction of the body. It seems as if patients can cope better with invisible damage than with destroyed appearance, as if dis-ease were more critical with respect to limbs than to organs, although this observation may not apply in every case. Possibly this situation is due to the fact that body-image in most people has a more external than internal character. It might be due to the degree of confrontation with oneself and with others: confrontation is more intense and persistent in cases of external bodily trauma. Yet one could certainly not assert that internal damage, even an injury perceived neither by observers nor patient, is without problems. Such cases also require attention to the emotional significance of the affected organ. This emotional significance is at root related to sociocultural norms.

Except for the relatively minor traumatic effects of the operation itself, removing an appendix or a tonsil hardly smacks of high drama (you don't even miss them; perhaps you'd be better off without them!). The operation carries very little risk. Emotionally speaking, these organs are only minimally significant, if at all. Consequently, coping with the absence of them does not even fall into the realm of a problem.

However, the opposite is true concerning, for example, the resection of a portion of the stomach or the removal of gallstones. In the first place such operations are clearly more critical. Moreover, these organs play a role in social situations, within and beyond the family. Both stomach and gallbladder affect eating, and their removal means a new diet. For some persons, meals are unimportant events; socially, they will not, therefore, have much trouble because of the operation. On those for whom meals play an important part in social and professional contact, a special diet will make an unmistakable impact. For them, coping with an operation affecting social exchange will cause trouble, and they will recover less readily. Greater difficulties are in store for those who have had a colostomy and must suffer the embarrassment of bags.

The removal of the uterus, which has a highly emotional significance—identified as it is by some women with their sexuality—will seem to some patients to end their existence as females. This reaction rests, of course, on the cultural expectations of a woman as wife and mother. Traditionally, after menopause a significant role for women was extinguished; they could no longer bear children. For women who have accepted this role, consciously or unconsciously, a hysterectomy similarly means being "over the hill": no womb, no worth.

But though loss of the uterus for many women is a miserable event, today women, and men, are able to accept new roles and meanings in their lives. Hysterectomy's threat to a woman's dignity and worth as a person has become much less problematic. In addition, surgical technology and anesthesiology have become so sophisticated that the secondary somatic effects of the operation have less impact than heretofore. But the most important point is that the role of women is changing in our culture. Although the uterus is necessary to bring children into the world, childbearing is no longer necessarily the central purpose of a women's existence. Finally, it has become very clear that the absence of the uterus has no direct effect on sexual experience. For some women, in fact, its absence affords freedom from anxiety about pregnancy.

Indeed, sexuality in our culture has more to do with external appearance than with biological function. The female breast has a meaning far beyond nursing children, as Philip Roth's novella *The Breast* so neatly explored. Sexuality, beauty, style, even politics (going braless) are all associated with the breast.

The certainty that she can no longer conceive tends to be less threatening to a woman in our culture than is the possibility of losing her femininity, friends, and sexual partner. Thus, many women are more seriously disturbed, experience dis-ease, after a mastectomy than after a hysterectomy. It is certainly valid to speak of a threat to femininity experienced in operations on the organs of the body, but the

Current breast-oriented culture and its direct relation to self-image ▶

Lejaby.
Das schönere ich.
Miss 18
Miss 18
Das elegant geschwungene, weite
Dekolleté verrät Pariser Charme
und französische Modellierkunst.
spürt ihn kaum.
Top 18
Die erlesene Motivstickerei
Emtex, Köln, Tel.: 5994027
Lintex C.P. 584, 1001 Lausanne
Lenitex, Wien, Tel.: 881293
The Wonderworkers
There are three bras in the Wonderbra range.
And every one of them works wonders for you.
The bra that began it all. (Illustrated)
The new, lighter Wonderbra.
It comes in sizes A 32-36, B 32-36.
The front-opening Wonderbra.
Created with a minimum 85% nylon content.
In A 32-36, B 32-38.
Gossard
Wonderbra
22 Hanover Square, W1A 1BS.
Nobody understands a girl like we do

Veeto Skin Smoother.
In the interests of a little sexual inequality.
Soft, smooth skin is a part of feeling feminine. That's why Veeto is made to be more than just a hair remover. It's a Skin Smoother.
It removes unwanted hair, of course. Removes it safely, gently and completely.
But Veeto does much more. Its rich lanolin softens and moisturises your skin while it smoothes away unwanted hair.
And it has the delicate fragrance of Spring apple blossom. To banish for ever the days of hair removers with a nasty smell.
Veeto Skin Smoother is a new generation of hair remover that understands what it means to be a woman. And, if it gives a girl an unfair advantage, so much the better.
Veeto
Veeto
Veeto
Veeto Skin Smoother-because you're a woman.
Weil man auch anderen schöne Aussichten gönnen soll:
Shorty ist der große Teen & Twen-Knüller. Mit extra großem Slipteil wie geschaffen für hot pants, Mini oder pur. Sitzt faltenfrei wie angegossen. Ist wahnsinnig transparent und hauchzart. Aus dem Erfolgsgarn Ergelan.
Verwöhnen Sie Ihre Beine mit
Ergee
INTERNATIONAL
Shorty
U, ik, wij allemaal hebben dagelijks Odorex nodig!
Voel u fris en zeker overal - onder alle omstandigheden. Odorex zorgt voor dat prettige, veilige gevoel. 't Is zo eenvoudig. Met de Odorex Stick Deodorant: even een paar streekjes. Wèg lastige okselgeur. Met de Odorex Spray in twee heerlijke frisse geuren 's ochtends even een wolkje onder uw armen. Odorex, huidfrisse zekerheid door een minuutje aandacht.
odorex
spray
odorex
f 1.70 en f 2.65
f 3.45 en f 4.95
Odorex

content of that threat has changed; the same holds true for the cultural meaning of *woman.*

Nevertheless, an alert physician or therapist will keep in mind that many men and women still define femininity in terms of the womb. Recall John Updike's masterful play on the word *woman* ("womb-man"), in his short story "Wife-Wooing," to recognize the extent of dis-ease a hysterectomy can cause. We may live in a breast-oriented culture, but strong feelings about the womb persist.

3. Social/Medical Indications for Dis-ease

In subsection 1. we considered requested dis-ease for easing a patient's life-threatening condition. In this third category we will touch on requests to ease dis-ease in social circumstances. After assessing the (moral) responsibility of the client, doctors perform some requested operations that do not alleviate life-threatening conditions. The plan is thoroughly discussed. To this category belong requested male or female sterilization and abortion. On the basis of full consent, "social" indicators (a terrible misnomer) lead to a medical or technical solution. Consult the bibliography for a more detailed discussion of this category, and for better terminology. The concept, however, is clear enough. A general finding in almost all follow-up research is that those who freely seek some destruction of their body for social reasons experience dis-ease, but they seldom harbor anger at the intervention itself. From our discussion, this conclusion would be expected.

There is a massive amount of literature on several of the problems covered in this chapter, although not on the general topic of dis-ease. We shall be content to offer only a representative sample concerning various aspects mentioned in the text.

CONCLUSION

Just as with any other topic, a description of dis-ease in all its forms includes exceptions. It is dangerous to generalize without attention to these exceptions, or, more precisely, the modifying influences. Even though the categories and responses to dis-ease we have described cannot encompass all possible exceptions and variations, and cannot automatically be applied to every individual, they nevertheless do

◀ *Norms presented as if related to presumed roles of women* adequately present tendencies. Comparison of circumstances and the most likely responses is possible.

It should also be mentioned that within each category of dis-ease, a greater spread of differences is present than our brief discussion could cover. These differences are due to characteristics of personality, intelligence, life experience, and so on. A substantial study of each of the possible variations would be necessary to do justice to the topic.

However, treatment of the general problem of dis-ease is minimal in medical literature, and even less evident with respect to individual differences in response. Although there are exceptions to this rule—which we will be citing in the pages to follow—medicine tends to focus on the scientific and technological categories of disease that have brought it so much success, particularly in the realm of infectious diseases. Is there a criticism in these remarks? Yes, if to focus on scientific categories means to miss the existential agonies created by dis-ease in body-concept and self-concept, for these, too, have to do with healing.

One could object that bootmakers must attend to their craft and physicians to theirs, but the real question is: What is the physicians' craft? Wiping out disease? Or healing dis-ease? As more and more data are collected regarding the impact of psychic experience and social relations on all forms of disease process, an exclusive concentration on the physical and measurable aspects of disease not only seems to neglect the humanity of patients, but also seems to be the source of diagnostic and therapeutic disasters (Duff and Hollingshead, 1968).

In the Netherlands in 1954, A. Querido introduced the concept of integral health care. In the United States, the similar concept of holistic health care (D. Tubesing, 1979) has captured the imagination of a significant minority of health-care providers. Both movements arise from a conviction that in medicine one cannot merely focus on the organism for clues regarding the genesis and treatment of illness. One must also deal with the spiritual and social context of the patient. As noted in our introduction, Western medicine has been dominated by the model of materialistic and mechanistic concepts of disease. What is more, these truncated notions of disease are considered an adequate, even comprehensive, guide to the treatment of patients and a complete salve in the obligation to heal.

Querido is not the first and certainly not the last to speak against simplistic single causality in conceptions of the disease process (see E. D. Pellegrino, 1979). In medical circles psychiatrists have been the principal critics of this kind of reductionistic thinking (T. Szasz, and many others). Perhaps owing to their polemics, however, their ideas have fallen on deaf ears, and the attempt to replace a single-cause theory of disease with a multiple-cause one has yet to be widely adopted; the single-cause theory usually predominates.

G. A. Foulds, also a psychiatrist, fulminates against this state of the art in which the terminology neglects real sources of disease: "We might therefore speak . . . of the Myth of Physical, or organic, illness. This is only the case, however, when we are considering the organism as an abstraction from the person, but the organism is necessary to, and included within the person. Thus no events can occur to the organism which do not occur to the person, in so far as the person includes the organism" (1976, p. 7). Thus Foulds holds that the person is a system in which the organism is only one aspect: "If the system undergoes a change which renders it incapable of carrying out its functions in such a way as to maintain that system, we might refer to it as ill or diseased" (p. 7).

In our description of disturbances we have emphasized that every dis-ease is more than a blow to the organism: it is also a blow to the system, to the person as a given whole. Repairing an organism is something less than the recovery of a person, of a human gestalt. Medicine cannot conclude its ministry by checking whether the organism has healed or not: it is the person who presents a condition and who must be healed, in part, if not in whole.

This does not mean that every physician should be a psychologist. It does mean that physicians and technicians should realize that their management of a patient is not an isolated treatment of a physical entity. Instead, it is treatment in which considered values hold sway, in which a human being is treated, a being who is *soma,* a sum of experiences and relationships.

A perceptive study by N. R. Bernstein, entitled *Emotional Care of the Facially Burned and Disfigured* (1976), demonstrates that medical care can encompass more than the usual (and technically excellent) care of the body; that psychological and social aspects must be included: "The burn patient cannot complete a stable body image. Too much physical pain, damage, and scarring persist, and too much medical therapy intrudes" (p. 55).

Drawing a conclusion regarding identity derived from E. Erikson ("unicity," continuity, and group solidarity), Bernstein opines: "Each of these is influenced by deformity, so that the person feels unique in a negative sense and the striving for continuity of experience is frequently interrupted by the intrusion of negative self-consciousness, surgical and medical interference, and social pressures to reject deviance" (p. 55).

With this, dis-ease is described. The world of meaning the patient possesses is, to a great extent, determined by the role of the healer, the healer's technical armamentarium, and his handling of the disease or recovery process. When real attention is paid to this world, then one can speak of an integral health care. Until then, medicine only heals disease.

3. Clinical Determination

One of the most important elements in the doctor-patient relationship is the process by which conclusions are drawn regarding the patient and the illness. It is also the most difficult to formulate adequately. On the one hand it is emphasized that diagnosis requires a continuous dialogue with the patient on many levels; on the other hand, it is emphasized that the diagnosis must be somewhat independent of the patient's condition, such that its conclusions result from the scientific knowledge of the doctor rather than from essential, but less sophisticated, contributions from patients.

Little can be advanced against these positions. Nevertheless, recent developments show that the relation of the patient toward the doctor during a period of physical dependency is becoming less a matter of psychological dependency and the patient's contribution is recognized to be a more valued component in diagnosis and treatment. The patient should have some "input" into the workup. This is most evident in primary health care, but it appears necessary with respect to specialized care, as well. Medical-ethics discussions of abortion and euthanasia, for example, emphasize the rights and values of patients in the decisions made. These and other ethical issues have contributed to our awareness of the value of patient contributions to medical decisions.

In this chapter we offer a description of the workup, the process of forming an impression about the patient's disease and its treatment, in which observations about the role of patients are included through a discussion of an authentic dialogue between both parties in the doctor-patient relationship. Our restriction is therefore clear: our observations cannot be applied to every case. Instead, they represent a continuum in which we present an ideal model for certain circumstances. Our model is primarily based on experience in primary-care settings (home health care as well as clinics), and surgical and gynecological divisions in a hospital. We begin with a schematic presentation of the process, after which we will discuss its separate components.

A. PATIENT, DOCTOR, PERCEPTION

With respect to the concrete illness in question, the patient's *subjective* experience is met by the doctor's hypothesis, primarily an *objectively* based scientific judgment. The doctor's hypothesis is thus essentially different than the patient's. The way the patient experiences the illness and the way the doctor renders judgments successively interact with each other during the course of diagnosis and treatment. We will examine the patient component of the process first, in accord with the schematic diagram proposed above.

1. Patient

(a) *Value System*—In order to detect an illness or other disorder it is essential that the patient be guiding his life according to a set of norms and values, expressed or unexpressed. By reason of these the patient first detects something amiss. We have already proposed that the patient's norms directly accent the symptoms, the meaning ascribed to them, and the consequences as he understands them. In fact, more than experience, circumscribed largely by norms, contributes to an awareness of dis-ease. The most important measure is the verbal and nonverbal presentation of realities within a concrete situation, a situation that calls forth a judgment about status. This status assessment depends upon experience, but the presentation is largely independent of experience.

(b) *Situation*—The circumstances surrounding the first inkling of symptoms influences the degree of importance attached to them. Is the patient at home in familiar surroundings? Lying in a strange street after an accident? Brought to the hospital, which is a massive, bewildering complex?—"hundreds" of people jammed in the waiting room of the public-health clinic or the bustling matter-of-factness of the emergency room both have enormous influence. The symptoms experienced at home that seemed so threatening are all relativized in the waiting room, where many others seem to be equally badly or worse off. Discussion of the symptoms with the doctor will therefore be relativized; both the discussion and the recounting of symptoms will be relativized by the doctor, who has seen—the patient thinks—many other such cases. As a consequence, there is a tendency on the part of the patient to dramatize the symptoms and their pain so that the doctor will notice that they are as genuine and special as the ones others

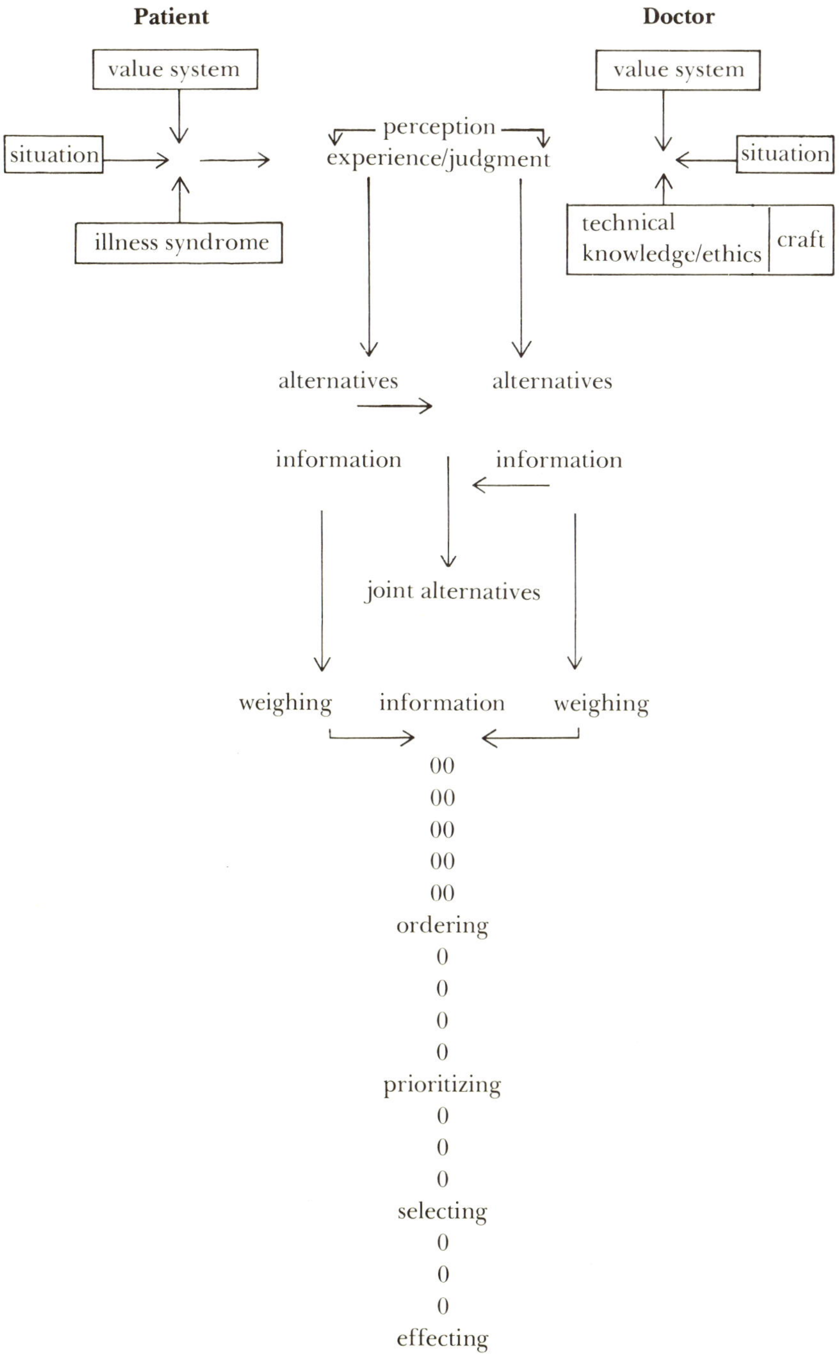
Patient
Doctor
value system
value system
situation
situation
illness syndrome
perception
experience/judgment
technical knowledge/ethics
craft
alternatives
alternatives
information
information
joint alternatives
weighing
information
weighing
00
00
00
00
00
ordering
0
0
0
0
prioritizing
0
0
0
selecting
0
0
0
effecting

experience. In other words, relativizing circumstances lead to a stronger demand for the doctor's attention.

(c) *Syndromes*—The form and content of the degree of dis-ease and the bundle of specific symptoms are most directly grasped in the introductory stages of the doctor-patient relationship, so that the doctor can form an initial impression. The ways in which dis-ease are grasped by the patient have been documented in the preceding chapter. All that needs to be underscored here is that these experiences are central to the presentation of symptoms by the patient.

2. The Doctor

(a) *Value System*—Just as with patients, doctors have a value and norm system that directs their life and determines their judgments. It is true that the doctor meets the patient as a functionary. But this function does not detract from the fact that the doctor is also a private person, not only encumbered with his cares and pleasures, but also infused with his goals and visions. He can recognize these just as patients can. In most cases these values do not surface, because they are not required by the nature of the doctor-patient relationship. However, the values become explicit in cases in which values can clash such as on the subjects of abortion and euthanasia, in which the doctor's values are inherently protected as well as the patient's.

(b) *Situation*—Confrontation occurs for the doctor as well as the patient, although in a different way. When the patient is at home he feels comfortable in his own setting, while the doctor is in a strange or at least different setting. On the other hand, being in a hospital can create in patients the feeling of being overwhelmed, because they do not fully comprehend its size and hidden organization; to the doctor, meanwhile, this is familiar "turf", so much so, that the hospital can have a dulling effect on his awareness of its impact on patients. Of additional importance for the doctor is that his setting encompasses a support system. This system not only includes the familiar routines and aids but also imparts support to the doctor through unspoken standards and environmental attributes, such that the doctor's function is given status and power. Aspects of the doctor-patient confrontation on the doctor's turf include the doctor's wearing his uniform while the patient wears the hospital gown; the examining table, at which the doctor stands while the patient lies down; the instrument cabinet, from which the doctor selects strange-looking items with obvious certainty while the patient can only guess their purpose.

(c) *Ethics*—The patient brings his symptoms to the relationship with the doctor; the doctor brings his theoretical knowledge and technical skill. There is yet another component, however, namely, the doctor's

Waiting room

professional ethics. Distinct from philosophical ethical theory, this system of ethics is a collection of standards and norms that describe the doctor's professional functions to the patient and society. Professional ethics is a network of procedural norms, agreements, and stipulations that has two desired effects: the patient is guaranteed a certain normative standard for his own security and the doctor is protected from unusual and extreme requests from the patient or society, thus establishing *his* security in the relationship. Professional ethics includes certain fixed activities (such as the standards of quality care), while excluding other activities (such as violating confidentiality). Although only infrequently, professional ethics can clash with a doctor's personal ethics and norms. Professionally justifiable requests for abortion, euthanasia, sterilization, and drugs can conflict with the personal vision of the man or woman who must function as a professional. These conflicts create personal ethical problems for professionals, irrespective of the ethical issues that arise between doctor, patient, and society. Suggestions that health professionals do away with their code, however, must be measured against the security guarantees the code provides for both patient and doctor.

(d) *Technological Knowledge and Skill*—Within both the ethical and technological realms, the doctor receives knowledge of the patient's complaints verbally as well as nonverbally. But if these complaints are too vague, too hard to classify, the doctor can attempt to get a clearer picture by employing an objectifying armamentarium. This armamentarium includes technical measurements and objective scientific knowledge about the symptoms and the patient's complaints. This process should result in an objective, nosological classification, a medical scientific translation of the patient's subjective complaints—a description of disease from the patient's dis-ease. Should such a classification still prove elusive, the doctor's impressions can then be checked against a specialist's, such as a radiological specialist or a biochemical analyst.

But to describe the process of decision making, reference to specialties is not essential. What is essential is how the doctor sorts out clear and obscure data by which he seeks objective support (through comparison with standards) for securing his impressions within a medical-technical schema of disease. His object is to arrange data in a nosological structure. Nosological closure (name giving) almost always implies a cadre of symptoms grouped as a syndrome; once a syndrome is identified one can usually trace the history from onset of the illness (etiology) and obtain indications for possible treatment (therapy).

What frequently happens is that the syndrome is unclear, some symptoms falling within it and some without. In the nosological sense, then, several possibilities or impressions must be considered. The doctor then must try several therapies or further tests to rule out various impressions. In this case, one cannot with certainty couple a syndrome with a particular etiology or be comparatively sure of a course of treatment.

From these considerations we can schematize the process of the workup as follows:

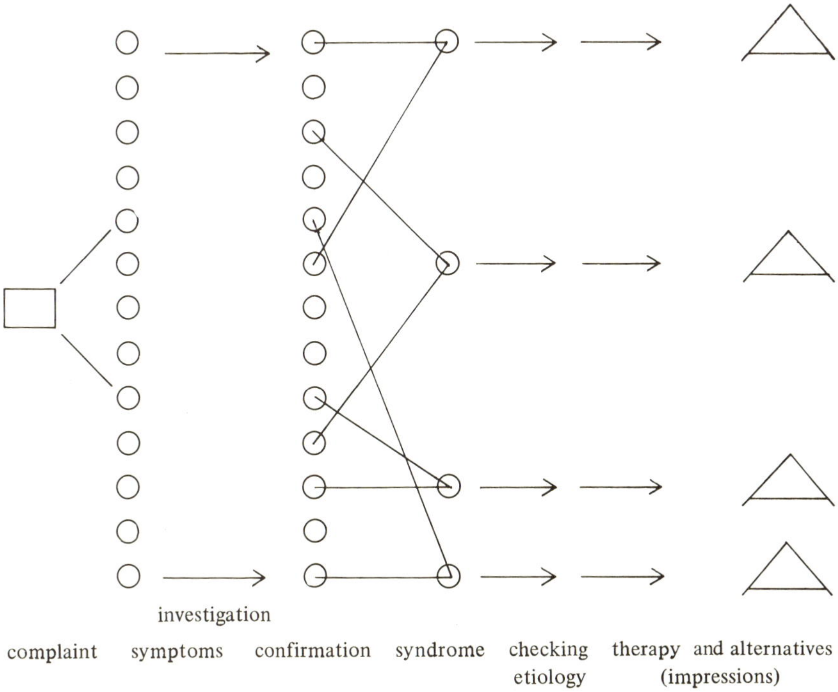

Nosological classification often leads, as we have said, to a number of alternatives, creating a so-called differential diagnosis. Because the system of medical classification is rigid, in the sense that it is based on a very strict causal line (cause—result—therapy), according to our schema one is faced not only with four possible diagnoses but also with four possible discrete etiologies and therapies. The choice can now be sharpened by resorting to further tests and, in some cases, trial therapies. During this period symptoms receive renewed attention or are approached differently, so that their importance within a set syndrome is either strengthened or ruled out. A more detailed discussion with the patient usually occurs at this point, so that certain etiological factors of some syndromes can be excised and, by consequence, certain syndromes and courses of therapy removed from consideration. Many

"Your number"

patients find this segment of the workup the most frustrating, because it appears to them that the doctor is stymied and is treating them by trial and error, when in fact a process of closure is taking place.

3. Perception

Before continuing to consider the process of clinical determination, it is important to note some parenthetical comments about perception. The way in which the process is to be considered further abstracts from the doctor-patient interaction—the way each views the other in the interaction and influence it. Thus, the structure of our consideration requires a discussion of material alterations arising from the interaction.

(a) *General Vision*—Either explicitly or implicitly present in the relationship, both doctor and patient have an overarching vision, a generalization, a generic judgment of each other. This judgment can vary from "the patient is necessary for my livelihood" to "the patient is a human totality who isn't functioning well right now and comes to me for help, which I can perhaps give him." Similarly, the patient's generic judgment can range from "the doctor is a good person, a figure of trust, in whom I can place my hope" to "the doctor exploits patients by listening too eagerly to complaints so he can get richer."

Thus, the "general vision" is a kind of stereotype that abstracts from the person here and now in the relation. It is an expectant attitude, which results *in fine* in the following judgments: "I was right" or "I was wrong."

(b) *Role*—As with generic judgment (distinct from *prejudging,* to which word we would attach the negative connotations of *judgment),* one can speak of the roles played in the relation as well as the roles persons assume at will. Both doctor and patient assume a role vis-à-vis the "other" on the basis of their generic judgment; that is to say, they take on a deportment toward each other that serves them best in the dualistic situation. As long as both judgments are maintained in the relationship, there is hardly a problem to speak of: both parties continue in the role each expects of the other. The tone and determinations in the relation do not change. The idea both partners have of the relation remains unchanged. There is no genuine problem even if both perceptions are negative—what happens in the interaction always confirms this negative judgment, leading precisely to the same determinations and no more.

Difficulties arise when either expectation creates dissonance in the other. It does not matter which party offends in this regard. Doubts lead to a desire to break the contract, despite the status of the doctor or the dependency of the patient. Clearly most desirable would be a "meta-communication," a dialogue about roles, judgments, and prejudices, which might reconstitute the relation on more congruent mutual expectations. Such a dialogue is rarely encountered. More often, both parties seem to resist each other by "growing into" the assigned role.

(c) *Status*—The doctor has his status, indeed, a very high status. To a patient with a slightly flattering generic judgment of doctors, the doctor acquires an even more substantial status, in part because of his historical standing in the community, in part because of his power, obtained as it is from presumed knowledge and skill with respect to the burdens of human life. Today it is clear that historical standing in the community is less important to patients than it once was, mostly because of urbanization and social dislocation. By the same token, the public stands in less awe of increased knowledge, because such knowledge nowadays does not undergird social status. In every case, medical knowledge is more critically examined by the public than it was in earlier times. Only the skill and art of the physician can guarantee him status in modern society. We will address this point in the conclusion of the chapter.

(d) *Dependence*—In addition to the actual dependence of the patient there is a projected dependency, chiefly related to the status of the doctor. Actual dependence arises from the fact that a seriously ill patient has no one but the doctor to whom to turn for help. Projected dependency has to do with a perception of power predominantly outside specific technical competency; it is power in a normative sense.

It is not just a question of projecting. There are many doctors who, on the basis of their art, attempt to acquire power over patients that exceeds the bounds of their calling or specific function, and which certainly is unacceptable to patients who object to it.

Finally, another aspect of dependency is indirect dependence, which appears during examinations (especially in the examination room); in waiting room, and while the patient moves from lab to lab on those colored lines in the hospital. It also arises when the patient, in the most literal sense, is subject to management strategy. One can detect an almost hangdog expression and dependent demeanor in patients during these interactions.

(e) *Interaction*—Interaction between the doctor and patient is largely determined by the perceptions already discussed. Information is passed verbally and nonverbally, intentionally and unintentionally. That this interaction only infrequently approaches a level of open dialogue ought to be made clear. The factors contributing to this problem stem from the fact that patients experience their complaints differently in the here and now. By the same token, the complaints are determined by individual perception and the level of doctor-patient interaction, such that their presentation can be positively or negatively influenced. Similarly, a contribution is made by the doctor through his perceptions, his manner, and the level of the interation at the moment; these in turn influence decisions about arranging the respective complaints in a certain order. The doctor is obligated to make decisions in the most objective way possible. With respect to the interaction, this means that in fact two persons with similar but not completely complementary goals interact. And they interact with wholly different attitudes with respect to each other, the interaction itself, and the problem (illness) to which the interaction is addressed. Small wonder, then, that complete openness in dialogue rarely occurs. The doctor-patient relation is thus governed by different social conventions and rules than the serious conversation between friends and acquaintances.

B. INFORMATION

We now turn to the following problem. In the dialogue between the doctor and patient the latter must try to make his complaints clear and orderly, even though he is a product of a social setting and unique experiences—family, schooling, work—all of which influence his perception and presentation. The subjective patient experience, expressed more or less in faulty personal language, must be the stuff from which the doctor forms an opinion. That is to say, from the everyday language of the patient the physician must translate the subjective experience of dis-ease into medical jargon and scientific classification: the disease.

The patient also furnishes information to the doctor tinged with an everyday suspicion of causes ("I've got pain in my side, here, and sometimes it appears all the way around to my back, here. I think it must be appendicitis"). Simultaneously, the physician also considers alternatives ("Where precisely in your side do you experience the pain? Do you have more pain in your back in the morning? Yes? Well, then, we shouldn't make too much out of this. I don't think it's your appendix, because if it were you'd have more pain over here"). Information is colored by what we think, what we conjecture. Thus the doctor's information about possible etiology is weighted by his desire to clarify possible diagnostic alternatives ("You've been drinking a lot, working overtime, and you've already had trouble with your gallbladder once before"). And physicians must translate patient language to gain an understanding of the complaint, but they are also constrained to translate their own medical language into terms comprehensible to the patient for a true exchange of information.

In this way both doctor and patient, acting in tandem, can arrive at the alternatives from which, through the doctor's linking of syndrome and etiology, the weight of probability comes to rest on an identifiable disease.

C. WEIGHING ALTERNATIVES

Weighing alternatives is at once an individual activity and a joint one. The patient offers his perspective on the newly articulated alternatives. This perspective includes his own "order of preferences," that is, an order that reveals what is most acceptable or endurable to him with respect to his values and life experience. The most threatening possibilities are, for the most part, considered last and furthest away in the range of alternatives. More tangible and less threatening possibilities are given prominence in this order of preferences. In other words, the patient cannot be expected to assess possibilities according to medical realities, but rather according to his subjective experience. The doctor tries to present a range of medical probabilities according to a weight of more or less clearly presented indicators. From this further tests and consultations are requested to gain better evidence. Both parties put their cards on the table, as it were: both present their perception of the range of alternatives, including their own criteria, often unexpressed, of the order within that range. Physicians should remember that patients have different criteria, sometimes resistant to the truth, regarding the order of possibilities at this point.

D. ORDERING, PRIORITIZING, AND CHOOSING

1. Ordering

The clinical-determination process reaches a more definitive stage when both parties seriously consider arguments for a jointly acceptable ranking of possibilities (one hopes they will succeed; often they do not!). In this phase the doctor should have gained an appreciation of the patient's life situation so that he can identify and understand the patient's priorities and bring the patient around to a more objective consideration. With this approach by the doctor, the patient gains some distance from his complaints, and the medical priorities can be examined more rationally. Gaining a more objective perspective is important throughout the process, but it is essential at this step. The success at distancing will have telling results in a joint "clinical judgment" during this phase. The doctor should not be the sole judge. The patient gains more and more distance from subjective complaints during the dialogue preceding this phase, and from viewing his case through the eyes of the doctor. Since prioritizing preferably rests on "objective" criteria, this is the only way to obtain patient participation in the process.

The step of prioritizing is real only if it occurs on the basis of "degrees of probability," and authentic only if the patient achieves some distance from those degrees high on the list. If the patient is not at this level of sophistication, the prioritizing done by the doctor will be summarily shut out, rejected. It will be all the more difficult subsequently to address that patient's objectivity and re-engage him in the process. It is therefore preferable during the clinical-determination procedures that the physician offer as much information to the patient as possible, gain as much as is needed from the patient, and make his information understandable to the patient. This means nothing less than active and joint labor; it is not achieved through passive objectivity about the patient. Nevertheless, the process is hard for most patients, because they must achieve distance not only from their subjective complaints, but also from their social situation, and even from their own bodies (Cf. E. Cassell, "Disease as an It," cited at the end of chapter two). With respect to this last point a great deal depends on the seriousness of the complaint, the period of time in which it appeared, the moment it gained the patient's attention, and its perceived implications, now and for the future.

2. Prioritizing

The joint effort to organize possibilities is the clinical imperative, the need to make a choice from among the alternatives in order to help the patient. Such imperative presupposes that the order or range of possibilities be ranked according to what must be done first, second, and so on. Thus, prioritizing has a pragmatic aim. Once again, information about actual steps of action must be passed on to the patient in understandable language. At this stage, for example, the seriousness of the required tests can further exacerbate the anxiety of the patient, even though the tests must be employed to gain diagnostic and therapeutic closure. If an EKG or simple blood test might furnish the same data as a cardiac catheterization, it makes sense to pursue the less drastic course first. When one can accomplish a real partnership with the patient in prioritizing steps of alternatives, then it is much easier to discuss and clarify the consequence of the course of action pursued with that patient. It is, in fact, not unthinkable that the results of the action steps could easily provide the basis for a reassessment of the jointly determined plan; both doctor and patient would be engaged in the reassessment as the results came in. A clash of principles in such a case would most likely be improbable.

3. Choice and Effecting

Once a prioritized schema is established by a ranking of alternatives and their test results, a definitive choice can be made. Only organizational difficulties should intrude on the list of priorities developed by the physician and the patient. In the final analysis these are assumed in the definitive choices: When can the tests be done? When is the operating room available? When can the patient get his affairs in shape to enter the hospital? And so on. Some changes in priorities may be necessitated by available space in the hospital. But these considerations are not essential to the decision-making process. Usually they have little impact on effecting a clinical determination.

REVIEW OF THE LITERATURE

The literature about the decision-making process in the doctor-patient relation represents three separate concerns: the doctor-patient relation itself, patient-oriented information, and the procedures for forming decisions. Although our focus throughout the chapter has been on the psychological aspects of these concerns and not so much on the philosophical, linguistic, and logical aspects, a brief review of all the literature is in order.

R. Kertész (1970) applied the model of transactional analysis to the doctor-patient relation. Participants in communication as seen within the theory of transactional analysis are labeled adults (open, deliberating), parents (closed, authoritarian, normative), or children (passive, dependent, listening). He then recounted the frequency of parent-child interactions, parent-adult, and so on, according to the familiar schema:

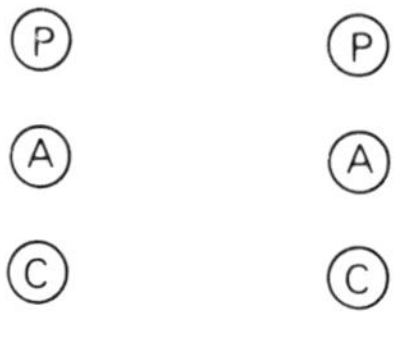

These data are important when we consider that clinical determination must advance on a level of mutual respect. A parent-child interaction reduces the likelihood of such respect and joint dialogue. Nurturing in the parent-child interaction seems to appear with greater frequency than in an adult-adult interaction, especially among specialists in medicine, including psychiatrists. The degree of patient responsiveness and the seriousness of condition sometimes determine the degree of medical paternalism, but often do not.

It is hard to formulate a negative generalization about clinical interaction from Kertész's study, because the ideal adult-adult relation, viewed by us as essential to clinical determination, does sometimes appear. Kertész describes the classic curative relation following the P-C mode as one in which feedback from the patient is seldom elicited and communication may be "interposed" (in the sense of substituted) by drugs and technical apparatus.

That alternatives to this classic relation do occur can be seen from a recent concern for a new understanding of medicine and a more historical comprehension of the sources of the medical model. The English psychiatrist A. H. Crisp, who spent considerable time on the doctor-patient relation, offered the following formulation of this newer vision of medicine:

> This view emphasizes a multifactorial etiology, still with a constitutional basis, but with experiential factors, interpersonal as well as inanimate, shaping and imprinting all aspects of body behavior with broad genetic limits. Psychic, behavioral and visceral responses become related in an experientially meaningful way to each other and to the environment, and some of them, through maladaption, may leave the individual vulnerable to breakdown and ultimately to disease if chronically or recurrently stressed (1970, p. 14).

Crisp suggests a multifactorial analysis not only with respect to the origins of disease but also with respect to a theory of the doctor-patient relation: "The nature of the doctor-patient relationship appears to be complexly compounded of a number of cultural, social and personal interacting factors" (p. 14). With this the problematic of the decision-making process is brought into another and broader perspective.

Multifactorial aspects are central both to the process and to the conditions under which it occurs. Rarely in medicine or clinical psychology is there an explicit discussion of the decision-making process, which is not so true for industrial or economic psychology. We should briefly take a closer look at these fields to which Crisp's observations are equally applicable.

C. L. Menting (1976), who builds his case on an earlier work by J. W. Thibaut and H. H. Kelly (1959), consistently attempts to make clear how the conduct of external organization and interaction between those concerned influences the process of forming decisions. He reveals a propensity for accenting external structure, especially as this relates to role expectation in the relation (Menting; Thibaut and Kelly). M. Mulder (1958) stresses the interaction itself, independent of content, believing the interaction structure is more important than the communication structure.

In this regard P. H. Admiraal's (1976, following S. Toulmin) distinction between causal conduct and rational conduct is interesting. He holds that everything we do has causes. And some of these have reasons too. It follows that rational behavior, behavior backed by reasons, displays elements of a learning process. Learning processes that imitate human conduct are seen to function with respect to the individual and the decisions to be made; they are processes that rest on individual experience in the foregoing decision-and-choice-loaded situations (in the industrial psychology literature these learning processes are mostly related to choosing certain products through advertising). Thus, in most decision and choice processes, goes the argument, individual experience and learned behavior are the backbone. However, this concentration on individual experience and learned behavior raises a valid question regarding the applicability of the processes to the doctor-patient relation. A great many patients have not "learned" how to relate to doctors, or how to participate in the clinical-determination process. For this reason, F. Hansen's (1972, pp. 195 ff.) model would presumably be better suited in these specific situations. In this model Hansen discerns the decision-making process as a series of conflicts in which each conflict, each moment of the series, can be studied from a number of different standpoints.

1. The circumstances initiating the conflict;
2. The amount of perceived conflict aroused at the onset of the process;
3. The acceptable amount of conflict;
4. The alternatives that are considered;
5. The salient value structure;
6. The beliefs relating alternatives with values;
7. The information acquired;
8. The choice principle applied;
9. The alternative chosen;
10. The amount of conflict immediately following the choice;
11. The extent and nature of post-choice processes;
12. Behavioral consequences of the choice (action taken);
13. Cognitive consequences of the choice (information stored in memory, modification of values and beliefs, and the like).

In this model, the amount of conflict is independent of the range of information, the options or alternatives present and clearly understood, and the endurance of either the conflict or the value system. After more intensive study, it seems that the model might be able to incorporate many relevant factors in the doctor-patient relation.

According to Hansen (1972), continuing the decision process depends almost exclusively on motivation. Resolutions of the consequent conflicts appear on the basis of cognitive processes and experience; were resolutions less problematic, the learning-process character of the doctor-patient relation would be clearer. The patient's cognitions, without doubt, have less to do with learning processes (for those are too minuscule to be perceived) than with the extent of information given. Thus, F. Hansen (1972) follows a general line of thought (like that found in Gagne) regarding other decision models, to wit: 1) problem identification (in our context, information is required for this component), 2) collection of information, 3) evaluation and concept formation (in our context, the illumination of alternatives), 4) decision, and 5) a post-decisional factor (a sort of evaluation after decision, important for the learning process).

Moreover, we should add at this point in the consideration a survey of the many different ways doctors and patients present themselves to one another, some of which have been covered in the chapter. These could conceivably be laid out independent of the distinctive background, with respect to external organization, environmental influences, and roles, which are emphasized by social psychology. But the patient is inexperienced in decision procedures with regard to his own suffering as a subjective datum; the doctor, by the same token, takes this suffering as routine and is much more object-oriented.

Hence, the doctor can easily orient himself to more traditional decision techniques, in the sense that H. A. Simon (1960) uses them. According to Simon for the doctor it is a question of the usual, administrative routine, and standardized work methods whereby medical decisions belong ("programatically") to routine and from which special procedures are developed. However, the patient's inexperience leads to decisions that are "momentous" and "poorly structured," mostly undergirded by "general procedures" or analogues from other kinds of situations. Even if the patient is familiar with decision procedures in other settings, in this situation he is unprepared and mystified by the subjective character of his own messages, the unfamiliarity of the setting, and the specific interaction with the doctor, so as, without some help, to be totally inert.

Yet Simon as well as Hansen and the other authors all emphasize the importance of conveying information that clarifies the decision and offers more "satisfaction" to the one who is deciding. Note here the psychological reason for the ethical obligation of informed consent. On this point there is more literature that relates directly to patients.

J. Skipper and R. C. Leonard (1968) have argued that involving parents in the clinical determination and management of children requires attention to relevant information about the parents' and children's relationship, especially the stress ("conflict" in Hansen's sense) arising from parent-child interactions. This attention has positive consequences for the child's recovery, including the child's behavior once home from the hospital: less fever, quicker healing after surgery, fewer complications, fewer nightmares. C. A. Lindeman and B. van Aernham (1971) observed the same effect in adult surgical patients: greater specific information before the operation led to less anxiety, less pain after the operation, fewer complications, and quicker recovery. An almost classic study is that of P. A. Tryon and R. C. Leonard (1966). In this study of gynecological patients, remarkably greater cooperation was obtained by increasing the amount of specific information offered to the patient, leading to a smoother and much more pleasant physical examination; both patients and doctors found this patient-oriented approach far more satisfactory than the usual one. An increase of information leads to an improvement of patient participation and decision making—in transactional-analysis terms, the P-C relation is replaced by the A-A relation.

The conclusion is inescapable. Information not only is essential to resolving conflicts (Hansen), to facilitating the decision process by setting alternatives in greater relief, but it also helps patients move from a subjective to a more objective stance, through which both physicians and patients can center on the issues with a similar focus. The interaction thus acquires an entirely different character from dependency. The patient may now work with the doctor in making a mutual decision, which for psychological, medical, and ethical reasons is essential.

CONCLUSION

By way of conclusion we should note that our interest in the subject of clinical determination focuses less on the logic of clinical judgment in the philosophical sense (cf. references) and more on the psychological effects of mutual decision making. The procedure described in this chapter is an ideal far from reality in many doctor-patient relationships, and we would be remiss if we did not touch on one aspect of clinical determination that we have only glanced before: power. Whereas the decision-making process is rarely described in the literature, power is even more infrequently treated, except as it appears in the question of medical paternalism.

The cause of this situation is not hard to find. Knowledge creates power, even as power obtains knowledge. This is almost axiomatic in medicine.

Knowledge of the life process and the causes of its termination, and knowledge of the art of continuing life in the face of threatening conditions, have given physicians enormous power and positions of authority throughout the ages in every culture. The witch doctor's position, with his feather dress and tinkling bells, is hardly worth distinguishing in this respect from the position of the modern physician, in his white coat, with his stethoscope hanging from his neck. They both have the ability to influence life and death. All other human beings share an inability to do this. The authority of the doctor, as a result, seems untouchable. Thus, patients who value their lives more than other concerns are ready and willing to submit to the doctor's knowledge and craft.

We do not wish to discuss here the misuses of the doctor's power over patients, except to note that such power must sooner or later have an enormous influence on the development of the doctor's personality. It is equally obvious that this power will consequently have its influence on the behavior of patients.

The distance between doctor and patient is largely determined by the former's art. Even when the difference in knowledge is not that great, the art still creates distance. Should the patient on these grounds overperceive the doctor's power and oversubmit to it, the relation tilts toward an extreme that is not, strictly speaking, necessary. The mutual expectations concerning the different roles in the relation create continuity and strengthen already existing distances between the parties.

In such an extreme form there is "no problem" with respect to decision; the "victim" knows nothing and can do nothing. At the other extreme, the doctor knows all and can do all. The decision lies with the knower, the one possessing all the knowledge. With him and him alone rests the decision. The doctor might see his authority weaken were he to involve the "submitter" in any decision, so he is little inclined to do so.

Despite the occurrence of this model in Western culture, some change is taking place. There are a number of reasons for this. First, although people still value their lives more than other things, prosperity and modern technology have contributed to questions about the *quality* of life: life must be conducted with a certain minimum standard to make it livable and worthwhile. The power simply to prolong life, therefore, is not always viewed as positive. Indeed, some negative judgments are currently made about those who unduly seek power.

Secondly, knowledge is widespread among the populace of Western countries; it is no longer the possession of a few, thanks to universal education, radio, television, and so on. Thus, the extremes in knowledge between the schooled and the unschooled have become noticeably less, and the faith in doctors' knowledge has to a certain extent deteriorated. The period of medical fairy tales is ending.

The doctor's art, of course, still should be emphasized in any comparison with patients. However on the basis of newly widespread knowledge, even the art is viewed more critically than ever before by a greater number of people. More so than in the past, the patient is able to draw comparisons, especially on the basis of information he has learned. He may even have some knowledge of techniques, albeit not a working knowledge.

In the third place, as a result of increased specialization, patients come into contact with a far greater number of doctors than was formerly the case. Patients therefore have more data upon which to base comparisons, even when these data stem merely from human contact. Consequently, the power of any one doctor over a patient has become diluted.

Fourthly, through the influence of social and behavioral sciences, the vision of man in the health professions has become increasingly integrated, such that one is inclined to consider more multi-causal and multi-conditional etiologies for disease than were possible within the traditional medical model, which was essentially materialistic. This developing vision has brought to light lacunae in the doctor's knowledge, and the absolute power of the doctor is accordingly diminished.

Finally, our view of society tends toward a universal spreading of knowledge and, therefore, of power. In this social view, any assumption by an individual of absolute power is implicitly suspect, because it impedes the ideal of freedom that is at the very heart of social development.

When a doctor assumes power, it is not necessarily deterimental to medicine. However the assumption of power should be coupled with increased responsibility. Normally, one in power does not have to answer to a subordinate. But one who professes to heal in our cultural context must be confronted with the necessity for responsible behavior toward patients and a defense of his insights about disease. This means that a more horizontal dialogue must be established with patients.

It is within this context that the process of clinical determination, with its emphasis on coequal dialogue and mutual decision making, has been presented in this chapter. It is presented as an ideal, with a discussion of variations and impediments. Medicine need not change. What needs to be changed is the way in which it is practiced.

4. Dis-Ease Workup

In chapter two we spoke of the first effects of dis-ease. We now turn our attention to the workup of dis-ease, focusing for this purpose on patients' assimilation of their illness. In addition to aspects that relate directly to the life-world of the patient, we will discuss a number of environmental factors variously influencing not only the way the patient experiences dis-ease but also the way he assimilates this experience. Describing these, in effect, creates a workup of dis-ease, an assessment for treatment.

A. DISCONGRUITY WITH ONE'S OWN BODY

As already suggested, the patient should be viewed as a whole person, an individual totality experiencing each instance of life. We found relevant to this view the phenomenological idea of gestalt and body-image central to subjectivity, as expressed in the writings of J. de Jonge (1956), G. Marcel (1958), and M. Merleau-Ponty (1945).

However, consulting the literature is insufficient both to perceive and to verify how patients experience their own unity, or how this unity is disrupted during illness. Clinical examples are necessary, because they demonstrate that patients feel incomplete, not the way they wish to be. A discongruity arises between what patients were before and what they are now: patients compare themselves with *how* they were, not *whom* they were, and find themselves altered in a significant way. Their picture of themselves no longer suffices; the previous image only calls attention to the ways in which they have now changed.

Incongruence is a temporal experience based upon what has occurred in the past. It is not only a present condition but rather is almost always related to a previously developed image about the self, which highlights what has been lost. Most of all, it is incomplete. Incongruence quells identity. It is a painful dis-ease of equilibrium and identity. Sometimes it can be revelatory, helping the patient find himself in a new status; even though this is unsettling, it is less unsettling than the painful disequilibrium immediately preceding. More often than not, however, this revelation does not occur. Instead, incongruity due to disrupted balance is difficult to overcome, precisely because it is not easy to place and carries with it no message. The patient is not in a state to discern the whys and wherefores leading to incongruence; he cannot fill the vacuum in himself from his own resources. In the patient's concrete world this demands an exceptional power of concentration on the processes occurring in his body. It is an ability he does not have, the ability to decipher the events responsible for his current condition of discongruity, his destroyed equilibrium. No balance can come from imbalance.

Moreover, there seem to be a number of mechanisms at work that influence the destroyed balance for good and for ill. Two of these mechanisms, guilt and aggression, play a large role in righting the patient's balance, being directly related to the concept of causality, to be discussed first.

1. Causality

We encounter a mistrust in one's own body in every sick person, in every injured patient. The body has come under the influence of unknown forces that cause disease or help cure it, impede or impel the processes at work. Even the expert has only recently been able to apply names to these forces; the patient may not as yet be able to do so. The expert is aware of a few more or less objective facts within his limited and very specialized point of view. From these he offers information about what has taken place or is now taking place in the body.

Nevertheless, even the expert can barely articulate what is going on in most cases. At this stage it is not clear which invisible forces are at work, or whether a certain process is in a downward or upward course. One wound may heal, another may not: no one knows exactly why. One kind of illness may be discussed as a familiar unity, another may not admit of such a complete description and keeps experts in the dark. The patient, meanwhile, though given certain information, is in most cases inexpert about such processes, and finds the course of events even more enigmatic than does the specialist. Another cause of this bafflement is that the patient often has only a weak awareness of his own body: he does not see what is happening under the bandages; he cannot "read" his X-rays; he only feels bad and suffers from vague impressions. He is the victim of a partially strange body that has taken over a portion of his life, pursuing its own course without appeal to his usual control.

With a healthy body one can experiment, one can command, one has it somewhat in control. One is identical to one's healthy body. With illness the body pursues its own path, placing itself beyond control. (That the processes automatically pursue their own course in normal circumstances is not important. One pays little or no attention to them—then they are assumed into the normal image. Only in illness do they become the object of attention.) One is overwhelmed by intangible forces; one cannot guess what game is being played, because the rules have changed. Confronted by a situation like this, one responds with suspicion, reservation, apprehension, anxiety, and mistrust.

The familiarity with one's identity, implicit in normal activities, is ruptured; that identity has fled, together with the healthy life. Shall I be cured, the patient wonders, and if so, how? Shall I completely recover from being a patient or remain visibly hampered? If the latter, what effect will this have on my life?

If I am to recover, the sick ask themselves, what is going on in my body? How long will it last? Will I die? For almost all patients this kind of uncertainty takes command of their life. They become preoccupied with what is not known and what will happen.

It seems to be a general rule that patients afflicted in this situation seek certitude: the cause. Patients struggle to gain clarity, to grasp what has happened to them. Perhaps the ability to grasp the process aids in removing a portion of its threat: by conceptualizing a cause, structuring can begin, a structuring that attains some viewpoint, that contributes some measure of recovered equilibrium, that creates some degree of relief. Indeed, certainty can offer relief even if it is negative (Rumke, 1954). This is a truth that surely applies beyond psychopathology.

Establishing a causal relation in most cases is easier for accident victims than for the ill. For the latter it is harder to identify a concrete cause, much less a concrete agent. Sometimes it is the patient himself; at other times it might be another, a group, or even society itself. While it is true that accident victims also ask "why me?," it is also true that they can answer the question by reference to a sequence of events. As a result they can direct their aggression toward the agent responsible in this sequence.

For the sick, however, especially the chronically sick patients with arthritis, cancer, the causal question is far more burning and persistent. The search for the elusive cause is so predominant that for them it leads endlessly to self-blame. The question "Why me?" seems to terminate only in "Because I. . . ." Speaking with patients, health professionals have seen to what irrational lengths patients will go in positing themselves as the cause of their illness. Self-blame, depression, and apathy often go hand in hand.

Sometimes these guilt feelings in the ill are portioned out to others in the environment. Thus, husbands of women with breast or uterine cancer often labor under self-doubt with regard to their supposed part in the course of events. We know of a not unusual case of a wife blaming herself years after her husband died of cancer of the spleen, because when they were first married she had hit him on the chest during an argument. This case and many like it demonstrate the power of the causal connection in tragic illnesses.

2. Aggression

With the possible exception of self-inflicted accidents (driving under the influence of alcohol), in which the cause is clearly oneself, accident victims direct their aggression outward, to a guilty party who can continue his life while they are lying in the hospital. The ability to make this causal relation offers the patient a concrete possibility to localize at least part of his discongruity, and almost forces him to pursue an equilibrium recovery.

The advantage this type of patient enjoys over the victim of disease is that he can direct his anger, his disappointment, *outward*. He thereby establishes and maintains communication channels with the external world, no matter how negative. Even an aggressive bond with the external world is extremely important during the period when introversion constitutes a real danger to every patient.

The ability to assimilate and express aggression is diametrically opposed to that of the patient chronically confined to the hospital. Aggression is "intentionality directed outwards" and is usually directed toward some object. It is goal behavior. But within the long-term hospital situation everything is oriented inward. Pain makes patients self-oriented; immobility impedes any tendency toward externally directed activity; fatigue inhibits action. The body's intention to express aggression, manifesting itself in muscular tension, might serve only to increase pain. So this path is also cut off. Finally, the concrete goal toward which the aggression should be directed, the object of aggression, is not present. It is outside.

The apparent advantage enjoyed by the accident victim is diminished by the degree of trauma and confinement, as in this case:

Case X

A fifty-two-year-old man had a fractured hip, the result of a coworker's mishandling of a dragline during an excavation. One afternoon this hospitalized patient suddenly requested a different doctor. That morning he had said to his orthopedic surgeon that he found the process of recovery was taking far too long and that the doctor did nothing but stand by his bed, pull on the

> pulley, and tell him that he must be patient. "But I don't give a damn. It doesn't do me any good. If this is a way to earn one's money, it doesn't work." The physician "had some words" with him, telling the patient he must stop complaining, that he surely must see that he was still alive, and that there were people who still wanted to help him, despite his "big mouth." The patient could help himself most by resting in bed and cooperating with the physical therapy when the time came. The patient's request for another doctor was put in a letter to the medical director, who in turn passed it on to the doctor in question. Two days later the battle between the patient and doctor was at an end; the patient was placed under the care of another physician. As it turned out, this relation was better, because the new doctor could explain to a somewhat rough and bellicose patient what was happening in his own language, telling him the truth without being belligerent.

It seems clear that for the patient described there was only one course of action available, verbal aggression. This aggression was most easily directed against the doctor on his case. The doctor was experienced by the patient as an adequate object of aggression, because the doctor poked, cut, amputated if need be. He thus seemed to take an aggressive stance toward the patient, and could be viewed as a natural extension of the accident.

However, a patient examines his verbal aggression after almost every exchange ("This man is trying to help me, make me better. Why am I doing this to him?"). Thus, a great deal of ambivalence about the doctor is felt, ambivalence that causes some confusion in the patient when he attacks the doctor. If this ambivalence is undetected by the doctor it leads to no solution of the problem; the patient might be fearful that the doctor will retaliate with aggression against other parts of the body. (N.B. A patient's relationship with surgeons is of a different order from that with internists, for the latter are not perceived as cutting into the body). Health professionals and physicians who can recognize and deal with patient aggression can greatly help the patient work out his problems. If, on the other hand, patients perceive that aggression is prohibited—when, for example, the patient's dependency on the doctor is stressed ("you had better be thankful")—they suffer greater risk of withdrawal and apathy.

3. Guilt Feelings

Just as an accident victim, especially when deprived of aggressive avenues, is beset by guilt feelings, so are patients who suffer an illness, only more so. For these patients, as noted earlier, the cause of their ailment is less clear than for an accident victim, and specific agents, or "guilty parties," cannot be identified. Again, it is extremely important that the causal process take place, so that patients can maintain external channels of communication, which are essential for re-establishing equilibrium. Many people with illness, unable to identify the agent of their misery, resort to looking for the cause in themselves. One could argue that such patients really are not beset by guilt, but rather by self-doubt, which is misconstrued as guilt when the situation seems ripe for it. Certainly, patients' self-doubt is often occasioned by the reality of their situation, but the unreal doubts that also occur are the culprits behind unreal guilt feelings in a deadly vicious circle. Both unreal doubts and guilt feelings feed on each other, as in this case:

Case XI

The patient is a fifty-nine-year-old woman with an advanced carcinoma; her central nervous system is involved to such an extent that she is now completely paralyzed. She is very depressed and withdrawn from her environment, husband, and children. It is especially difficult to establish any contact with her. As a child her pastor and parents had often warned her against the dangers of masturbation, a serious "sin" that would lead most certainly to a number of diseases. Yet since she was seventeen years old she had not been able to control her impulses and became a "sinner" a number of times. She is possessed with the idea that God's punishment has now been visited on her and that she has let both God and her parents down, not to speak of her husband and children. She should not have married after her "mistakes," and is now convinced that the disease she brought upon herself will be passed on to her children.

While it may be true that the eventual discovery of "the" cause may result in some peace ("I know it now"), the circle is only closed. The accent now rests on unreal doubts about oneself, thus strengthening self-directed tendencies and *prohibiting* communication outside of oneself.

This "self-anchoring" seems to occur most in patients faced with many unsolvable problems. Thus, the man who blames his lung cancer on the fact that he smoked too much and the arthritic patient who blames his disease on a chilly house where he lived are more "approachable" than the patient with metastatic carcinoma of the uterus who places the blame of her disease on two sexual contacts she had with friends before her marriage. The former guilt feelings are slightly more realistic than the latter.

A similar thought demands some further discussion before the conclusion of this section, the idea that one's sins and guilt can be passed on through generations. This bizarre idea is often encountered in depressive states. What makes the idea dangerous is its certitude—patients acquire a closed mind about such a causal chain and are thereby all the less approachable. Such patients are all the more prone to misinterpret events in their environment as verifying the idea. In this way the patient's self-respect is often heavily chained to the actual course of the disease.

To conclude: Despite a patient's compliance while the treatment regimen is going on, professional attention must consider the very real possibility that the patient may not actually be so tranquil and agreeable. The patient may be filled with aggression and guilt feelings, which contribute to the dis-ease.

4. Ambivalence

The aggression of the accident victim is directed outward, the aggression of the sick inward. Both suffer the vulnerability of ambivalent feelings about themselves as patients. Chief among these are the urge to lay bare their feelings, on the one hand, and the concomitant fear that an inaccurate interpretation of their feelings may contribute to increased risk in which their bond of communication may be broken or anger may be directed against them as patients. Among the sick one finds the fear of this risk so inhibiting that they tend to redirect the aggression as guilt feelings and self-doubt, both of which contribute to their apathy and, in some cases, suicidal depression.

What we wish to emphasize, however, is the presence of a fundamental ambivalence; perhaps it would be better to call it an existential ambivalence in which one category of patients overcome the ambivalence in an outward show of aggression, and the other category of patients focus on themselves. Both the ambivalence and the direction of feelings are influenced to a great extent by external circumstances.

5. Egocentrism

Ambivalence occurs not only in feelings about oneself and the environment. It also occurs with respect to one's temporal perspective.

The past is most often experienced through the routines of life, the humdrum marks of daily existence. But these marks, though commonplace, are in fact very important, for they contribute familiar, recognizable landmarks to one's existence. In so doing, they also guarantee a measure of security and peace in a changing world. One can put one's trust in these landmarks; the certainty of one's existence is assured by them. How else to explain the consternation when the lights go out, or the water stops running? Or notice how upset people get when the train they take every day does not come one morning. For the patient *all* these secure facets of existence are unalterably changed during an illness. They cannot be used in the usual way.

Only the self remains. However, even about the self, doubts occur. The body that normally circumscribes the self is no longer what it was; it has become an unknown in the equation. What can be done with it now? What is going on in the body?

Such uncertainties, such undermining of one's existence, often impede any use of past experience as a guide to the future, particularly those past experiences that are necessary for creating some security. Existence has now become too uncertain, too fraught with question marks, for any useful attempt to establish a sense of security based on either the past or the future.

A number of unsettling factors lead to a crisis that for most patients issues in the question "Why me?" Among the factors are existential uncertainty and its threat; ambivalent feelings, which often cannot be expressed; and mistrust of one's own body, even though it still represents a part of the self. This many-sided crisis of the "I," the self, leads to an even deeper question than the one about the cause of the accident or illness, though it, too, is based on an effort to obtain some causal responsibility. This deeper question is "Why have I," this person lying here, been "chosen" to bear this burden? It is the most fundamental question the sick or injured will ever ask themselves during their impairment, and they must wrestle with it, even though there is no answer. Whereas in the search for the cause of a concrete condition one may be able to find an answer—real or imagined—it is much more difficult to discover an answer to the question "Why me?" The question strikes a blow at the base of one's existence, because it is a question about the very existence of an "I," as well as about the meaning of existence in a more general sense.

Not every patient, of course, can formulate the question so clearly and so consciously wrestle with possible answers, but all patients are confronted with the crisis contained in the question and undergo the feelings accompanying it. One patient may pursue the exisentential question "Why me?" with "What is the meaning for me and for others?" Another may brush the question off, and in an exalted and carefree manner attempt to demonstrate to himself and others that the problem means nothing to him.

Not to flee in the face of this question means that one is placed in an essential confrontation with oneself. For some, the confrontation can lead to a foundering sense of reality, almost a psychotic episode. For most, however, the question usually focuses on misperceived ideas of guilt and sinfulness. And for others, the confrontation can even be quite salutary—camouflaged by the commonplace "You only go around once in life," the question exacts an assessment of one's life, which can teach patients life's importance in their day to day existence. In this case, an illness can be a profound learning experience.

During the crisis the patient may try to address the important external affairs of life but is always drawn back in on the self. Thus, he or she tends to become depressed and excessively preoccupied with the self. There is no period in the process of an illness when the concrete environment means less, or, more precisely, is of such relative unimportance, than during this crisis phase. The strong self-centeredness characterizing this period, the intensity of ego preoccupation, not infrequently means that things once valued in the environment have diminished in importance. These things are dismissed, sloughed off in favor of ego reconstruction. Sometimes patients lose so much awareness of the material environment that "healthy" persons in the surrounding may not learn of the question with which they are grappling. It is as if the patient had an intuition that the environment contains no response to the question, cannot answer it, is incapable of providing any meaning in the face of it.

The intuition is correct. Persons who are healthy tend to answer this sort of existential question which is always concerned with the worth and meaning of existence by saying something like "You shouldn't bother so much with questions like that. Everything will be all right." How often does this question threaten society with a direct challenge it would rather ignore?

Actually, it is inherent in the crisis that the patient direct the question as far as possible to himself. The response of others cannot and will not be so meaningfully placed in what is really a reassessment of one's life and a reorientation to its deeper values. Often both dying and convalescing patients come to a subsequent awareness that immersion in this question was the most positive event experienced during the course of their illness.

B. ENVIRONMENTAL INFLUENCES

A number of environmental influences have bearing on the experience of the patients. These are manifested both in the hospital and during subsequent recovery, as well as in the first period of assimilation of dis-ease and its sequellae. Although the influences outside the hospital do not have as great an impact as those inside, the degree to which the various factors affect patient recovery changes constantly.

First of all, the patient situation varies from case to case. Secondly, it is difficult in the extreme to identify which factors may be operative and to what degree they may be exercising a role. In the third place, the influence of these factors on the conduct and life experience of the patient is not just a case of current impact, but is also part of an ever-changing interaction, which may occur over a span of years. As a result, one might assert that, given a different, more serious condition or set of circumstances, these external factors might have had an altered impact, so as to be more sharply focused and identified. We will nonetheless discuss external influences under the following four headings: 1) physical aspects, 2) sociocultural aspects, 3) human aspects, and 4) ethical and religious aspects. Our purpose at this point is simply to identify the problem areas, rather than to conduct an extensive analysis. Some of the gaps can be filled by our discussion of the literature on this topic.

1. Physical Aspects

The physical aspects that influence the workup and treatment of a disease, and the accompanying patient feelings already identified, fall into two general categories: a) aspects specifically bound up with hospital conditions and b) relevant aspects identified in the world outside the hospital.

(a) The physical set up of the hospital is, of course, dependent on cost factors, the imagination (or lack thereof) of the architect, and efficiency as perceived by the professional staff. It seems that room and passageway organization and choice of colors are seldom considered from the standpoint of the patients.

The hospital stay for many victims of acute illness begins in the intensive-care unit (ICU) or coronary-care unit (CCU). The patient may first gain consciousness in a sterile white environment filled with monitors, blips, and IV tubes. In a primeval forest of alien forms, the patient encounters an unmistakably serious condition in himself, other prostrate patients, and decisive people clad in white, bustling to and fro.

Case XII

A verbal account by a patient:
. . . And then I came to, and I could just make out the clock in the corner . . . It was three o'clock . . . But everywhere there were tubes and buzzing . . . and then I went back to sleep, and I thought I had been rudely jerked . . . then I was awake again and it was only five after three . . . That evening the kids came to visit me. They all had those white coats on, so I didn't recognize them at first. I said to myself, now what's up? . . . That afternoon my wife had one of those coats on, but somehow it didn't register with me. But the kids! That just seemed crazy. Later I understood, but

> at that moment! . . . You know, you look around at all the faces on the other beds and you think, you know, that this looks just like Buchenwald . . . Now you know that it's not going well for you but you don't see it so clearly, you don't see that you look just like all these others . . . God, what happened to me to put me in this ward?

Have we ever really asked what effect this bewildering new world has on the patient recovering consciousness, especially as the patient may not, or may just barely, realize what has happened? Obviously, technical assistance is essential. But what of the effect of the organization of the room, particularly the arrangement of beds and apparatus?

We raise the question without posing an answer, even though it is clear that the ICU creates shock in the patient, especially when he sees all the other prostrate forms in nearby beds. This shock can be severe, at least for a short time, when the patient first gazes at the relatively singular spatial configuration of the room or ward itself.

Of course the shock of waking up in the ICU is just one kind. Shocks of a different nature are presented by the endless hospital halls, from admissions to treatment rooms to nursing stations; the many closed doors to rooms that bear no significance for patients; even the optimal size of the sick rooms. None of this is familiar to the patient. How much thought, for example, has been given to the color scheme, something quite often accented in other areas of life, especially the way it might affect the state of the patient? Are colors such as green, yellow, brown, red, or blue less functional than the omnipresent white? Only a few hospitals (and these are mostly children's hospitals) have paid attention to color as a factor in the total treatment of patients.

Again we offer no answers here. We only note that the question needs to be asked. That the question has not been asked implies that authorities and designers have neglected to consider that the hospital may be home for patients for weeks and even months. The efficient, cost-effective modern building is so uniform and impersonal that it is almost impossible for individual patients to recognize their own personhood, to test it, and to recover it.

(b) *Outside the Hospital*—The world outside the hospital, though of a different arrangement or order, is also unmistakably an impediment to the sick, impaired, and handicapped. The U.S. Department of Health and Human Services (formerly HEW) has decreed that all public buildings and institutions receiving federal funds make provisions for the handicapped, in an effort to overcome some of these impediments. But the fact remains that streets with sharp curbs, even at corners, and steps up into streetcars, trains, and buses can be insurmountable barriers to some people. Add to these the often monumental flights of stairs in subways, office buildings, stores, and government institutions (though these last are changing) and one can readily see that an impaired person cannot participate in the usual human activities of a municipality without special assistance. In effect, then, the world outside the hospital also creates dependency.

It is painful to realize that a structure—stairs or a sidewalk—that to those of us who are healthy represents a means of access represents to the patient or handicapped a barrier. Every obstacle requires a request for help (though often there is no help). One's dependency is thus doubly reinforced. We will discuss these problems in greater detail in chapter seven.

2. Sociocultural Aspects

A hospital has its unique culture, and the sciences functioning within a hospital create their own subculture. One can thus draw a distinction between the hospital and the external world.

(a) *Inside the Hospital*—Every culture is identified by thought and conduct based on principles of value, norms, and agreements that govern social interaction between members. The hospital is just such a culture, although it operates within a broader social and cultural matrix. In other words, it is a subculture. The way it is governed, the way it is managed, and the way in which leadership is exercised within it reveal manifold norms and agreements, some explicitly formulated and others simply assumed by its members. The overriding norms relate to the professional codes of medicine, nursing, and allied health care; they are handled by an interdependent ethic. On the one hand one may assert that the patient's welfare depends on his acceptance and trust (or nonacceptance and mistrust) of this fundamental ethic; without doubt, many patients do place trust foremost in their relation with the hospital staff. On the other hand, situations arise in which the desires of patients, seen from their personal value system, are not (or no longer) congruent with the value system of the hospital. In these situations, when the patient may be asking existential questions about his or her own values, one finds a cadre of assumed hospital values that are either hard or impossible to articulate. Questions of abortion and euthanasia are the most obvious examples, but many other questions patients have about their illness or injuries can easily be interpreted as questioning the implied value system of the hospital. They may be very legitimate questions and dealt with as such, but often they are classed as evidence of mistrust, because hospital personnel cannot articulate the implied values that the questions threaten.

(b) *Outside the Hospital*—Every form of social life has an aversion to

"My wheelchair is my life." —Space is truth

sickness and injury. But many rituals exist explicitly to lend this aversion a degree of social acceptability.

Compassion and care, among other feelings and behaviors, are socially desirable responses. But these responses cannot always overcome taboos and attitudes about certain kinds of diseases and injuries.* Every social group and its corresponding subculture relegates to the sphere of taboos its set of disease categories.

Currently cancer is one such disease. Its name often may not be mentioned to those with the disease, and patients with cancer suffer from an isolation that exceeds that for patients with other illnesses and complaints. Obvious amputations also seem to call forth an unexpressed aversion and patients with serious disfiguring injuries (burn victims) have to cope with an almost constant aversion by others in society. Sometimes this aversion, visible and measurable, is covered up with socially accepted behavior (Case XIII). But this overcompensating behavior can usually be detected by victims.

Case XIII

John was a carpenter who had suffered a job-related accident that left his face, among other things, scarred by burns. This twenty-one-year-old man was in the hospital for more than a year; when alert, he fell prey to profound dejection and depression. Before the accident he had enjoyed a large circle of men and women friends. But when he was at last permitted to go home for the weekend, only one friend stayed with him there and came on subsequent weekends visit. Whenever John suggested they go to the movies (where it was usually dark) his friend always had some excuse not to go. Finally John gave up his requests and stayed at home. He did not even want to go out. Expecting additional skin transplants, he did not want to go home at all. "Here in the hospital they treat me well, even visitors, because they expect to see rare things here. But no sooner do I leave the building, then people stop and stare at me. Children shriek their heads off and run away from me as fast as they can. No, let me stay here longer."

It is not important at this point to determine what the background to this attitude is. Rather, it is important to note that patients experience a wall between them and society outside the hospital, a wall they cannot

*These attitudes are sometimes so differentiated that aversion occurs not only toward a specific handicap but also toward its cause. Thus, disabled war veterans enjoy more privileges offered by society than do those invalids suffering a handicap from some other cause, such as a job-related injury. Moreover, veterans disabled during "popular" wars, such as World War II, receive more honor from society than do veterans of unpopular wars, such as the Vietnam war.

seem to pass through. While in the hospital this implied value system seems abrogated, because it cannot be articulated without violating the basic ethic of care for patients: at the hospital one can relate to the person *as a patient,* with all the attendant gradations, without forming those socially determined judgments automatically evoked by the sight of an injury outside the hospital.

3. Human Aspects

Persons around the patient not only are bearers of the social norms that play a part in their contacts with the patient. They also have the potential to develop a more personal relationship whereby the collective norms are pushed into the background, though not completely diminished.

(a) *Inside the Hospital*—The relationships patients create in the hospital are mostly with medical professionals. These persons usually restrict their contact with patients to their professional duties. For the professional as well as the patient, it is not difficult to perceive that any personal bonds between helper and helped will pass—the professional can always escape back into his or her official role, which the patient knows, and the patient will probably leave the hospital. Moreover, the patient is dependent on the professionalism of those who assist him, and the professional is reluctant to extend friendship to the patient, because he or she is expected to treat the patient with professional objectivity, with which a personal bond might interfere. The patient, for his part, wants some personal contact with the professional; he may try to reach the human being behind the professional mask.

(b) *Outside the Hospital*—Once home, personal contacts with family, acquaintances, and eventually coworkers have the greatest import for patients. Although not every person in this context carries collective social norms, such norms usually play a role in contacts and relations outside the hospital.

It becomes essential, therefore, to place personal relations above social normative behavior. Another crucial point regards the degree to which the sickness or injury is identified by the patient with a specific cause within the family or at work. If it is only indirectly linked, the cause will not be employed as blatantly as is a direct cause in the manipulation that some recovering patients practice. If there has been some causal connection (real or imagined!), ambivalent relations easily result between the sick and injured and their social context, an ambivalence beyond that found in normal, healthy relations. Projection of the cause onto family or work conveniently enhances any ambivalence already present, and the subjective distance of the patient toward family and work is so great that it makes it extremely difficult to discuss or resolve the conflicts. Probably in such cases a complicated and intensified process of aggression and guilt develops, such that neither the patient nor his healthy associates can grasp the facts from an objective perspective.

These situations become especially problematic when the cause of illness or accident can indeed be attributed to working conditions toward which the patient already had ambivalent feelings. Such cases usually result in the worker's suing the "responsible party," his or her boss. The patient marshals a record of supposed injustices, including the accident, in order to gain redress, such as a lifetime income from disability payments or a lawsuit. Emotional manipulation of family members is not uncommon. In these instances the patient—consciously or not—does not intend to achieve complete recovery—manipulation would then be impossible.

4. Ethical and Religious Aspects

Ethical and religious aspects lie on a higher plane than the principles composing social norms. Here it is not a question of social norms, but rather one concerning the intrinsic values of life and death.

(a) *Inside the Hospital*—There are very few institutions within the health-care system where life and the possibilities of life are not addressed. One can posit without fear of contradiction that the fundamental principle of health care, including the norms found in professional codes, rests on the view that life is always to be held more precious than other things. Apart from current discussions regarding extreme situations, such as the role of euthanasia (for the most part these take place outside the walls of the hospital), the overriding value of life is the primary principle. And the patient is aware of that. Even patients who are unconscious or in such a state that they can barely think for themselves know that their life is held dear. Again, the question arises of discussing implicitly held values and ideals with the patient. Both the patient and family should know what values are to predominate. The "Patient's Bill of Rights" (a required promulgation of all hospitals about the rights of patients) is a first step toward such an articulation, but it hardly encompasses the religious values of the staff, even in a religious hospital.

In addition to a vision of life and death there is a view of sickness and pain. In some sectarian hospitals there is a long tradition of identifying the redemptive character of sickness and especially pain, with the result that medication for labor pain was not given to certain categories of patients, such as unwed mothers. Thus, "religious" views can be falsely incorporated into negative judgments about the patients. The question of the meaning of suffering is still real today for these and other hospitals, involving courses of treatments indicated on the basis of an unexpressed attitude toward suffering. However, only rarely is the personal view of the patient addressed.

(b) *Outside the Hospital*—Explicit and implicit views of life and death are not confined to the hospital, even one with a religious support system. They also play a role outside the hospital, albeit in a different way and with less capability of explicit utterance. Doubtless, these views are an element in the patient's surroundings, especially among family and friends. Not infrequently the views of others are adopted by the patient and incorporated into his own world view; as such they are quite identifiable. Sometimes they interfere with the patient's judgments about his or her condition (see chapter eight).

Throughout the chapter's second section we have offered only a brief discussion of the four categories of environmental influences on a patient's adjustment to a condition, as they occur both within and without the hospital. It is obviously not crystal clear how each internal and external factor affects an individual patient, and to what extent and when during illness and recovery it influences each person. For this reason, we have posed only a few questions, of a general nature. Note that individual aspects will have a greater or lesser effect according to the patient's ability to cope with a condition and the feelings it provokes. Because the effect is totally dependent on the patient's ability to recognize the external factors and either accept or reject them with respect to both himself and his condition, it is essential that patients be given the opportunity to recognize all such factors. Actually, there are two requirements: to make as explicit as possible the external factors that have an impact on the patient's condition and existence, and to explicate norms and attitudes as much as possible, so that they can be communicated to the patient. These constitute the minimal requirements for the health professional concerned with the workup of patient dis-ease and the treatment of the whole person, as opposed to a mere organ system or disease entity.

REVIEW OF THE LITERATURE

The literature on the dis-ease workup, beyond simple casuistic discussion or promoting opinions without an experimental basis, is very hard to find. And yet, the topics involved offer a fertile field for research. The literature is discussed under the two main headings of the chapter.

1. Discongruity With One's Own Body

One of S. Fisher's studies is *Body Consciousness: You Are What You Feel* (1973). Despite the popular title, it treats an important point, namely, that body-image and self-concept are inseparable aspects of what it means to be human.

At the start of this chapter we introduced the term *incongruence.* The term can be found in C. R. Rogers (1961). By it he means that a person no longer experiences the self as before. Rogers does not apply *incongruence* to patients suffering a physical disease, although they obviously experience it, because they can barely recognize themselves in a damaged body. We have extended the meaning of *incongruence* to cover such patients. Recognition and self-perception are themes directly related to the problem of discongruity and are long overdue as objects of psychological research. Some experiments already done suggest that a loss of proportion presents difficulties in self-recognition. Fisher amply summarizes the experiments to date on the question of self-recognition and self-perception. Among others, he mentions E. Deno (1953), who photographed a group of youths and then asked them to pick out their pictures in which the faces had been masked. Only thirty percent were able to identify their pictures.

H. G. Wolff's famous studies (1950) on recognizing parts of the body, hands, and profiles, demonstrated that emotional reaction hindered recognition.

Also important for our point are the studies by A. C. Traub and J. Orbach (1964) that involved subjects' reconstructing their image using variable mirror images. Only a few "normal" subjects were able to construct an exact picture of themselves. But even more than do the subjects in these studies, patients find their bodies differently constructed with impaired or altered functions, functions that they cannot as yet comprehend. The body is thereby "stolen," and it is covered up throughout the day, such that the usual form and function are hard to retrieve. The feeling is analogous to the experiments in which persons no longer recognize themselves, and cannot identify their own bodies.

We suggest that there are two paths the patient might take. The first is that in which the self-concept fades; the patient becomes alienated from the former self through loss of body-image, and faces the trials of living within a distorted self. Incongruence is direct, almost tangibly present, and the self is irretrievably lost. Seen from the perspective of Merleau-Ponty (1945), the meaning structure of the subject is lost. Instead, dissolution occurs toward both objects and subjectivity, so that the meaning structure appears to be almost invalid. The body-subject-in-the-world, Merleau-Ponty's very definition of man, loses its meaning. The patient suffers a wound, as it were, that prohibits new acquisition of meaning with respect to the world of objects as well as the self. This is not an easy challenge to overcome.

The patient's second path is denial of the illness. In so doing, an enduring relation between the self and the former body-concept is established. Discongruity in this case appears at moments when the patient must face the discrepancy between the maintained body-concept and reality. Such discongruity is observed, for example, in amputees who formerly functioned out of a body-concept in which the amputation had no place, but must now, on the road to recovery, face up to the missing limb. We have already mentioned the phantom-limb syndrome, in which patients experience pain in a missing member. I. C. Kolb (1959) offers a summary of research on the syndrome. The observations of T. Szasz (1968) are equally important in this regard, as is the research by J. H. Jarwis (1967), who found among 104 women that twenty-four percent discovered phantom-breast sensations after mastectomies.

Both Szasz (1968) and S. A. Weiss (1958) propose that the experience of phantom members has to do with nonacceptance of the member's loss. Thus, the experience of phantoms indicates patients attempting to reexperience the trauma in small doses. In other words, patients are actually delaying a renewed body-image by postponing the completeness of the trauma. Hence, whereas patients in the first category, who release their previous body-image, tend to suffer uncertainty and depression, patients in the second category, who hang on to a familiar body-image, tend toward denial of the real situation.

The first group usually accepts their situation; their problem is to overcome the disability by giving it form and content. The second group opts for comparison of future possibilities with a sense of self that is maintained without compromise; their problem is reaching an adjustment in their sense of self. In the experience of surgeons and orthopedic specialists, phantom pain seldom if ever occurs in patients for whom amputation was experienced as freeing them from a body member that was causing difficulties. The same is true regarding patients for whom an amputation represents a renewed ability to negotiate obstacles. Amputation in this sense is seen as a door to greater freedom rather than as a destruction of body possibilities (e.g., gangrenous toes which confined the patient to bed are removed and the patient can now get about on crutches).

On the questions of causality, aggression, and guilt, one finds little in the literature. Although their importance is not unknown and they are implicitly mentioned in some works, rarely are these topics sufficiently amplified to account for a specific dis-ease. We now turn to the workup of the emotional aspects of disease.

As articulated by J. D. Campbell in his article "Attribution of Illness" (1974), every person has a strong tendency to deny sickness, and thereby to misperceive the growing signs of illness in him- or herself. Persons are much more able to recognize the signs in others to observe that "He looks a little peaked today." There is a tendency to maintain an adequate self-picture in the person's perception to the social world; the self is perceived as a valued object to be protected and enhanced. A threat to one's health is a threat to personal equilibrium. To become sick represents a dissonance that we would rather ignore, especially in ourselves. Such dissonance occurs in the first phases of illness recognition covered by this chapter: after "recognition" of dis-ease, the patient looks for its "roots," and must then "admit" these in the moment of interrupted self-allusion. The usual order of events, the routine, is interrupted, either suddenly or with creeping inexorability. In this phase the patient experiences the first part of the career of the disabled (C. Safilos-Rotschild, 1970). Safilos-Rotschild agrees here with T. J. Scheff (1967) and Szasz (1961) that not only does disease or accident contribute to a situation of interrupted self-allusion, but also the medical diagnosis determines to a great extent the situation in which the patient finds himself. At the heart of this view is choice. The accident victim, of course, has no choice. But once the medical diagnosis is enjoined, neither does the victim of illness. Choices are then taken out of patients' hands and placed in the health professional's, for they are almost always determined by the causes and conditions of the disease, suggesting, as they do, what remedies to employ.

Our interest remains in the process that leads to the judgment that "I am sick," the first clinical moment as it has been described, the process leading to a medical diagnosis, the environment, and especially "relevant others" (cf. Campbell, 1974). This interest leads eventually to the findings of C. H. Elledge (1948). Others do indeed play a role in the process, but as circumscribed by the moment in the patient's life when illness must be recognized or when an accident actually occurs. They accent the patient's past and the current significance of the event: the patient's future plans, past influences on these, and the crisis point at which the patient now stands. An adolescent succumbing to polio must endure an entirely different disease history from a fifty-year-old woman who faces a permanent stiff leg resulting from a compound fracture.

In addition to these differences, there are social factors. M. Field's (1967) view is that illness not only interrupts the ordinary pattern of living, it affects the person's feelings about himself. Something happens to the ego of the person who feels his customary way of coping with life is slipping from him. Little can be found in the literature on our observations about aggression and guilt feelings in patients and families, but Field's overweening pessimism regarding the feelings of the patient's loved ones may serve as an illustration: "They are reduced to the status of helpless onlookers . . ."

Apart from more general treatments by Field and Campbell, it must be said that most studies are based on some form of casuistry, coupled with the particular view of the author. An exception is a little volume by V. M. Naylor and D. Michaels (1961) that deals with research on cancer patients. Following a breakdown in trust regarding treatment possibilities—usually after some initial successes—the cancer patient has little time for preoccupation with the future. Instead, the patient is interested in the past and, above all, the present. This result supports our contention that the sick, more than an accident victim, are burdened by guilt feelings and must confront the past in order to gain some clarity about them. Mental suffering and emotional difficulties are more significant for cancer patients than for patients with other diseases because they more frequently attribute the cause of their illness to past reprehensible behavior.

Egocentrism in patients can best be expressed by the comment of one of the patients in Naylor and Michael's study: "There's too much time to think." *In fine,* there are few obvious conclusions in that work, but at least it was based on the experimental method and empirical research. For some professionals such a gem is still worth much more than extensive observations and personal experience.

2. Environmental Influences

The first of these, the physical environment of patients, has not, as we have suggested, received the attention it deserves. There is very little material on the topic. One can, of course, find publications on hospital construction and costs, but these are seldom related to the important features in the patient's experience. G. Fieret and J. Bergsma (1979) made a survey of literature concerning patient experience and architectural *design,* they found several interesting articles containing nice ideas and ad hoc descriptions, but only a few follow-up studies offering data to substantiate findings. M. Proshansky (1969) represents an exception to this rule, as his *Environmental Psychology* includes studies related to the hospital situation. We also should mention D. Canter (1977) and his hospital-evaluation studies, and L. M. Wilson (1972), who explored the influence of environment on the incidence of intensive-care delirium, finding that an absence of windows results in an increase of fifty percent over less sterile environments. J. K. Skipper et al. (1964), although not directly on the point, formulate some hypotheses related to architecture as an influence on communication between patient and helper. Nevertheless, this terrain is still a fallow field for clinical-psychology research.

With respect to sociocultural influences on disease process and handicaps, a bit more can be found in the literature. R. A. Scott contributed the article "The Construction of Conceptions of Stigma by Professional Experts" to a volume edited by D. M. Boswell and J. M. Wingrove (1974). The professional operates out of a multitude of norms and values, of which he or she may be aware in the beginning but in due course pushes into the background. This process occurs such that practicing experts can rarely articulate these norms on the scene. This means that not long after the process begins it seems no longer possible to foresee the consequences of professional decisions on the values of patients. According to Scott there are a number of influences on professional normative behavior, but only rarely consciously formed. Among these are cultural values infusing the life of the professional ("expert"), the profession itself, the organization in which the professional practices, and the "material conditions," or the kinds of patients with which the professional deals. An additional contribution in this area is by J. E. P. Menzies (1974), who holds that nursing is infused with implicit social conceptions. As a consequence, it is practiced within a convulsive social system, which serves as a self-protective cover for nurses who would otherwise be overwhelmed with stress. M. Field (1967) looks once again at the dependency of hospital patients with consequent regressive impulses. Independent of all physical- and technical-treatment dependencies, such as those described by Richardson et al. (1964) and many others, it is not unthinkable that the greatest dependency of all lies in the *value system* from which the treatment springs. R. A. Scott (1974) also underlined this problem, which reaches monumental proportions precisely because the value system in question is very difficult to articulate. We have noted, in addition, that this dependency is increased in environments where the albeit remote possibility of articulation is hampered by inadequate communication with the patient. We should also mention E. Goffman (1974), who uses *value system* in a different connection, and describes the doctor-patient interaction as a form of "informational-control," that is, interaction in which helper and patient preselect and filter information given to each other according to their own value (or selection) systems. Real communication then requires a dialogue between the doctor and patient on the norms of information selection, as well as an exchange of that information.

Obviously, medical institutions are not the only place where this problematic situation occurs. Daily life contains the same problems, perhaps amplified, for the escape hatch provided by the nonhospital surroundings leaves plenty of room for inattention and denial. Goffman (1963) has paid particular attention to this arena. He emphasizes two conditions, among others, that lead to value clashes. The first is the visibility of the handicaps, in a discussion of which he almost cynically observes that it has less to do with visibility than with the ability of the environment to perceive! The second is the degree to which the "stigma" is known to us, that is, possesses some identity. With respect to the first condition, problems occur in the communicability of the meaning of the handicap, which is a continuing problem for the patient. With respect to the second condition, the problem lies in getting people to acknowledge socially determined norms and judgments usually hidden in the background of "stigmas." Clearly this personal knowledge, identity possessed with respect to others, adhers from the patient's standpoint to a very small group of persons. Also, as patients have reported (Goffman, 1963), the experience of "stigma" is accompanied by a loss of friends and acquaintances, and dwindling relations with coworkers during the period of acceptance.

S. Richardson (1964) emphasized the social isolation and consequent deprivation of handicapped children. In relating this phenomenon to adulthood, Goffman shows how isolation places children in double jeopardy: there are both the loss of relationships to cultivate, upon which to ground one's life, and the over-protectiveness toward the few relationships that survive, causing them to become excessively intensified.

"Whether or not the person has adjusted to his loss, he will experience difficulties in his relationship with non-injured people" is one of the conclusions of a study conducted by T. Dembo, G. L. Leviton, and B. A. Wright (1970). They propose that the way the handicapped person handles social relations depends on the degree to which he or she has accepted the handicap.

Finally, we should note a remarkable phenomenon. Through a study done by R. C. Comer and J. A. Piliavin (1975), it is clear that irrespective of social isolation of handicapped persons by so-called normal persons, the handicapped comes through this experience in a sounder state than the "normal," healthy person. There is a noticeable tendency to ascribe to handicapped persons properties of friendliness, probity, honor, and greater intelligence than "normal" persons. The belief in such attributes diminishes the minute one becomes handicapped, oneself. According to the authors: "normal" people tend to form myths about the handicapped ("He has gone through a lot; she has had to overcome many trials"), which are reduced to realistic proportions when one becomes handicapped or gets to know a handicapped person better (also see Goffman, 1974). But, ironically, the authors have also observed the striking tendency simultaneously to ascribe to "being disabled" a lower social value by both normal and handicapped persons; this is eventually "normalized" by "normal" persons, but it continues to hold its "lower" connotations for the handicapped. A European study would be required to determine the extent to which these authors' results depend on American cultural values and to what extent they are grounded in broader cultural values.

As mentioned a number of times, an important difference exists between the relation of patients to generally held social norms and values and to more personally based relationships. Inasmuch as the patient enjoys an "identity" (Goffman, 1974), he will be treated as a person, evoking modified social values and content of personal relations. It is this very personal relationship that allows us to speak of the different implications of a handicap. A. Farina et al. (1968) view this expressibility as essential to the promotion of the concept of identity, even as the exaggerated value placed on it is being reduced, as already mentioned, to normal proportions. It would be well to question to what extent Farina's research can be extrapolated, as his study was done on students under his instruction, which might reduce its validity. Moreover, his concept of "stigmatized" was not clearly related to a specific value judgment. In this respect, Comer and Piliavin (1975) represent a more valid study.

We now turn again to Dembo, Leviton, and Wright (1970), who explicated the way in which a handicapped person relates to surroundings on the basis of self-acceptance: "When the person devalues himself because of his loss, he will feel that his non-acceptance by others is largely justified. He will agree with the other group members that a non-injured person is more valuable, more likeable, more worthy." In the opposite case, the disabled will have less difficulty taking his place in the group, whereas in the first instance there is a tendency by the handicapped to insert himself in the group by passively accepting the role of needing less assistance in order to gain acceptance, and to agree with the judgments of others in order to maintain this acceptance.

The stance of patients toward family and work is more or less determined by their place in primary personal relations. C. H. Elledge (1948) offers ample observations on this point from the view of a social worker. Safilos-Rotschild (1970) focuses on the work place. Field (1967) makes more specific observations about family life. We should note, however, that these three studies occur within the American context, in which problems of the disabled are related to economic pressures on the family almost bankrupted by health fees. By contrast, this situation does not occur in Western Europe and Canada, where medicine is socialized; the results of studies of the patient in his social context in these countries may well be different. There are very few American studies on disability not related to economic factors within the American cultural system. An exception is that of T. M. Cole, R. Chilgren, and P. Rosenberg (1973). Their special interest was in sexual problems of the handicapped brought into the family context. On this subject they are in congruity with K. Hesseling and A. Verkuyl (1972), who enjoyed great impact in the Netherlands with their study *We Are Not Made of Stone.* Cole, et al., inaugurated a program of sex education for patients with spinal-cord injuries and social workers in the field. For a number of days they underwent a training program consisting of films, dialogues, and group discussions on the difficulties raised by the subject for both groups. What emerged was that the social workers, the "experts," appeared completely misinformed about the sexual condition of their patients, while the spinal-cord-injury patients gained a measure of clarity about avenues of sexuality still open to them. The typical lack of professional help (in most cases none was given about sexuality at all) left patients with only their own basic sexual understanding and whatever savvy they could muster, right or wrong. Neglect of such an essential area is a good example of the implicit norms that are currently in operation!

Finally, the meaning of ethical and religious norms with regard to illness and handicap can best be found in specific theological literature, especially the studies by thinkers such as P. Sporken and J. Faber, and the wealth of articles and books on terminal illness that have sprouted up in recent times. We need not elaborate on this point.

CONCLUSION

In a Dutch article entitled "Psychosomatics and Cognitive Processes," P. A. Vroon (1975) explores the importance language can have for the onset of psychosomatic disease. Description of a certain organ and sensations associated with that organ concentrates both thinking and feelings on the organ (as in the case of pain). Calling attention to a certain organ over a period of time creates a certain tone, like wearing away a stone with drops of water, resulting in an unwarranted concentration or reflection on that organ or feeling. Examples abound:

"What's wrong with your stomach that you drink so much?" "Why do you always slouch? Stand up straight!" "It's all in your head." In this context Vroon recalls an observation by R. Linschoten, who used to speak of a "dictatorship of language." Within this approach it is possible to reflect on the acceptance of dis-ease and its workup. The "dictatorship of language" operates here, as well. We should discuss what can be called the "fear of classification": the unbridled classification of patients is a phenomenon accompanying differentiating cultural values and its effect is not intended.

Western psychiatry is a textbook example. Long accepted, psychiatry has entered daily speech, in which the terminology has acquired negative cultural connotations: *psychopath, hysterical, degenerate, schizophrenic*. Modern psychiatry has in fact come almost full circle from employing these diagnostic categories, because it has begun to notice that once a label is applied to a patient, the patient becomes permanently stamped in a medical record that sometimes controls both place and progress of further treatment. If a patient is labeled a psychopath, attitudes and subsequent treatment seem to follow from the label, and breaking out of this odium is almost impossible. "Psychopath" is not an uncommon diatribe in daily speech.

The health care system employs many labels and classifications, all of which put a patient in a medical yoke. There are categories of "easy" and "difficult" cases, for example. Removing tonsils or an appendix and setting a broken bone are cases of little importance medically; they are "easily" done and few problems are encountered. The simplicity for medical personnel leads quite naturally to the assumption that patients must also find them simple and straightforward: "No Problem" is that rubric under which these patients must endure their trauma. Thus, in cases that present little or no challenge to medical technology there is almost a complete lack of sympathy for the meaning of the event for the individual patient. The same misperception confronts a patient complaining of a nervous condition: "You don't have anything except a case of nerves." The patient returns home with the knowledge that he has "nothing." However, this "knowledge" may be quite different from the more specific formulation. "There is no medically indicated reason for my condition." The two are quite different, of course.

Many patients have the same experience upon hearing that their complaints are psychosomatic. Social etiquette requires that the sick (and sickness) are not to be taken seriously; the patient must not become morose, so that he can recover quickly. Popular thinking about psychosomatic illness has reversed from earlier rejection of its validity. It has led to the notion that, for example, stomach disorders and asthma are *automatically* psychosomatic and therefore inconsequential. It is almost impossible today to have a "normal" stomach or bowel disorder! Clearly, our use of language rejects claims of pain and related appeals for sympathy. A long-term complaint will meet with even less acceptance than a sudden one.

The general problem is this: categorizing has a direct effect on the environment in which the patient will be treated by coupling expectations with the classification. A stomach patient remains such for a long time, perhaps for the rest of his life. The environment will always target previous stomach disorders in offering advice about any current problem—"This or that, we have seen, will be good for your stomach." Almost as common in this category is the person who has suffered a minor heart attack. It is known that loved ones develop refined techniques to control the ex-patient ("Don't go out alone," 'Don't lock your bathroom door," "Don't smoke," "Keep calm at all costs"). The result of such solicitousness is that necessary activities are reduced to inactivity, and the patient remains a patient; the environment, as it were, fossilizes the patient's condition by concentration on the diseased organ. The patient will do well if he or she can break out of this paternalism. Implied in this advice, of course, is the importance of preparing convalescents for this situation and involving the support group (usually loved ones) in the preparation. Conversely, an inappropriate preparation would be attaching a taboo to the word *heart,* for example; anxieties and fears would unnecessarily be linked to *heart,* leading to a negative preparation. The classic heart taboo almost has a life of its own, which health professionals should be aware of in order to help patients.

The iatrogenic effects of categorization herein discussed will not occur in every case. Nor when they occur will their effects always be so serious. On the other hand, no one can break out of the categorization completely. The environment contributes to this harnessing of patients. The words of Szasz, "to reexperience in small doses," apply here in a broader sense. The patient's disease remains with him for a long time. It fixes him in the patient role long after the disease may have waned.

5. Pain

Your pain is the breaking of the shelter that encloses your understanding
—Kahlil Gibran

Pain has many meanings. Observing it sometimes has dramatic effects. At other times it irritates us or makes a humorous impression. The enduring effects on those who suffer pain are, at the very least, twofold. First, those who suffer pain cannot pay sufficient attention to others; pain is a signal. No matter how that signal is perceived, thinking of others or of other things becomes immersed in the appeal for self-attention that marks the pain signal. Secondly, pain is a signal that carries no real advice about response. It creates confusion. One of the important reasons for this is that the phenomenon of pain is so difficult to convey to others. Others in the environment have difficulty rating the degree of pain a person suffers, they cannot feel the pain one suffers. Grief and fear are feelings that can be shared. We can sympathize with another's grief, actually experience it within us. On that basis we provide a bond both toward the one grieving and towards grief itself. Pain calls forth an analogous response, of course, but to a far lesser extent than grief. Even though one may attempt to express the extent that another person suffers pain, one has no real access to that event, the actual suffering of pain. If sympathy is based on feelings we have in the presence of feelings that others have, then a response to pain, unless we suffer the same pain, is one step removed from sympathy.

Having pain leads one who suffers, as a consequence, to feelings of isolation. One must face the pain, in real terms, alone. No one else feels that pain. As grief builds a bridge to others to overcome isolation, pain must cross that bridge at the same time in order to elicit response. Grief is the bridge for sympathy with pain.

One who has seen many persons in pain and worked intensively with them comes to the conclusion that it is impossible to speak of a "pain patient." Every generalization in this regard seems incorrect and forced. Naturally, one can observe that almost all patients experience some degree of isolation in their pain. But this only serves to increase the feelings of powerlessness in the observer. For this very reason, pain intrigues us all the more.

A. PAIN AND ITS EXPRESSION

Pain is intriguing, is enigmatic; it poses questions for which there are no answers. Nevertheless, we will try to discuss a number of aspects of pain, because it is so central to the concerns in this book.

First of all, we should examine the phenomenon called discrepancy. Both clinically and otherwise observed, discrepancy seems to occur between pain and its expression. It is an observation anyone can make. Patients complain of severe pain in a part of their body for which the health professional, even with the most sophisticated instruments, can find either no or only the slighest objective basis for any disorder. By contrast, other patients suffering from a serious injury or swelling offer no evidence of pain, even though their injuries lead us to suppose they are in profound distress. We can press this observation to even greater extremes. We can include patients with severe complaints of pain in a limb that is no longer present—the phantom-limb syndrome. At the other end of the spectrum is the ice skater who has fallen hard on his rear. From our own experience we know how painful that can be! We rush to help. Yet most such victims suffer this pain with a smiling grimace, intended to signal pain but also its cover-up. The effect is merely ludicrous—everyone laughs, and the skating resumes.

Not only is discrepancy possible to observe in others, it is a datum of our own experience. Each of us knows from experience that we cannot identify, at least in every case, a measured account of the relation between an objective cause of pain and its experience or expression. Yet another experience can be noted here. It is the experience of those who work in an urban health-care clinic in which an international cast of patients is daily present. The medical workers would all be prepared to state that it is almost impossible to predict how a complaint will be presented and the degree of pain that accompanies it, even when an objective medical disorder can be discerned.

B. THE EXPERIENCE OF PAIN

In general, pain can be grasped, as it has been of old, as both an event and a signal, as a sign that in and/or to a body something occurs that possibly threatens that body. The range and intensity of the signal seem largely variable.

On the one hand, variability occurs in the cause of pain, which can also vary in its seriousness. On the other, a high degree of variability exists in the way in which pain is endured and expressed to others. Experiencing pain is obviously a very personal event; enduring it rests on individual qualities and intensities of feeling that are largely unpredictable and untranslatable. The question of variability seems to some to suggest that the victim may not wish to transfer the experience to others. This point relates to personal stances toward pain, as well as to the meaning pain may carry in one's experience and environment.

For example, is pain considered inevitable or triumphant? This is a distinction drawn by F. J. Buytendijk in his study of pain (1957). In the first case there is a certain degree of acceptance. Pain is seen as inescapable: knowledge of this allows some distancing, making acceptance possible. The perceived triumph of pain, in the second case, is an attitude in which pain gains control without any perspective. Suffering pain is a complete experience of its presence, without any distancing. Pain has won.

An author by the name of A. Kossman (1973) presents both forms in his account of a mishap that almost took his life. He describes his suffering thus: "I lay there unable to sleep from thirst and pain, and yet I was not awake either. I rambled on to myself. I knew that I was lying there at night but had no idea in whose room. . . ." (pp. 31-32) Later in his account he says, "I never complained about the pain to Ida or friends, and the nurses never betrayed to them my constant wailing" (p. 33).

These two forms of pain are present in a phase that seems far removed from pain's signal function. But this observation depends on whether the signal can acquire one function during the course of an illness and another in relation to the environment.

A child first experiencing pain is completely preoccupied with sounding an alarm to those around him. The child acknowledges its dependency. An adult, on the other hand, can ignore the pain as proof of independence—"I won't give in to it, or I'll look like a baby."

The thesis that pain may have different and changing functions in relations between persons is an invitation to explore some relational aspects of pain.

1. Suspicion

What meaning does pain have for the self, for one's body? Pain signals an unusual occurrence, whatever that occurrence may be in itself. Pain appears and calls attention to that spot in which the event occurs and to which it does not normally belong. Thus, pain calls for some distrust or suspicion in the body. What is going on? What is happening to my body? Attention is suddenly paid to the fact that one *is* a body, that one depends on one's body, that one is dominated by the body. The less the pain is localized and identified, the greater the suspicion.

One walks, stumbles, and suddenly suffers a pain in the ankle. Inasmuch as it is a precise pain, one can grasp the cause in the tentative diagnosis "That's a really bad sprain!" One tries to stand and the pain is worse. Then suspicion enters: "It isn't broken?!" Suspicion about one's ankle grows and is put into a larger perspective: "How can I get home and go to work in the morning?" The experience of pain is here and now in this ankle, but suspicions about this joint are placed in a temporal perspective: the consequences of the suspicion. Is there perhaps a relation between the experience of the severity of pain, the degree of suspicion, and the temporal perspective brought to the occurrence?

Pain causes a distance from one's own body; the body-experience is mobilized and intensified. The body-subject is at least partially converted into a body-object: one moment one *is* one's body, the next moment one *has* a body. But it is now a possession one mistrusts even while commanding! Note that children do not reach the degree of distance from their body adults do; a child with pain is much more overcome by that pain in his or her total being. Yet children, too, can acquire some distance. When a child suffers some physical injury, he or she immediately turns to the affected part, looking at it in a new way, and holding the injured part as if it were an object. If the child forgets the pain and then looks at the part again, a new outbreak of tears occurs. Distance breaks down and the whole unpleasant experience comes to the fore again.

An adult distances rationally. While also looking at the location of the pain (like the child), the purpose of looking is different—it is to arrive at an objective causal identification.

Suspicion continues as long as the cause is not identified. Upon identification relief from suspicion is observable. Watch the patient's look of relief when the doctor—especially after taking a while—announces that she has found "something" or discovered "it." Even if the medical findings are too general to be classified, some relaxation occurs. It is undoubtedly a product of our culture that identifying a cause means to the patient that something can be done.

If the causal identity has not been found or not conveyed to the patient, suspicion about one's body grows as the pain continues or intensifies. In most cases this acquired uncertainty is imposed on the self: one is no longer identical with oneself. The relation between body-image and self-concept no longer possesses the consistency it once enjoyed—a discongruity arises between concept and reality. Continuity is destroyed, above all with respect to a future perspective. To quote C. R. Rogers, the "organized configurations of perceptions of the self" have become jumbled.

The truth about oneself also undergoes modification. One no longer recognizes oneself in the present conditions.

Thus, pain signifies disharmony, discongruity, and the beginnings of dissolution. Buytendijk writes, "The natural expression of pain . . . tells us how much an immediate experience of pain can be endured without disharmony and powerlessness in the face of the distinction between the 'I' and my corporeity" (1957, p. 16).

pain

pain now
i am pain

she comes
a slow creeping fog
invisible, ethereal
slinking
through the caverns

a treacherous
misty season
mated to my
body

my own autumn

peace just now
as my body
unfaithful groom
slept

i know she
waits there
she belongs to me
she will make it clear
my peace
will not remain
a void.

2. Coercion

Buytendijk calls the coercive character of pain "a kind of task" to be endured. The coercive character permits the patient, on the one hand, to create some distance while objectifying the experience taking place, and, on the other hand, simultaneously to incorporate the pain in a renewed sense of self. In other words, such a patient can make a place for the pain; the patient is not conquered by the pain. Rather, some working relationship is created with its inevitability.

By turning a threatening irritant into an objectified inevitability, this working relationship with pain allows one to pay little heed to the disastrous influence pain can have on the concept of self. Nevertheless, the patient often finds it extremely difficult to maintain such a relationship with pain. It is a challenge, because pain can sometimes last for years (chronic arthritis, for example). If the patient is successful, however, he or she creates at least a livable situation without losing self-concept.

Of course, there is also pain to be endured for only a short while, such as at the dentist's, after an operation, during childbirth. What makes these instances easier to accept is the localization and foreknowledge of the cause. Pain in such cases can be tolerated because it is perceived as an unpleasant side effect of a positive goal.

3. Suffering

As Buytendijk suggests, suffering pain in restlessness, protest, and rage is a sort of passive acceptance of its triumph over us. For then we have admitted that pain has conquered and the battle is over. One who suffers in this fashion is overcome with pain. One's experience is only of pain, no more and no less; there is room for nothing else. Pain conquers all other considerations. One's whole body and whole self seem permeated with pain. The patient will betray this condition in describing it: he or she will not say, "I have pain here," for there is no longer an "I" that "has" pain. Instead, this patient will only say the equivalent of "Pain, pain, pain." The suffering is underscored by moaning, groaning, and even screaming.

The self, taken over by pain, no longer has control over events. There is no channeling of efforts, no differentiation, no localization process. There is just total pain. A Kossmann calls it "an overall pain, a complete pain."

"The patient suffers terribly and *is* only that suffering. There is only pain. In fact, without any other perspective, only a pain-filled now exists," says Buytendijk (1957, p. 154). He further states that pain such as this lacks any meaning. And because this suffering so transforms a person, we can no longer offer a human response to it. The patient is so taken up with his pain that it remains questionable whether we can communicate with him in any way except through that pain.

Pain of this intensity will eventually kill a person. Fortunately, with the aid of drugs, the intensity can be reduced, so that some objectification of it is possible.

4. Denial

Pain denial seldom happens in accidents, large or small, when it is clear to every onlooker that there must surely be an associated pain. We rule out cases in which the wounded claims to have no pain but is biting his lip; such cases are not denial but a form of coping. By denial we mean cases in which patients do not seem to suffer pain when it obviously exists.

This form of denial occurs, indeed, when patients know they have pain but do not acknowledge it or permit themselves to experience it. Possibly they are concerned with hiding the conviction that they have been stricken with a terminal disease. In such cases patients are totally unaware of the negative consequences for self-concept this conviction carries.

An example of this denial is the woman with a rapidly enlarging growth in her breast that she daily confronts, but who sets her mind at ease because she has no pain (will not let herself feel pain); she "thus" concludes that the growth is not serious. Denial results from fear of a reality that is (perhaps) known but not accepted. Unfortunately, denial appears in those patients, perhaps hardly aware of it, who have proclaimed a faulty self-diagnosis to themselves.

E. Kübler Ross deals with a similar mechanism in her study *Living with Dying* (1969), which is directed to the area of terminal disease. She points out that denial works like a buffer against unprepared shock. Such denial offers the patient an opportunity to summon a sense of self as a defense against the shock. Shock, itself, is like a stupor from which the patient gradually recovers. As the patient does recover the natural response to the problem will be denial: "No, it is just impossible." The reason for this denial, she suggests, is that all persons secretly or unconsciously consider themselves immortal. Only with great difficulty do persons come to see that they, too, must do battle with death.

Thus denial includes a vague consciousness of pain yet a gradual disclaimer on grounds of unacceptability. One can speak here of a mechanism for strengthening and supporting one's self-concept. In the last analysis, however, the mechanism is ineffective and perilous when it continues too long, as in the case of the woman with a tumor in her breast. (This mechanism should not be confused with the appearance of an *absence* of pain right after an accident, as we have already noted earlier in the text).

5. De-dramatizing

De-dramatizing pain is yet another aspect of pain that is influenced by others. In fact, it arises closer to home than denial, in day-to-day relations with others. We take it to mean a process occurring when persons are dependent on positive values in their environment for self-acceptance. There are patients, even though in severe pain, who will not "reveal" it, not "act like children," and "will just not let anyone know." The last phrase is an accurate representation of what happens in these instances. One will not admit pain to another while simultaneously revealing how one will not be brought down by that pain. This is a more subtle mechanism than denial. The latter is governed by self-delusion, often to protect self-concept. The former, however, is governed by positive social values. Hence the context, a less personal sphere, can influence de-dramatizing pain.

The process is demonstrated when one breaks one's leg while skiing on a winter vacation. The same pain and cause—icy conditions—occur in this instance as do when one breaks a leg crossing the street. Yet the first instance is usually put in a jocular mode, in which the plaster cast is touted as a trophy (people complain if the doctor does not use a cast!), while the second is classified differently, with considerable compassion extended to the victim. Without doubt, anticipation plays a role here, as perhaps does the "status" of the accident—it is a far greater slight to self-acceptance to suffer a "stupid" accident on the street than to take on the challenge of the slopes.

Thus, another factor, discussed under dis-ease, comes into play in a nondramatic display of pain: the causal agent. One is oneself the cause of a winter-sports accident. But an accident on the street may involve some other causal agent, stronger than oneself, that aggressively (guilty or not) attacked one's person.

Finally, there are those kinds of pain that provoke embarrassment and humor. A toothache is a good example. Not only do others chuckle at the poor soul holding the side of his face, but the victim himself can be seen grinning and bearing it even in the presence of real pain. "He laughs like a man with a toothache" captures our ambivalence about this sort of pain. It is an ambivalence caused by our inability to deny the pain or disguise it, our attempts to gain distance from it, and the awareness that, while unpleasant, it does not represent a real danger to life and limb. It is also, in the case of toothaches, localized in the very place so essential for communication.

6. Dramatizing

Dramatizing that accents and intensifies the expression of pain is another environmentally related factor. An appeal to surroundings is made in this instance, too, less as a result of positive values than as a desire for warmth, some extension of direct contact from others. In dramatizing pain, so obvious among children, dependency needs are emphasized; self-acceptance remains in a passive-dependence mode. Dramatizing can be influenced by the context in which the pain is suffered, such as injuries received during a game, when expressions of pain are more pronounced than the injury usually warrants. The presence of spectators in this case undoubtably intensifies the expressions. Additionally, the spectators' interest in the game's continuing, their own blood lust, and disappointment when it has to stop mean that the injury had better be serious! Further, it is not out of the ordinary to find dramatization in cases of "guilt": when one is responsible for one's own injury, dramatizing the pain may disguise this responsibility; if others are responsible for one's injury, such dramatics can emphasize their guilt. Many a doctor can testify to this as a football player with a broken bone arrives amid fanfare at the emergency room, surrounded by friends.

C. FIGHTING PAIN

The impression exists that patients preoccupied with themselves, more concerned than others with their own body and illness, suffer greater feelings of pain than patients who "put up a real battle" (which almost literally describes what takes place). Conversely, patients more oriented to surroundings seem less preoccupied with their pain. They feel, perhaps, that the pain can be "dissolved," even though its intensity is such that at times there is no escape. Among other things, a battle with one's pain means that the patient will maintain some interest in the surroundings and in others who can help. A special case of this occurs in terminal-cancer patients, for whom the intensity of pain can often be overwhelming. By fighting the distress with certain pain-killing drugs, a condition can be created in which the patient is both more comfortable and, above all, able to communicate with others. Such special formulas permit deadening the pain without a loss of consciousness, whereas most anesthesiologists usually work with preparations that, in combination, produce dizziness, hallucinations, and a loss of consciousness. Without such drugs, the battle against pain would issue in inchoate consciousness at best.

Here, also, one encounters things that highlight the roots of pain. It has already been mentioned that pain can, on the one hand, have a cohesive effect and, on the other, it can lead to dissolution (actually, pain is a continuum, ranging from a call to others for help to an occupation with oneself dissolved in suffering). Most patients experience depression upon completing a struggle with pain. Confronting the void (lack of pain) created by this victory is a difficult project for many patients, leaving them with an emotional vacuum. "Something happened in my body that puzzled me and over which I had no control"—this statement by a patient is accurate. Maybe, too, this awareness reflects the meaninglessness of suffering underscored by its vanquishment. Or it may have something to do with the locus of suffering and illness in the patient's life plans, especially if pain is related to sin and penalty, and undergone to make suffering meaningful. Finally, the emptiness may well be the result of having grappled with the fear of death as directly presented by the pain, and now absent.

It has become clear to us that battle against pain, with the use of pharmaceuticals, has become for many a healing achievement, even though the existential roots of pain have been dissolved. The same is true for the patient in question, the observer, and those wishing to gain some insight into the phenomenon of pain.

We opened this chapter with a quotation from Gibran about pain. It is difficult to see, at first glance, how pain can in any way "break open" our understanding. Physiologically speaking, it is an abhorrent reality. Yet its power to overwhelm not only our daily existence but also our very sense of self can assist us in recognizing the healing power of—and our profound dependence on—others. But dependency alone is not the lesson. The fact we have bodies and will die eventually is the lesson. Being aware of this through the experience of fighting pain and winning contributes to our understanding of what it means to be human. Odd as it may seem, cruel as it may sound, to have experienced pain is to have gained wisdom.

REVIEW OF THE LITERATURE

In the preceding section we have made some points about pain as a phenomenon and a number of notes about everyday clinical experience with patients in pain. We now turn to insights from the literature. This literature can be overwhelming, so we have concentrated on just a few key works. In order to create some order in this review, we employ the categories suggested by Szasz (1968). There are, he suggests, physical pain and psychic pain, both of which stem from a special model or vision. Finally (!) there is the patient's pain.

1. Physiological Views

Pain has been studied by physiologists, anatomists, neurophysiologists, and neuroanatomists. For some time it has been the object of concentrated study, which explains why so many experiments have been done and theories formed. Every theory establishes the necessity to undertake many experiments aimed at destroying the validity of other theories and supporting the present one.

M. Callens (1972) states flatly that the specific perception of pain is due to damaged tissue. The pain-sensitive receptors are the nerve-endings of the (myelinated) III nerve fibers and the (nonmyelinated) CdR, or IV nerve fibers. Different pain modalities (sharp or continuously dull) are dependent on the distinct conduction speeds of the so-called III and IV fibers. The simplistic account of pain perception and conduction described in Callens's text seems almost perplexing in light of current controversies.

W. Metz (1964) serves as a corrective, because he compares the major findings and theories in physiology. It becomes rapidly evident from his perspective how complex the matter really is, even within the realm of physiology. We should point out that not a single physiological theory can be supported by anatomical studies (cf. G. Weddel, D. C. Sinclair, and W. H. Feindel (1948). Anatomical studies such as M. von Frey's (1922) indicate that conceptual models of specific pain receptors are quite literally invalid. It is clear that the last word has yet to be spoken on this problem.

An important contribution seems to be the "Gate Control Theory," developed by W. R. Melzack and P. O. Wall (1968). "A gate-control system modulates sensory input from the skin before it evokes pain perception and response" (p. 33). The authors develop this point: "The fast and slow-conducting fibers in peripheral nerves activate opposing mechanisms which, together with descending central neural influences, determine the amount of input transmitted from peripheral fibers to dorsal-horn transmission cells in the spinal cord" (p. 33). This view makes apparent the profound influences cybernetics has had in recent years on the development of physiology, psychophysiology, and neurophysiology.

The problem of pain also demonstrates the many steps taken to clarify the "structural" aspects of the mechanisms in the process of pain conduction. This development requires, for example, the contributions of biochemistry, even though these belong to the applied rather than the theoretical sphere.

Another discovery made possible by reading Metz (1964) is the incredible inconsistency of results yielded by physiological experiments on pain. The results seem to vary from author to author. It is not uncommon to find authorities switching to theories against which they previously contended. The literature is therefore characterized by entangled controversies. K. M. Dallenbach (1939) established this confusion as antedating the turn of the century (such as the controversy between W. Blix and A. Goldschneider). It does not seem to be abating as the Pain Congress of Paris in 1967 made abundantly clear.

The fact that pain is physiological is obvious. How it comes about, however, is very much a matter of debate.

2. Psychological Views

Pain as an object of psychological study can be traced to the research into psychophysiology conducted by W. Wundt about the turn of the century and later to the independent focus on pain developed by phenomenologists. In 1954 Merleau-Ponty included pain in his studies of perception and behavior, raising the research to philosophical considerations of human conduct. The 1957 study of Buytendijk is unsurpassed in comprehensiveness; P. Lersch (1960) based his findings on the study. Lersch asked to what extent pain should be considered a result of emotion or a state of mind. According to him, pain is chiefly experienced as a state. But it also has a relation to an object. Pain can only be experienced through something that causes pain. Here Lersch targets pain that is caused by a certain part of the body; the body "gives" us pain. Externalizing pain in this way, and claiming it corresponds to some "state," is certainly arguable. Perhaps the only conclusion can be found in the statement Buytendijk makes to the effect that the essence of pain is to disorganize.

Less speculative than Buytendijk's work are experiments psychologists have conducted in recent years. Those by T. X. Barber (1969) showed how pain is a variable of suggestion and explored the cognitive aspects of the perception of pain. Thus, R. E. Nisbett and S. Schachter (1966) claimed that knowledge about pain-perception processes, even when these are inexactly represented (in this case, they proposed that pain was a side effect), actually contributed to the dimunition of pain. The same result was obtained by R. J. Bandler, G. R. Mandaras, and D. J. Bem (1968). Cognition, in their thesis, plays a controlling role in the endurance of pain (refer also to our previously mentioned observations that knowledge about the cause of pain contributes to a patient's obtaining a degree of relief).

Certainly, an important result of recent psychological experiments is the possibility of pain adaptation. Classically put, pain is considered a warning signal ("Hence, pain is non-adaptable"—Dallenbach 1939),

[Buytendijk p. 7]). However, warm and cold experiments conducted by J. D. Hardy, J. A. Stolwijk, and D. Hoffmann (1965) and repeated by Kensalo (1968) lead to a different view altogether. F. A. Geldard (1972) also comes to the conclusion that because too few experimental methods are suited for an experimental study of the adaptation process, the warm and cold experiments demonstrate adaptation to pain "quite decisively."

One must, in the final analysis, conclude that physiological research directed toward discovery of general laws has not as yet reached this goal in its own domain nor in relation to anatomy. Psychological experiments, partially aimed at revealing the inconsistencies in physiological findings, can trace a few influential factors in pain perception. No other general statements can be formed at this time.

* * *

"Between knowing and living tension exists, both a disharmony and a strain; it is experienced as painful when one questions the meaning and essence of one's experience by turning to science." This is the introductory remark by Buytendijk in his chapter on pain in the sciences (1957, p. 7). It is a convenient motto for our next attempt to put some perspective on pain.

We have focused on the patient and pain. We have also given a modest account of what physiology and psychology—the sciences—have to say about pain. We have held that clinical experiences and scientific findings asymptotically approach the same point, though seldom support one another completely. We should ask ourselves anew, given this poor track record, whether some other approach might offer a better chance to acquire new perspectives on pain. Without deluding ourselves that we can solve the discrepancy in many opinions about pain presented by the medical model and survival instinct, we will seek some other approach. We will position some guideposts that might lead to a discovery of such an approach.

1. Historical Shifts

A first guidepost is an aspect that offers the lowest grade of evidence among the considerations to follow. Because we do not enjoy eternal life by which to pass judgment on changing pain perception over the centuries, we cannot claim direct knowledge of these changes. With the help of literature, however, we can unearth some suggestive, though inconclusive, data. J. H. van den Berg (1960) is convinced that during the last 150 to 200 years a shift has occurred in feelings of pain. He bases his stance on, among others, R. Leriche, who in turn formulated a theory of shifting perception from differences in pain perception between racial and cultural groups. However much van den Berg's well-organized presentation may, in the last analysis, be doubted, this does not necessarily mean that his thesis of a historical shift is entirely wrong. Van den Berg's argument that greater sensitivity to pain occurred in the period around 1780 because its description can be found rather extensively in literature of the time is somewhat more convincing than other points in his book. Even this argument, however, seems undermined by his own observation that it would be difficult to deny the presence of analytic descriptions of pain in literature prior to that time. For example, Saint Thomas Aquinas 500 years before the 1700s offered an almost classically phenomenological description of pain accompanying fear in his discussion of impediments to a voluntary act. H. H. Beeks' descriptions (1974) of mental illness in the Middle Ages and the wide use of scourging during that epoch suggest that pain was more integrated in daily life, with, perhaps, some other significance than that found around the 1800s. It might be that the struggle against pain was more difficult in earlier periods, although physicians in the Middle Ages did have an armamentarium of analgesics. Seifert and H. K. Beecher suggest a coupling in Western culture between the perception of pain and the possibility of overcoming it. Abstracting from arguments pro and con, we are inclined to accept van den Berg's position that one distinguishing aspect of the eighteenth century was that it paid more attention to pain than had previous centuries, this being only one of many distinctive features of the period. Whether individual pain perception was in any way markedly different than in prior epochs is a question that must go unresolved. We simply have no evidence.

2. Racial and Cultural Distinctions

R. Leriche, so justly memorialized in later theories, was not alone in his opinion that pain perception varies widely among different races and different cultural levels within the same race or nation. Several studies reported by L. W. S. van Eps (1954) also support this conclusion. These studies all noted the remarkable ease with which primitive women seemed to give birth; giving birth apparently offered hardly any pain, as opposed to the experience of more enculturated women. Thus van Eps cites a study proporting to show that small, almost anemic women in the wilds, have a much easier time with childbirth than do Hottentot women.

However, a careful study of the observations he cites in the studies between "primitive" and "cultured" women brings van Eps to the final conclusion that all tales about great differences belong to the realm of fables. The same pain occurs for birth in all races and peoples.

Recent contributions by J. van de Koppel (1975) support van Eps' conclusion, offering the possibility that it might be applicable in a broader context than heretofore realized. He mentions that certain Bantu tribes in Central Africa express their pain more noticeably than the inexpressive Pygmies, but that this does not mean that they suffer less pain than cultivated whites. The problem contained in all such claims and comparisons is the impossibility of comparing pain perception with differences in pain expression and coupling both with the inescapable subjectivity of the observer. More experimental research is therefore welcome, and we can find it in M. van Woodrow, G. Friedman, A. B. Siegelaub, and M. E. Collen (1972).

These researchers measured pain tolerance using a very accurately conceived descriptive analysis: the object was the Achilles tendon. Their conclusion is that whites tolerate more pain than Orientals, while blacks occupy an intermediate position. Furthermore, they state that men have a greater pain tolerance than women and that tolerance of pain is reduced as one ages. These results directly contradict current mythologies (van Eps, 1954).

Another important study is that done by B. Winsberg and J. C. Greenlich (1967), who tried to acquire insights into the pain accompanying childbirth. Three hundred sixty-five patients were observed by independent obstetricians and nurses in groups mixed according to race and sex. Later, the observations were tested against the patients' own awarenesses. What appeared was that there was a high correlation between different observations by sex and races, and no distinction could be drawn between the experience of black and white women. Indeed, it appears that the highly qualified observers, who had had much experience helping those giving birth, tended to ascribe less pain to the women than they themselves found they experienced.

M. Weisenberg et al. (1975), who conducted a study of pain in a dental clinic, found little if no distinction in pain levels (although they did discover that there was a wide divergence of anxiety about the procedures!).

Obtaining solid evidence for pain comparison appears to be almost impossible. Note how M. Zborowski (1952) analyzed and compared the difference between the expression and the experience of pain among a number of cultural groups. He wisely confined himself largely to description—rarely did he reach any "hard" conclusions.

3. Influencing

We have already mentioned the study by Nisbett and Schachter (1966) in which ruling cognitive suggestions seem to influence pain experience. Bandler et al. (1968) argue that perception of one's reaction to pain heightens one's experience of that pain. (Note how we try to divert a child's attention from the place where it hurts; "not looking" reinforces the child's natural tendency to neglect the locus of pain.) They also conclude that the theoretical possibility of escape, in the sense that the pain is not necessary, seems to intensify the pain more than in situations in which there is no escape. This is nothing other than a more passive resignation to the pain. Finally, L A. Copp (1974) studied the attitudes of patients toward their pain, their "coping style," and the ways they came to grips with or attempted to alleviate their pain.

According to D. Siegele (1974), who accepts the gate-control theory of Melzack and Wall, there are only three categories possible for the way in which pain may be influenced. 1) "sensory-discriminative" influence, 2) "motivational drive," and 3) "cognition activities." These categories, paralleling the three experiments mentioned below, are not solely theoretical distinctions, but can be employed clinically. We can see this in research conducted by nurses in a number of clinical settings.

Among such studies we will single out those done by F. E. Schmitt and P. J. Wooldridge (1973), A. M. Putt (1970), and C. A. Lindeman and B. van Aernam (1971). All examined the effect on patients of a good emotional preparation for an operation. It appears that a significant drop in pain levels occurs, as indicated by decreased need for postoperative pain medication, if: 1) patients are informed they will suffer pain after the operation and are told what kind of pain to expect ("sensory-discriminative influence"); 2) patients are allowed to relax and be cooperative, discuss their anxieties with others and ventilate fears to the nurses ("motivational drive"); and 3) patients receive clear instructions on how best to conduct themselves after the operation, even information about their projected motor status ("cognition activities").

These authors note their finding that there is a clear correlation between the presence of anxiety and the experience of pain. An exception to this is the finding of M. A. Breughel (1971), who could not reach a similar conclusion about correlation. Nevertheless, reducing anxiety in patients leads to a reduction in pain levels in virtually all other research analogous to that cited.

With regard to the aspect of pain we call "influencing," it is important to underscore the fact that, for once, results of laboratory research seem to be confirmed by clinical studies; only Metz (1964) found a lack of coordination between laboratory and clinical research.

Of course, given the current state of the art, his finding could be valid for other areas than research on pain. Thus the rather dismal record on coordinating laboratory and clinical research means that translating laboratory experiments on pain to the clinical context is precarious. For one thing, the life-threatening aspects of pain are siphoned off in such experiments; subjects and researchers alike know that the items studied are, in fact, controlled. Such controls cannot be reproduced clinically when matters concern real illness and/or wounds. For another, the time perspective in the laboratory experiments do not reflect the real course of pain in a patient.

4. Adaptation

The problem of translating and transposing laboratory or controlled experiments into clinical terms, and vice versa, belongs to a facet called adaptation.

F. A. Geldard (1972) is convinced that adaptation is inconceivable with respect to the original conception of pain (adaptation goes counter to the survival principle, the warning that pain signals transmit to the entity in question). However, adaptation is, in fact, quite conceivable in the laboratory. More than that, it is demonstrable. The most famous demonstrations in this regard are the hot and cold experiments. (Moreover, the discussion of pain also includes "impression" and "feeling." Hence, aspects of the discussion involve the anatomy of pain receptors, as, for example, in J. D. Hardy et al., 1965). It seems one can become accustomed to painful warm and cold sensations. The same adaptation can be found among subjects pricked with needles (Dallenbach, 1939).

R. A. Sternbach (1974), however, finds nothing of this possible adaptation among chronic pain patients he describes in a pain clinic. Adaptation conceptions are no more fitting for him than they were for M. von Frey (1922), who dealt with a totally different matter. For Sternbach pain in a chronic pain patient has a necessary and integrated psychodynamic function for his existence, such that only psychotherapy aimed at this function—and thus at the pain—could have any influence on it.

Thus, Sternbach comes to a similar conclusion as Metz (1975). The concept of adaptation to pain at either end of an extreme (such as hot and cold) is fine in theory but does not seem to apply in practice. This becomes apparent in clinical pain studies. The concept of adaptation is so seldom verified clinically that we must state that laboratory and clinic are still too far apart on this issue to draw any valid conclusions.

5. Therapy

In addition to laboratory and clinical studies, therapy can shed yet another light on pain phenomena.

The very first psychotherapeutic work on painful arthritis occurred long ago. The ninth-century Arabic scholar al-Shafi'i wrote of a "therapy" that was very effective about A.D. 400: Abu Bakr Muhammad ibn Zakariyyà Razi treated Sheik Amir Mansur ibn Nuh ibn Nasr using aggressive confrontation methods for the latter's extremely painful rheumatoid arthritis. Razi was the famous author of the twenty-five volume *Al-Hawi,* on medicine.

Of course, since that time things have developed a great deal with respect to both psychotherapy and chemotherapy (which we will not treat here). C. J. Glynn and S. Folkard (1975) conclude from their experience with pain patients that pain intensity and reporting varied between introverted and extroverted patients (using Eysenck's scale), while for all groups of patients definite daily oscillation in intensity occurred. Ten p.m. was recorded as the worst time. The authors relate this finding to what R. T. Conroy and J. N. Mills (1970) called "circadian rhythms," oscillations of physiological states over a twenty-four hour period. Yet the authors found no complete parallel between physiological undulations and the experience of pain.

M. Bond (1975) considers the difference in pain experience between different personality types (introvert and extrovert) to be a matter of different responses to analgesics.

The importance of such therapeutic findings is that although the relation between bodily disruption and pain is indeed present, certain other factors unmistakably play a role in the experience and handling of pain, factors such as personality traits. Another example is found in Metz (1975). One of his more extreme lines of thought is that pain should be viewed completely from the perspective of a communication function, such that psychotherapy is necessary to address its endurance.

Sternbach (1974) offers a detailed report of his therapeutic work with chronic patients. He begins with a "contract" drawn up with the patient whereby the patient must make a decisive commitment to be free of pain or have the pain greatly reduced. After having established individual goals of the therapy, the program begins. The starting point of the entire program of operative conditioning is first and foremost that the pain condition of the patient is to be changed; that is, the way the patient *uses* pain in his behavior in relations with others. According to Sternbach, only after a change in pain behavior can there be an alteration in the experience of pain.

In Sternbach's treatment it is essential that the usual manner of expressing pain and gaining attention will not be honored. Quite the contrary. Special attention is given to reacting during the conditioning, such that individual attentions are used to gain a different "orientation" by the patient. The purpose is to demonstrate to the patient that in spite of the pain personal functions are in many respects still possible.

Up to this point Sternbach works in almost the same way as W. E. Fordyce et al. (1973). However, Sternbach now introduces a form of group therapy, wherein patients each describe the way they handle their pain in interpersonal relations ("He has to describe his pain game"). Sternbach also adds a consideration of defenses made possible by surgical and chemical interventions (antidependency). The purpose of the whole effort is to make clear to the patient that the pain need not define one's whole life as an inevitable given. Thus, the patient does an injustice to himself or herself by regarding the pain as a central feature of existence. When this point is made, strides are possible.

About the sixth week, a definite improvement is noticed. A ceremony is now conducted in which the patient (ex-patient) is given a certificate notifying all that a chapter of the patient's life is closed and a new one beginning. The patient can now be known as a "pain expert" if successful, despite pain, in changing the direction of his or her life, or a "perpetual pain patient" if some clear "headway" has been made. The certificate represents the achievement of a desired state, but also serves as a reminder whenever the patient glances at it. The overwhelmingly positive results of the therapy lead to decreased pain, lowered intake of analgesics, and a remarkable increase in activities.

D. SUMMARY

Nothing is more difficult than to arrive at well-rounded conclusions about pain. Nevertheless, some conclusions can be drawn, though perhaps tentatively, from sources in the literature and descriptions already discussed.

1) There are many kinds of pain in which there is a direct relation between anatomical disturbance, physiological dysfunction, and pain experience: "pain that belongs to the body" (Szasz).

2) There are types of pain that do not have any clear basis in the body: "psychic pain" (Szasz).

3) No matter in which category, the ways in which pain is experienced by the individual patient and the ways in which it is expressed are part and parcel of an individual, personal stance, which

makes generalizations particularly difficult: "the pain of the patient" (Szasz).

4) The ways in which individual pain is experienced and expressed are influenced along mechanical (operative), medicinal, psychological, and social lines.

5) With regard to psychological and social influence, the following factors play a role in every case: personality traits, in the sense of introversion or extroversion; relation to the self; relation to one other and to others; and context, cognition, anticipation, and adaptation.

6) Under the influence of the factors named in 5), the patient can alter attitudes with respect to personal pain on the basis of insight and conditioning (learning another behavior).

7) On the basis of insight into another "pain behavior," the experience of pain can be reduced even to zero, or given such a place in overall existence that diminishes its previous overriding rule. Thus, some improved quality of life becomes possible in that pain is given a back seat.

8) Without doubt, pain has a signal function, not exclusively in the sense of survival (bodily signal) but also in the psychosocial sphere. In the latter case it calls attention to a degree of dysfunction that is not only physical.

9) Pain can be discerned, if the foregoing conclusions are valid, in such emotions as sorrow, depression, and aggression.

10) Just as emotions such as aggression, depression, and sorrow at their most intense are interchangeable, so is pain.

CONCLUSION

Pain is always possessed by the whole person, or the whole person is possessed by pain, just as one is afflicted or happy as a whole, or affliction or joy takes possession of us.

Hence the notion that pain is "only" a form of communication is as incorrect as the notion that pain is only a result of pain receptors and an atavistic alarm signal. In many instances pain can be an important warning signal, but in just as many other cases it can also fulfill a function of communication.

It is not an accident that these notions of pain normally seem to be divorced from one another. As I. Illich (1975) declares, it is a technological society that holds no truck with pain, that is no longer prepared to accept pain as a subjective given. "One must break the habit of considering suffering an immediate part of contact with reality and instead consider every tiny pain as revealing one's relation to applied science" (p. 130). He calls our contemporary life style "cosmopolitan society," a technocratic system, in contradistinction to "culture," reserved as a system of meaning.

Insofar as suffering is pain, for many within cosmopolitan society such suffering loses its subjective significance; they forget that for others such suffering may still reflect meaning. For technocrats depression, for example, must be treated with drugs. On the other hand, notions that pain is merely communicative neglect the fact that one possessed by pain turns in on himself such that the meaning of being alive and being an individual can be revealed. Pain is a means in communication, a signal for help: the one who sounds the alarm must do so on the grounds that persons seem further apart from one another than they ought to be. It can also be a signal, even a dramatic signal, by which one can manipulate the surrounding (the pain game). In each of these cases pain is clearly distinct from emotions such as sorrow. Although in the deepest sorrow one can turn in on oneself and grieve, such that sorrow is a highly personal and subjective experience no one else can wholly follow (no one can immerse himself in another's sorrow), one can also share one's grief with another, influencing and possibly manipulating that person thereby. With pain, however, what is found most often is that it merely produces doctor's estimates on the amount of medicine to employ to insure the patient sleep and inure him to discomfort. (Although it should be noted that in the technocracy mourning over the loss of a loved one also produces, rather than compassion in others, a quick retreat to Valium to insure the mourner some peace. Something is certainly lost in such a technocracy.)

Pain treatment, pain medication, requires much attention in a technocracy, a technocracy in which new pain clinics appear every day. Pain requires attention because it has lost its meaning; the subjective significance of pain for a person's existence is rapidly vanishing in the West. Instead, we focus on the absurdity of pain and daily invite measures to combat this meaningless obstruction to the quality of life. Every culture, says Illich, teaches "the art of suffering," and that suffering is an art. But the medical establishment teaches "that suffering is unnecessary since pain can be conquered by technology" (1975, p. 133).

Illich notes further: "Society forms, in a certain sense, the personhood of one who suffers and structures the ways wherein he experiences his own physical pain and injuries as concrete" (p. 134). This view leads Illich to the seemingly contradictory observation that "widespread use of pain suppressants raises the question of painful stimuli" (p. 138).

We can easily place ourselves in the view Illich presents. But this or a similar viewpoint must also lead to some unfavorable consequences. Must, then, pain suppression be stopped? Must patients be subjected to suffering unbearable pain? Even to raise such a question seems inhumane. Yet it does make sense to follow up on Illich's views and ask what character pain control must take on. There are persons for whom a certain degree of pain, like deep sorrow, can indeed be meaningful. Should the question not be raised on their behalf?

On the other hand, many persons are condemned to suffer "meaningless" pain, in the sense that the pain results from a meaningless cause. The young man smashed in a car accident, a mean-ing-less con-se-quence of our "technocracy," is a good example. He would have enormous difficulty finding some significance for his pain; the cause is as absurd as the result. It is the mechanized society cited by Illich that is the "cause" of such meaningless events. Thus, it is also the society that is responsible for the meaningless pain the victim must suffer.

The cancer patient who endures serious pain for an additional year of life because of eight palliative operations is not only a medical success; he is also a victim of technocracy, for whose suffering the technocracy is guilty. How meaningful is pain for those for whom life's prolongation means nothing, can have no real significance? Although a culture may, in fact, lend subjective meaning to pain, sorrow, and suffering, what meaning can it supply to meaningless causes of pain?

Treating pain patients knowledgeably is especially difficult for health professionals. They have little basis for dialogue, often because health professionals cannot discern what meaning the pain may have for the patient. Significant? Meaningless? Precisely this uncertainty leads to an attempt to rapidly alleviate the pain or at least the pain signal, no matter what meaning the pain might have for the patient. Often this response is inadequate. As one speaks with patients about their sorrows and joys (preferably the latter, if possible) one can also discuss their pain. Listen to them, listen to their pain, give an ear to the signals, to the calls for help. Pain cannot be transferred but it can be communicated. Listening thus, one can then discern what patients intend with their pain, what place the pain has in their life, what meaning they attach to it. Only in this way can one transcend medical-technical categories and experience another's pain as an emotion, as a way this patient exists as a person. Only then can one determine what course of action must be taken against the pain. Recall that pain is a means. One must treat it with an eye to the end as well as the means, especially the goals of the patient.

Pain can be lonely, but it can also be a lifeline thrown out to others. It makes no sense to destroy the lifeline. Indeed, it should be grabbed.

6. Other Aspects of Illness

We have discussed dis-ease as a disturbance in the body and the self; the process of forming a clinical judgment by translating that dis-ease into a clinical entity; and developing a workup that will address both the dis-ease and the scientific category of disease. In the preceding chapter we turned to the tripartite division of pain to note that health-care professionals must deal with its significance for the person as well as its physiological presence. We continue now to discuss other features of illness that are easy to neglect in the total care of the patient: What it means to be bedridden and to be weary. Departing from our previous organization, we will discuss the literature and draw conclusions under each of the two topics, since they are somewhat disparate.

A. THE BED

Hospital patients spend most of their time in bed, as do those recovering at home. In most cases this is appropriate, but it also represents an unusual kind of confinement. This confinement of a patient suggests a few topics for consideration often neglected by health-care professionals.

1. Space

It is an idea of Merleau-Ponty's that the meaning of space is given to me by my body. As one grows, space acquires a different significance. As one sets off in a car, space is given yet another meaning (Kwant, 1968). Development of this idea led to the notion that the body stands in dialogue with the world primarily through movement, a concept that Buytendijk (1948) studied extensively.

In most cases, the hospital patient is forced into immobility. The maximum action radius of the body is confined to the covers on the bed. In the "dialogue with the world," then, the patient is assigned a passive role. One could also argue that the dialectical element in the relation between subject and environment is reduced to a minimum. The patient is dependent, biding time, not really active with respect to the environment, although this does not imply that he or she is disoriented but rather that in gesture and movement the orientation cannot be translated into any number of the usual physical activities.

Van den Berg (1963) described confinement to a bed by noting how after two or three days the bed begins to smell. The odors of cloth, bedsheets, covers, pillows, and pyjamas are all part of the tiny abode of the sick. This abode becomes a kind of continuous interpreter of the patient's condition that itself becomes vapid and stale. The patient is forced into passivity and dependence. Everything must be done for him by others. Not only is physical contact with surroundings seriously limited, but also one's contact with one's own body. Daily hygiene, the daily encounters with one's body, however minor, that maintain that contact, are now taken over by others.

The demands of the toilet become dependent on the preparedness of others, who come to assist by bringing chamber pots and emptying them. Patients feel ashamed to confront others so directly with such personal matters as excrement. The usual privacy is lost.

This shame is not circumscribed by others, but spills over into oneself, toward one's body. The man who hopes he will not experience an erection while being bathed, the woman who hopes she will not have her period while in the hospital both suffer this kind of shame. Nothing seems left to the person. It is as if one has "abdicated" whole portions of the self. In this shame and enforced inactivity a distancing from the external world appears, a distancing from one's own body. The sick estrange themselves, even from their own bodies. In this way the bed reinforces the dis-ease that has placed them there. In a literal sense sick persons can no longer be sure of themselves, can no longer recognize themselves through their usual posture, their customary and characteristic movements. They can no longer reconnoiter space; they can no longer make conquests of something that would contribute to their sense of wholeness. Space becomes something alien, unconquerable, no longer to be used.

Their posture, movements, the manner they use to deal with space become ceased activities. They are trapped, as it were, by inactivity. As Buytendijk (1948) emphasizes, the very notion of movement implies functions of vital relations and values, of kinds of behavior and of circumstances, of position and place, of action and reaction, as objective realities. Thus, for the sick, the normal realities are to a great extent cramped, focused on the bed; proportions of reality are altered. The significance of the environment is changed, because the body's relation to space has been curtailed.

In fact, the body itself becomes part of the newly curtailed environment. It becomes an object from which the self is dispossessed. Over the long haul even shame diminishes. Personal and intimate matters are hardly experienced as such; they too are abdicated. One is no longer a body; rather, one is confronted by the fact that one *has* a body. That there, that which is covered by sheets and blankets, is mine, seems to be mine—a patient might think, "I not only have a possession but others dispose of the body not as I will but as others will."

This distancing between the body and the self sets up a one-sided dialogue between a prone body, about five to six feet long, and space, which can no longer be measured. Moreover, the body is not only constrained but it is constrained in an unnatural horizontal position. Accustomed as one is to move about in space vertically, being horizontal signifies a serious encroachment on the perception of spatial arrangements around the bed. Chairs and tables are now at eye level. A book cannot be read by glancing downward but must be held above one's head, so that reading results in a stiff neck. One encounters persons entering the room at navel and hip level and above; the rest of their bodies are below one's field of vision!

Faces of persons standing next to the bed are also distorted by the supine posture, because normally we do not view the underside of chins. To look someone in the eye is virtually an impossibility, unless that person bends over. In doing so, however, the person only emphasizes the unusual position of the patient, because the standing person must bend almost ninety degrees to look the patient in the eye. If the visitor neglects to bend over, the patient must be content to stare into the visitor's nostrils, a less than satisfactory form of personal exchange. Eye contact can be made if the visitor stands at the foot of the bed, but this creates a distance, which reduces its effectiveness—the visitor has to shout to be heard! We always listen to one another with our faces level. But a bedridden patient must listen to a voice above his head; it passes over the patient's normal hearing height, unless the visitor sits on the bed. The supine patient, in turn, converses upward toward the ceiling, away from the ears of bystanders not normally positioned. Mutual comprehension is certainly not enhanced in this arrangement. Gradually, of course, patients forced to lie for many days become accustomed to this new situation, but not so totally that it does not cause some difficulties.

When the time comes for patients to begin to acquire some mobility, a new problem surfaces. Earlier learned perceptions of space, the distance between things, the quality of material resistance, all have drastically changed. Not only does the newly mobile patient have trouble with space, he is also directly threatened by an altered percep-

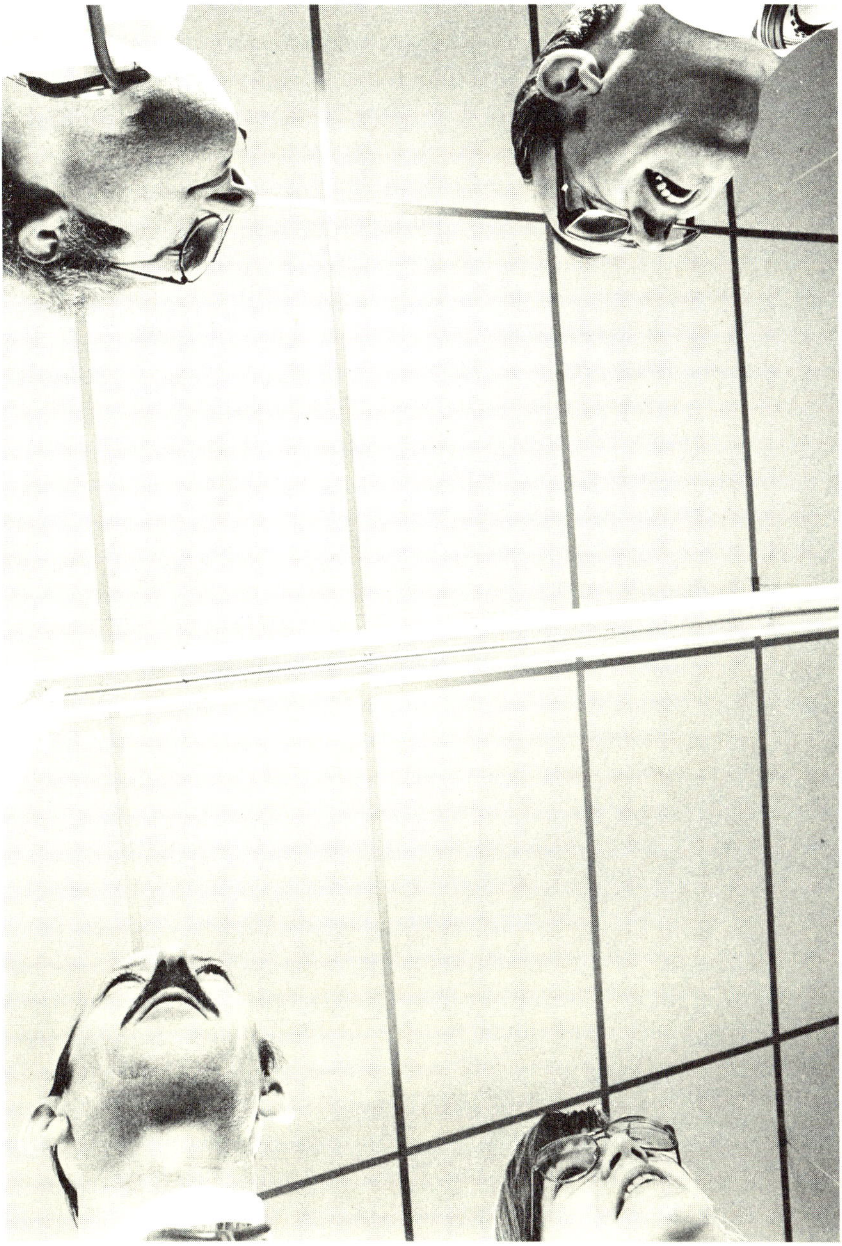

Visitors

tion of that space. The physical dialogue between the body and surrounding space has become so one-sided that it is a real challenge for the patient to reconstitute former perceptions.

The floor seems slippery. The chair seems far away to legs unaccustomed to walking. Will they fail? How far it seems to reach the bed again! Many patients express anxiety and misgivings about being able to stand again and the strength of their muscles. Readers can test these feelings even if they have never been bedridden by recalling the strange sensation after roller- or ice-skating when the ground is once again solid under their feet. Although physical exercise like this is quite different from lying in bed, one's sense of space and movement has definitely been altered and it takes a few moments to recover learned perceptions.

In *The Clocks of Bicètre* Georges Simenon (1963) describes the illness of one Maugras, who was afflicted with a paralyzing stroke. On the day he was to get out of bed the following happened:

> "What . . .?" he wanted to protest. The professor told you yesterday that you must get up for a few minutes. He reached out for his robe and his slippers. The attendant put his muscular arm around his shoulders and nurse Blanche helped him to stand up. Suddenly, there he was, standing straight. Anxiety came over him when he, startled, realized that he was supported by only two legs.
>
> "No, don't relax . . . grit your teeth and keep going . . . you shouldn't be afraid to fall . . ."
>
> Minutes later he sat in the wheelchair and reported: "He had the feeling that he veered to the right, that his body tilted, that he still listed off-center, and that he should go about in the wheelchair." "You'll get used to it soon enough," the nurse said. (p. 173)

He groped, noted that the distance had changed for his legs, and looked for obstacles where there weren't any.

The results of altered perception are noticeable not only during the first days of recovered movement in the hospital room, but also during rehabilitation as the circle of activities broadens. Patients newly released from the hospital can be quite anxious about crossing a well-marked street: it seems too busy, and most of all, the distance looks impossible. A few simple queries reveal that more than half of newly released hospital patients have the feeling that their homes and bedrooms have shrunk and acquired almost shrieking color!

2. Communication

Communication is the process in which information between a sender and a receiver is exchanged. Information in the form of spoken words and senses is exchanged, of course, but there are also nonverbal signals, which are conveyed in and through the properties of the body. In order for good communication to take place it is necessary to have a good "dispatch" as well as a good receiver.

We are accustomed to speaking in a horizontal direction. Usually mouths and ears are on approximately the same plane. Thus, as noted earlier, it is exceptionally difficult for patients to acclimatize themselves to vertical communication, to converse from below to above.

Should the visitor eventually sit next to the bed, the patient's head must be turned in a highly complicated way in order to communicate. At best such a position is unnatural and consequently tiring.

Noting the obvious technical problems this situation presents for verbal communication can only lead to the recognition that mutual comprehension will fare no better. In most cases one must consider the patient's fatigue, in every case his or her physical weakness, the doctor's haste, the presence of nurses and other professionals around the bed (especially in teaching hospitals), all of which do nothing to decrease the technical obstructions to communication. Instead, they accent them.

Add to this the fact that nonverbal communication, in normal circumstances a possible aid to verbal comprehension, in this situation is reduced almost to zero. As the patient looks upward at chins and nostrils, he cannot perceive the finer imitative musculature in the visitors' faces, which normally contributes to conversation. Because facial expressions of those around the bed are almost always hidden from the supine patient, this horizontal listener must rely even more than others on verbal statements (which in any case are made to and fro above his head).

On top of this the postures and movements of those standing around the bed are, from the patient's perspective, completely altered. They appear in a vertical plane. Interpreting them creates new difficulties and possible misunderstanding.

With respect to himself, the patient is even more inhibited. His body is covered, perhaps most of it is constrained. Thus it no longer contributes to nonverbal communication. Sometimes he can use his arms to emphasize a point, but he is accustomed to using them horizontally; suddenly he has to use them in a vertical plane: not from front and back, but from below to above. Estrangement in his emotions about self and body can only be enhanced by such odd and unaccustomed usage of his arms. Meanwhile, the bystander can only mimic what is going on in the patient, but this responsiveness, however well intentioned, goes on in a vertical field, not a supine position.

In ethology a supine posture betokens submission or subjection, a recognition of defeat. The patient lying horizontally is nonverbally "read" as having given up; he has nothing to tell; he is finished talking.

For the patient, then, verbal communication has been made difficult and nonverbal communication has become almost impossible. One often hears the charge that communication between doctors or nurses and bedridden patients is riddled with clichés. Perhaps this problem stems from the barriers that being bedridden constructs to an authentic exchange. The same holds true of visitors to patients, perhaps even more so (F. Dresen, 1975). There is so little that can really be discussed, and there is much that hinders.

CONCLUSION

Watching a visit to a sickroom one can observe visitors' heads turn this way and that in search of a familiar face. An average of one in six seems stunned by too much white. Sometimes visitors will retreat, because they did not find "their patient." The patient, of course, is only a head on a pillow; the rest is covered by clean sheets and blankets, so that recognition of a totality is reduced. Hospital regulations prohibit the patient's lifting his head from the pillow during a visit, especially if one is seriously ill or the victim of an accident—if one tries to move a bit, personnel will caution against it. Here is where the first of many communication difficulties begins. If a number of visitors arrive, the room becomes crowded. Matters of intimacy and trust can hardly be discussed; privacy has vanished. The patient moves his head from left to right to visitors on each side of the bed, so that none feels slighted. Dissatisfaction after the visit is unanimously expressed by both the visitors and the one visited. Fortunately, after recovery one can usually rectify these problems.

B. FATIGUE

A common complaint of those who are sick for long periods is fatigue. Usually the complaint comes as an unanticipated and even surprising problem, as almost always tiredness develops without any strenuous activity; paradoxically, the complaint usually surfaces while one is still wedded to the bed, the very means by which one ordinarily overcomes fatigue. And yet one gets tired, and shows symptoms of weariness. Obviously, tiredness is an accompanying symptom of certain illnesses, but this fatigue is of a different order. Hospital fatigue is clearly identifiable: a dull, slow motor activity, shuffling walk, slowly moving arms, head bowed low, rounded shoulders, a gaze without the usual intensity, a desire to sit almost immediately after standing up, the desire to get back into bed when one is forced to leave it. There is one clear inference: One is much more weary than the existing condition should warrant. Many patients are ill prepared to put this experience into words.

The patient might remark that he feels listless, does not have any interest in what is happening. He would rather go to sleep, but can't. Above all, he often notices that he no longer has any interest in things going on around him, especially beyond the hospital walls. Even reading the newspaper is too much. Do we have here the well-known phenomenon of regression? Regression is the resurfacing of infantile dependency in functions such that every responsibility for behavior is laid at the door of being a "patient." Regression as a hospital phenomenon seems to have been borrowed from the school of psychoanalysis (see the discussion J. C. B. Bremer [1972] conducts about, among others, the ideas of E. Dichter). However, the ways in which the phenomenon of fatigue presents itself exclude the specific characteristics of regression. That the fatigue exists is unmistakable, for its signs can be observed behaviorally. The phenomenon is thus a reality, even though it seems to have no causal link with the physical disease. Consequently, one cannot find a direct logical clarification using only physiological evidence.

Resolution of the problem seems better served by examining the experience of fatigue in subjectively living through "something" than by examining fatigue itself. Herewith the very kernel of the problem is laid bare: What exactly is fatigue? Does it have to do with physiologically measurable alterations in muscle strength, which, among other things, can be noted by increased levels of lactic acid? Or does it have to do, instead, with feelings occurring independent of muscle-strength conditions? Does it have to do with both? The character of this problem is barely distinguishable from the problem of pain, owing to the similarities in questions about the role of a physiological base.

Abstracting from what can be observed from patient behavior, and the fact that feelings of fatigue cannot have stemmed from undue physical activity, we must still search for further clarification. It is possible that patients complaining about fatigue are trying to communicate by these feelings something other than what we normally construe by fatigue. Observation of individual patient behavior leads to the following possible clarifications of the feelings they present.

1) There is indeed a physical basis for fatigue. Being sick, being in a hospital, creates certain feelings that can be expressed by weariness, by increased muscular tension: uncertainty, anxiety, doubts are frequent stressful emotions that usually lead to physical reactions. It can be shown that women who have had to stay in the hospital during their menstrual period in many cases have had increased tension, more

intense muscle strain, and increased heart rate. These are physical symptoms that often are not noticed by the patients themselves, but it is nevertheless not improbable that such increased muscular activity contributes to its usual physiological result, namely, fatigue. Because the cause of fatigue is misperceived by the patient as lying in a deviation from normal physical status (his illness) and not sought in his own strain, the stress situation, the strain, is further fostered. By consequence, fatigue gains a continuing character, making it difficult to combat. A direct result of this combination of unnoticed muscular activity and continuous fatigue is the high frequency of sleep complaints in the hospital. In reality, patients sleep relatively well, but owing to continuous tension no actual rest results, causing further strain and biomedical disequilibrium in the muscles. One is not refreshed upon awakening. In fact, the patient may feel wearier after sleeping than before going to sleep. The patient then interprets this feeling, wrongly, as not having slept well.

2) Ennui may be another source of patient fatigue, although it is also a complex phenomenon. Ennui or boredom means undergoing an intense emptiness between structured events in time. Structured elements in Western society include going to work, eating meals, and making arrangements often accompanying meals. In short, all appointments by which we conduct our lives from moment to moment are part of this structure. Our conduct is guided to a great extent by the upcoming moment lending the behavior its significance—persons act for ends, not only long-term goals, but brief high points in the day. Every hour a significant portion of time is devoted to these structured events: discussing business from four to five-thirty, drinks, dinner at six-fifteen, and TV at seven. Very few of these moments are available for the hospital patient, especially during recovery. Time is usually organized around the working day, when one is going strong. Orientation toward these structured moments is therefore especially difficult for those patients confined during recovery. Instead , the hospital structure takes over. The patient is oriented toward waking up, washing, breakfast, lunch, supper, and lights out. Because we usually attach meaning to structured moments in daily life, patients attach more meaning to these hospital routines than they warrant.

Case XIV

Fragments from the diary of a sixty-year-old patient admitted to intensive care after an automobile accident, and now recovering: 12/22: . . . You stayed for a while. Talked about being comfortable. Lunch was brought again. Spinach, stew, potatoes, and peaches. Visit ended. Got around a bit but felt out of sorts.

> Temperature 39.2, up some. No sense hanging around for 12 hours, so went to bed.
> 12/23: A nervous night. In and out of bed. Couldn't keep my eyes closed to get any sleep. Just told the doctor that I had a bit of bronchitis and couldn't get enough air. Asked him if I could sleep on my side. He didn't have any objection. So I'll take a little nap this afternoon. It wouldn't do for me to sleep now because you are coming. Going to sleep is hard for me right now because my lungs feel so tight.
> 12/24: Sleep was again not worth talking about. My breathing is also not really great, but the doctor says it is coming along fine. Looked forward to lunch and visit. What a visit it was! Jerry talked the whole hour about his house. It sounded good.
> Afterwards I sang a carol and hit the sack and slept till morning.
> 12/25: First day I felt just stuffy. Sat in the chair but slept. The Sisters sang midmorning, but I didn't hear them. Sat again to wait for lunch. Looked through magazines and papers. Still isn't good. I can see the titles allright, but when I try to read a story the letters dance. Hey, there's lunch now. What was it? A good portion of rabbit, potatoes, not mashed, peas in a decent sauce. I think I'll go back for a little nap until you come.

Among societies less concerned with emphasizing time and for whom space is much more important, ennui is clearly less prevalent. In even less Westernized societies, the phenomenon is virtually unknown.

Hence, one speaks of intentional activities of patients, which are really not intentional: walking to and fro, waiting for coffee, eating. None of this is actually structured and productive in the normal sense. Possibly men (for whom time is usually more structured than for the many women who do not work outside the home) suffer greater tension than women when time is converted into a meaningless vacuum. What is actually "said" in complaints about fatigue might be the combination of nonintentional activity and consequent strain. At least partially this combination leads to fatigue in the physical sense described in 1, above.

3) As a hard-working doctor once said: "I am never really tired. I am only tired if things do not make sense anymore. This is a hint that complaints about fatigue are often used as an escape." Presumably, this insight offers a clarification of fatigue closest to the concept of regression, in the sense that both can be seen as attempts at escape. Escape is actually not influenced by the content of the situation, but by the feeling of being conquered by it. In most cases there is an overburdening of diverse pressures, feelings, and emotions that are unsettled, cannot be integrated. Because they seem overwhelming, they often create a desire to flee: a tendency to withdraw from the multitude of

unsettled feelings and the responsibility that is part of those feelings. As a soldier can get weary of the violence of war without any strictly physical exhaustion, so, too, the patient can become antipathetic from too many impressions. Thus oppressed, the patient will screen himself via his fatigue from any further engagements, and entanglements. Such screening and withdrawal, turning in retreat back in on oneself, are certainly comparable to regression in a psychoanalytic sense. However, in manifesting itself as fatigue, such screening takes on a character that can fall into the category of social acceptability. As a legitimate social behavior, despite features shared with regression (especially escape), fatigue leading to withdrawal should be considered primarily a social rather than mental problem.

REVIEW OF THE LITERATURE

Literature on fatigue is slight, especially if one concentrates on physiological studies of work capacity. One book in that field, *Physiology of Work Capacity and Fatigue,* by E. Simonson (1971), certainly deserves mention, not least for its abundance of references (1,500) and diverse contributions. As a psychological reality, along the lines proposed in the chapter, fatigue has hardly been noticed in the literature. By drawing a distinction between normal and pathological fatigue P. Chauchard (1966) does shed a little light on the subject, but unfortunately, the attempted demonstration suffers from a lack of clarity and discipline. He includes chronic fatigue in his pathological category. In addition to illness secondary to fatigue there is also fatigue as an illness. Even though he further distinguishes neurotic and psychosomatic fatigue, his clarification nonetheless rests largely on somatic and biological bases. On these grounds Chauchard also notes the likelihood that chronic tension leads to a chronic increase in (toxic) waste material, which in turn can lead to chronic feelings of fatigue.

S. H. Bartley (1945) is remarkably more careful in his study of fatigue. In an article written with E. Chute he inventories the concept of fatigue from many standpoints, thereby clarifying its many connotations. This is an important article for the clarification of concepts and the determination of the limits of ideas. Among many of his significant caveats he notes, "(a) 'Fatigue is an organizational concept.'—"Fatigue always pertains to the whole person, and should be regarded from the standpoint of the individual's internal organization rather than merely from the standpoint of his available energy" (pp. 169-174). This view, in which fatigue is related to the (dis)organization of the individual as a whole, is further developed in Bartley's volume *Fatigue* (1965). In the 1945 work he notes further: "(11) Fatigue is personal. It has been said that fatigue is dependent upon personal attitudes. Fatigue is consistent with the individual's long-term ideas, goals, etc., and with his evaluation of himself. It generally arises as a phenomenon meaningful and relevant to a situation in which its elements are only a part" (p. 173).

Bartley (1945) finds that fatigue ought not to be linked with its ultimate cause, precisely because it has such a complete and unique identity of its own. Thus, it is incorrect to speak of work fatigue, muscular fatigue, battle fatigue, and so on. This is especially the case when "fatigue arises from conflict" (p. 172), whenever irreconcilable tendencies are present. "Conflict cannot be avoided in active situations. Fatigue commonly develops when action is thwarted" (p. 173). Further on he adds, "Fatigue, like other functional concepts, acquires meaning only when it is viewed in light of the dynamic situation in which it occurs" (p. 173).

To this should be joined the interesting view developed by P. S. Blitz and A. van Moorst (1976) that led them to postulate that fatigue is less a condition and more a mode of perception. By way of conclusion from this postulate, the authors develop a line of argument similar to Bartley's.

In *Fatigue* (1965), Bartley concludes that there are, in fact, three ways to approach fatigue: 1) as a direct result of used energy; 2) as a problem of process organization within a human body, and 3) as a relational problem between organism and environment (in which perception is included, among others). For the patient all three forms play a role. In this chapter we have shown by supposition that there is no direct relation between activity and fatigue. I. H. Gross and Bartley (1951) have made these data hard by conducting a "housekeeping" experiment. In doing certain household chores (cleaning rooms), it became clear that the subjects' attitudes toward the work were far more significant in creating fatigue than was the objective difficulty of the work (P. S. Blitz and A. van Moorst: Motivational strength determines how long one can tolerate fatigue).

Add to this Bartley's view that fatigue often arises in conflict and that fatigue, because it leads to inactivity, actually increases the duration of the conflict, and one finds a great deal of overlap with observations made in the hospital. At the same time, one crosses over to the phenomenon of ennui, even less apparent in the clinical-psychology literature than is fatigue. Ennui is treated like a stepchild.

W. Luypen (1951) says of ennui, among other things: "In the first phase of its appearance ennui is not experienced as shock or impact, but as a slowly swelling feeling of shiftlessness and paralysis. Without violence, without shock, without irritation and without consternation, but wary and even fatal, almost inconspicuous and yet tenacious, it makes itself master of the I, paralyzed and *dis-organized* such that it offers itself as a victim and with a sigh knows that 'I bore myself'" (p. 13).

As a conclusion of his detailed phenomenological study Luypen arrives at the following formulation: "All assembled facts reveal only continued dissatisfaction of one or more strivings such that this dissatisfaction comes to dominate the psyche. Comparison with the rise of impatience reveals, then, a special mode of striving concerning us here, namely, its inward-modified character. Ennui is thus to be viewed as an effective reaction of a steadily insistent dissatisfaction dominating the psyche in terms of an inward-modified striving" (p. 93). In this view of ennui, the notion of conflict appears once more.

Ennui can lead to drowsiness or sleep (legitimate withdrawal), or to destruction, "in which ennui obtains its maximum dominance" (Luypen 1951, p. 93). The tendency to destruction accompanies want, seen earlier as the cause of a "ceaseless feeling of emptiness" (p. 93) in that it appears to "eliminate that feeling" (p. 93). The pattern of this evil, this destruction, is blocked from view in the hospital situation, for a number of other plausible reasons (see pages 100 *ff.*). The patient cannot give vent to his aggression. He becomes bored. "[Fatigue] is simultaneously a defense against a powerful aggressiveness in [this neurosis] and is often seen as an important element in mechanisms to check it" (p. 93). Almost at the close of his article R. Puyol (1962) adds this very important note: "Fatigue is often seen in a feeling of incapacity, inhibition or retreat from action, such that the energy of the subject should be seen as employed in [defense] rather than that action is considered dangerous by the subject" (p. 24).

We have therefore come full circle. The patient's situation leads to dissatisfaction, unhappiness, to conflicts that are beyond his power to resolve (wanting to go home but waiting for something wholly unclear to happen). This causes tension. Disproportionate muscle tension leads to chronic fatigue, since there is only minimal motivation to accept and integrate these feelings of fatigue. Both fatigue and subsequent ennui are legitimate escapes from a situation in which aggression and destruction are impossible, not only on the basis of invested energy but also on the basis of a relation of organism to situation. This only intensifies fatigue (Bartley, 1965). It is therefore no surprise that in the research of L. F. Pride (1968) and later S. B. Foster (1974) an important physiological indicator for the degree of stress suffered by patients was the Na/K (sodium/potassium) ratio in the urine. Na/K is a by-product, excreted in the urine, that is produced by lactic-acid formation in active musculature (P. Chauchard, 1966).

Without much fear of contradiction, one can therefore claim that stress, frequently occurring in the hospital, results primarily from conflicts patients experience, because they cannot resolve the conflicts on the level of their individual "organization" (Bartley, Luypen), given the hurdles the hospital presents for the sick.

CONCLUSION

Seriously ill patients are often weary. Diverse categories of patients have at least one symptom of fatigue. The largest category of patients suffers from a form of fatigue barely related to their illness and more obviously resulting from their enforced stay in the hospital. This form is characterized by waiting, anxiety, uncertainty. Fatigue and ennui seem both to stem from conflict situations.

One conclusion of this chapter is that although hospitals are geared to minister to the sick and injured, they are less suited to long-term care of those who must remain there as a result of their illness or injury. Waiting, for example, is often characterized by an inability to articulate that for which the patient waits. Anxiety and uncertainty are also often related to ignorance and lack of information.

Conflict seems to arise on the one hand in the patient's ignorance and on the other in his dependency (he cannot walk away; he must be careful not to express his aggression). By contrast, waiting for something or someone that is known is tiresome but not unbearable.

Actually, it is surprising that "persons" are not extinguished by the corporal and spiritual inactivity imposed by the hospital. Absolute passivity influences the process of recovery, for both good and ill. Corporal and spiritual activity have a demonstrably positive effect (J. Bergsma and G. Rullmann Schadee, 1975). Informing the patient and involving him in treatment have a similarly positive effect on the process of recovery. In enforced inactivity, on the other hand, the person wrongly perceives that being a patient is more important than being a person. The essential element of conflict for a long-term patient is resistance to the fact that he has been reduced to a *patient.* The activities and responsibilities normally ascribed to him as a person are withheld by the internal divisions of an efficiently run organization.

7. Permanent Handicap and Chronic Illness

Having described and discussed the workup of an encroaching illness, we can turn to a further discussion of the processes of treatment. There are only three possible outcomes of illness: 1) the patient recovers after a brief or longer period and can take his or her place in society as totally healed; 2) the patient recovers to some degree but is now hampered by some permanent handicap and must face this in order to be reinserted into society; 3) the patient does not recover, eventually dying of the illness.

Many of the difficulties discussed in this book apply to the first outcome. Our intent in this chapter, however, is to focus on the second and third possible outcomes, looking at permanent handicap and chronic illness (in the next chapter we will concentrate on dying). First we will treat the phases of the process in which patients confront an unwelcome discovery: they must live the rest of their lives with a permanent handicap.

A. PERMANENT HANDICAP

The patient, confronted during his treatment with the permanent character of what has affected him—a handicap—seems subjected to a psychological process that occurs in phases. This process sometimes seems to parallel the process of medical recovery, yet at other times to possess an entirely separate dynamic.

The four phases of the process resemble those identified by E. Kübler-Ross (1969) among terminal patients. Just as with the dying, it is important to emphasize that there is no absolute and rigid unfolding of the phases. Different aspects of these phases can appear at different times. The importance of distinguishing phases in the process stems from the fact that each requires a distinctly different and specific response from the environment with respect to the whole disease and recovery process. We will describe phases progressing from resignation to opposition via depression to acceptance. We will now look at each of these four phases separately.

1. Resignation

In addition to the previously described reaction to an acute incident, such as an accident or the discovery of a serious illness, when it dawns on the patient that his or her problem is grave and implications still lie in the future, there is almost always a (short) period of what can best be described as resignation. Accompanying the event or discovery there is an immediate abdication by the body and its "tender"—the person—to the expert.

J. H. van den Berg (1963) put it this way:

> The start of a serious illness is a cessation, a halt. One's usual life is cut off and another kind of life takes its place, whose structure one does not know. Weary of affliction and suffering, one can in no sense survey this new life. One can pay so little attention to its implications that no form can be given this new reality. One does not take hold of this new life. Instead, one undergoes it: Beaten, bewildered, rebellious, or even fruitlessly acquiescent. It is an experience of an all-out surprise attack. The sick person can scarcely put it in perspective (p. 11).

The patient is often already put in an alien situation as a result of the event. Admission to a hospital seems only to reinforce this alienation. He is, thereby, so thoroughly bewildered that he completely distances himself from his body. It is such a total passivity that care for the body is now the responsibility of the expert: this body is now the focus of health care. The patient is deemed powerless. He cannot do anything meaningful (except offer small bits of information about the thing, the body) that could in any way improve his condition. He easily hands over control of his own body. Resignation seems to stem most from powerlessness; perhaps being overpowered would be a better way to put it. Resistance and defense by the patient are minimal if not negligible. The degree of dissolution during this period is at its height, as is the patient's affect.

Clearly, the way in which the environment—the experts—responds to this condition of the patient is often extremely important for subsequent developments in the illness process. It determines how the patient will relate to those around him (cf. chapters three and four).

Because of his permanent injuries the patient does not recognize his passivity; but recognition of this passivity is necessary to inaugurate a partial recovery. Not recognizing passivity means that the patient has been summarily relegated to a role in conflict with his usual function.

The negative influence of this on winning back self-acceptance is evident: alienation from himself is unjustly continued; uncertainty is left unanswered; and his passivity is cultivated by those responsible for his care. Unless the patient possesses such strength of character as to escape, he will succumb to this dependent and overpowering role expectation.

Note well, however, that not every patient manifests resignation. Its presence depends largely on what takes place during the hospital-admission proceedings. The resignation seen in many patients during these first moments, sometimes when the patient is scarcely conscious, often leads experts to surmise incorrectly that the patient "is somewhat depressed, but not yet completely aware of the consequences of his condition." In fact, the opposite is often true. The patient is much more aware of his condition and its future ramifications than the experts and family may think (or will allow themselves to think in their avoidance of unpleasant realities). Resignation is more aptly ascribed to the fact that the patient indeed sees the consequences of his condition but that these appear so multiple and complex that he simply cannot put them in context. As a result he cannot gain perspective on them in order to divert himself from the overpowering force their recognition entails and for which he has as yet no response.

Perhaps in the act of handing over responsibility to the experts there is also an element of not wanting or being able to confront reality. Thus, in an attempt to escape one burdens others. The dissolution between self and body then is continued as a form of self-protection.

2. Opposition

Opposition is a feature found in almost every patient. In some it arises just once; in others, in phases or periodically; and in others still, as chronic behavior. The cause of this phase—characterized by physical and psychic unrest, a tendency to verbal aggression (discussing, complaining, grumbling), and criticism of experts and others—is not always the same.

A first instance could be a situation comparable to that discussed in 1, above. The patient is thrust into a role expectation with which he cannot identify. Imposition of this compelling expectation is often no longer accepted by the patient, especially since it requires passive and dependent behavior. The patient may well have had a hand in creating the expectation, but now he seeks greater input into decisions about his treatment. He can no longer accept the ways he was forced to function and now tries to create a renewed self-realization through opposition. In terms of psychic health, this opposition must be viewed as a positive contribution to a disturbed self-acceptance. All too often, however, those responsible for care misperceive opposition. Instead of seeing it for what it is, a renewal, they consider the patient in conflict with their treatment plan. The patient is labeled "difficult" or "unruly." This label can only lead to an extension and hardening of contrary behavior, precisely because the experts misperceive its meaning, just as they can misunderstand a depressive reaction of the patient (to be treated in the next section).

It is more difficult to deal with opposition resulting from a patient's unhappiness with the healing process. Usually this dissatisfaction stems from the length of time it takes, thus making time an important factor in addressing the problem.

A patient's perception of time rarely parallels the time necessary for the body to heal. Even if adequate information about recovery has been given, to cover all eventualities, for a number of patients the period of time is so great as to seem insurmountable. In some cases, opposition originating from aggression is aimed at specific persons, in other cases, at the total situation; one might even encounter opposition to a body that no longer does one's wishes (an extreme form of discongruity between self and body). Most often, however, opposition is directed against the care givers (doctors, nurses), who, in the eyes of the patient, have failed to bring about the expected recovery of the body. In these cases the principal features of opposition are mistrust of expertise and of the experts' commitment.

Opposition in this form can be channeled into positive results by increasing the quality and quantity of information given to the patient. But it is this form of opposition that plays most on professional feelings of commitment and the emotional content of doctor-patient relationships, creating a difficult underlying relation between helpers and helped. Thus, the helpers often miss the real meaning of the patient's criticism, taking it merely as a personal attack.

Certainly no less difficult to master is opposition out of desperation, in which the patient comes to oppose his own inability to cope with the realities of his total condition, no longer endurable and no longer capable of being integrated. Often undirected aggression is a sign of desperation in a patient unable to deal with poor recovery, admissability of inevitable consequences, the stay in the hospital, and separation from family. Rational arguments and considerations no longer work. The patient has heard them all and they carry no weight.

Patients manifesting this kind of opposition to their condition—their existence as trapped by their disease—come to reject all the facets inherent in this entrapment. Incongruence in their very existence is of such a degree, dissolution has taken on such forms, that the patient is unable to organize distinct and various realities in any kind of normal perspective.

Perhaps uncertainty about the future contributes to this wholesale dissolution ("What is going to happen to me?"). Perhaps the central feature is mistrust in the information conveyed by specialists "(So they tell me, but so what?"). At any rate, it is the *total* stress situation that the patient can no longer accept or bear. Certainly, ability to bear this stress differs widely from patient to patient, because it depends so much on personal variables. These variables, in turn, permit helpers in some cases to understand the "mistrust offensive" and continue to sympathize, and in other cases totally to miss it ("Why does the patient get so agitated?"). Most often the variable is the patient's strength of character and insight into his condition. When these break down, health professionals counter the patient's rejections with some of their own. The form taken by this opposition has an impact on the difficulties experienced by both the specialists and the family.

The caregivers' apparent impotence in the situation plays a large role at this point. Because the patient can no longer appreciate the caregivers' function, since their arguments lead nowhere, an ambiguous atmosphere is created. This situation, in turn, can lead only to disguise and cover-up by the care-givers in treating the patient. Lack of truth telling, whatever its ethical status, then leads the patient from opposition to depression, which is certainly a less desirable state. Thus, the professional's inability to grasp what is going on in opposition—an inability predicated on both patient and care givers—becomes the master of the healing relationship.

3. Depression

Depression is a direct outgrowth of the scenario sketched above; that is, situations in which opposition is inadequately handled. The impossibility of giving one's condition a meaningful form and content and the inability to direct one's opposition in a constructive way most often are avenues to depression. Strain, silence, slackening of tempo, lack of cooperation in one's management or active attempts to sabotage it, aversion to communication—these are the symptoms reflecting the fact that the patient is seriously frustrated in his external relations and is turning back in on himself.

Inherent in depression are guilt feelings about oppositional behavior and despair about one's condition, either because it cannot be completely grasped or because it cannot be put into a true future perspective.

Depression means that the patient is more or less unhinged. He is cutting himself off from usual relations in order to solve his discongruity on his own. When the discongruity is so great that it is the actual cause of the depression, when the discongruity predominates and self-acceptance is minimal, a real solution to the patient's problem is hardly possible.

One always detects in these depressions an inability—coupled with a seeming lack of desire—to permit the environment any influence, and the impossibility for the patient of gaining a grip on himself. In contrast to the resignation phase, in which responsibility is handed over passively to another, in depression all influence that the environment might have had is curtailed. The environment is shoved away, no longer accepted, no longer trusted, no longer considered a partner in management of the disease. A vacuum about prospect is created. Sometimes aggression against the self rushes into this vacuum, out of the false impression that one's outlook for recovery will improve with such aggression. Frequently the patient is tempted to commit suicide, because the physical situation augers ill; these temptations only strengthen the depression and can lead to increased agitation. Among the few remaining questions the patient directs to those around him is frequently a central one: "Can you help me commit suicide?" "Why don't you put an end to me?" The usual rational arguments offered in response to the questions are ineffectual, no matter how often they are given. The questions confront the environment with its own powerlessness. This confrontation, in turn, produces inadequate reactions, in the sense that poorly handled aggression results from the care-giver's insecurities.

Because of this dynamic, an empathic and supportive environment stands a better chance of offering some possibilities to the patient than an environment obsessed with treatment plans. The reason is simple. Except for specific technical and nursing care, there is really nothing to "do" about chronic illness. More than medical intervention, such illness calls for support.

4. Acceptance

By *acceptance* we understand an active engagement by the patient with his illness, its incalculable challenges and future limitations. Thus, acceptance is not a passive submission to an illness and its process. Rather, it involves an integration of the event in the life plans of the patient. To reach this stage demands that the patient has gained a certain degree of self-acceptance. The break-up between self and body must have been largely overcome. In every respect the body will have become subject again, rather than object. A primary condition for this change is that the patient has been fully informed about his status; he must be convinced that he has been given every ounce of information available. Doubts about possible information withheld or inaccurate facts make it impossible for the patient to establish the required relation with himself for a reconstituted integration.

Two important points follow from this consideration. First, one cannot properly speak of acceptance in any complete sense. Instead, we refer to "a degree of acceptance," since in any given situation complete integration is impossible, precisely because an end phase has not yet been obtained. The second point is that ethical arguments regarding truth telling usually are derived from moral principles. However, as indicated above, the guiding principle behind truth telling ought to be, at least in part, developed from what is best for the patient. Without the truth about their condition, patients are deprived of an essential tool to move from depression to a degree of acceptance, to grow from personal discongruity to a renewed integrity.

As the patient moves toward acceptance, some indicators become apparent. Acceptance is characterized by a sense of peace, active cooperation, and ready agreement with the management plan for the challenges and limitations accompanying the illness or injury. Any changes in the recovery process or in relations with the environment (a chance negative remark by the doctor or spouse, for example) can result in a relapse. The first steps toward acceptance are especially critical, because there is a shifting balance of factors that can be tilted. A negative imbalance would cause a retreat into the preceding phase.

5. Dealing with a Handicap

As we mentioned prior to our discussion of the four phases, emotions found in those phases and attitudes toward them do not occur in a lock-step way. Instead, persons can flip back and forth among all four phases. To emphasize this point, we will briefly discuss how patients come to deal with their handicap.

(a) *Developing Consciousness*—Persons encounter themselves as a gestalt and function in space experienced as a gestalt (see the points already developed on this topic in chapter 6). The patient in his bed encounters himself only as a destroyed gestalt. The schema of the gestalt has been broken. Not only has this been broken, by the sheets and blankets under which the patient lies for so long, but the body gestalt of the handicapped has also been broken: the existing balance represented by his previous gestalt has ruptured only a little while ago. Not enough time has yet elapsed to repair it. In addition, the effects are not yet visible. In fact, he may not always feel this rupture. But he does have some idea of it, some initial awareness, even though it may not have dawned completely on his consciousness or its effects may not as yet be fully comprehended.

Indeed, the first crisis has been weathered. But the rupture of the body gestalt was hidden in that crisis as only one of the features of the crisis. It was no more than one aspect. Its complete extent is not yet manifest.

It seems that at this stage, in spite of a certain degree of acceptance, mechanisms of recognition still remain to appear. The reason for this lack of recognition may well lie in the fact that the dissolution has been so thoroughly complete. The body is fully experienced as an alien object, in no way one's own. Consequently, the damage is experienced as remote or, alternatively, as repellant. Thus, for patients in this condition it is not I here, the self, that has been damaged. It is that, there, that nonself, that repellant object, that has suffered harm.

Sometimes even this act of recognition fails to appear in the course of a disease. The only way recognition is made possible is through the great struggle between the self and the object/body. Such discovery also accompanies being covered, tucked in, or the sensation that a missing portion of the body is still present (phantom-limb syndrome). As the general picture improves, repeated indirect confrontation with the body due to necessities (such as injections, bandage changing, and so forth) demands a subjective struggle with a relation that can no longer be denied, a relation wherein one "possesses" a body (Marcel). Of course, this relation is still one of "possession" rather than being. However, the broken gestalt is so intrinsic to the person that the confrontation already obtains a greater importance than that of other kinds of possessions.

As a sequela to structural damage, decreased function is hidden by functions performed by and inherent in the health-care environment such that its full import is not yet realized. It is only one aspect of a destroyed body organization, one facet of complete dependence. But when the patient begins to take over some functions himself, when he must confront his status directly, a different kind of intrusion on the self occurs. This intrusion is a requirement, a demand that the self confront a destroyed gestalt. This is the moment, perhaps shockingly sudden, when the patient first "realizes" what has actually happened: the familiar body-image can no longer be employed, because it simply cannot be summoned to function as it once did. The patient with an amputated leg first notices its complete implication when he tries to get out of bed or sit in a chair. He now experiences, for the first time, that something is really amiss: a part of his body he took for granted is now lacking, so that he can no longer manage such simple tasks as getting seated or even maintaining his balance.

A patient with a colostomy who wants to get out of bed and go to the bathroom on his own will realize suddenly that it is no longer possible. The new situation is comprehended only when someone else takes over this function by emptying and replacing a bag attached to his abdomen. The first mobilization of handicapped patients is almost always accompanied by the first real discovery of the extent of damage. Often it is followed by a new, though shorter, period of opposition or depression.

This setback of patients is related to their inability to integrate such first complete confrontations with the malfunctioning self. The setback seems to foster additional evasion of the confrontation and a renewed denial. Buytendijk (1965) says: "The trusted relation with our surroundings, usually taken for granted, in which we find our place and through which other things are placed, is our organized space. We are at home in this space. We stand and walk in it with balance and certitude. It gives meaning to our situations" (p. 7). He speaks here of a "coherence" between persons and the world. For the handicapped, this coherence has suddenly vanished at the very moment that they must "stand and walk." The gestalt body and gestalt space no longer cohere. Discongruity within patients is followed by discongruity between them and their situation. A new crisis occurs.

The new crisis sometimes lasts quite a while, especially because it occurs in a recovery period, which requires and offers content for renewed confrontation with an impaired body-image. Although recovery is aimed, of course, at learning to manage, reshaping a new body-image, the process is made possible only by repeated confrontation with what is missing.

(b) *Revaluation of Functions* — A patient attending to his handicap discovers that it is not just a single part of the body that has been functionally affected or altered. Rather, it is clear that he experiences the whole body as damaged. The gestalt, the configuration, has been broken in its totality. That is how it is experienced. The body is a damaged body. It is broken, severed, definitively disfigured. It can no longer function in familiar ways. This very definitiveness looms large for the patient. The future looks grim because it is invincible. An inability to grasp all the consequences for the long run makes the patient fearful and dispirited. He cannot easily project living with the handicap into the future, because this new body is not yet known. One could also infer that the realization of a handicap simultaneously produces initial estrangement. A full realization of handicap implies a lack of recognition, an experience of a strange new object to which one is irreconcilably attached and bound. Having a handicap and being handicapped plunge one into chaos.

Not only the body but one's entire identity has been destroyed. The body is no longer recognizable; consequently, neither is the "I," the self, one's identity. "Who am I?" "What shall I become?" Depending on background, every handicapped person experiences a more or less severe identity crisis. Beethoven, going deaf, wrote his *Heiligenstadt Testament,* in which he predicted his imminent death, years before the actual event. With deafness his identity as a composer was severely damaged. A major effort at reconstituting identity was required. It demanded the highest forms of human spirit.

Erik Erikson is the one who popularized the notion of an identity crisis in youth. He described it as follows: "A state of acute confusion usually becomes manifest at a time when [the young] individual finds himself exposed to a combination of experiences which demand his simultaneous commitment to physical intimacy, to decisive occupational choice, to energetic competition, and to psychosocial self-definition" (1968, p. 166). Recovery takes place in the formation of a new identity.

The basis of a new identity for the recently handicapped lies in the act of discovery of a new body. Discovery of new possibilities follow as a matter of course. Precisely because the former body-image as a whole has been destroyed, the patient can now discover a new body-image: all aspects of the body are altered against the backdrop of a broken gestalt. Nothing is as it was. Everything acquires a new place against this altered backdrop. If ever Piaget's distinction between objective and subjective space were valid, it is certainly at this juncture. If space presents difficulties to a healthy person, the same space is viewed by the handicapped as filled with stumbling blocks and overwhelming obstacles. He is insufficiently prepared to overcome them. Relation to the obstacles is in no instance what it once was, or as good as it was. Objective space has not changed. Only the way the patient now takes in this space has changed. Thus, coherence in objective as well as subjective space must be newly acquired. As a consequence, the patient's discovery must be directly not to one feature of his corporeity but rather to the totality of embodiment and surroundings. Steps in this discovery, unlike those of a baby, rapidly follow the first tentative *experiments.*

Even if the patient is not yet ready to take these quickening steps, the process of revalidation by caretakers encourages the patient to begin experimenting with his new body as soon as possible. Possibilities and impossibilities must be probed. The problem, of course, is that the patient has just recently experienced the "now," and must project possibilities and impossibilities against a dreadfully unclear future. The physical therapist and rehabilitation specialist do indeed know what lies ahead; they know the challenges an individual patient may have to face. Sometimes the chasm arising from differences in temporal perspectives between helper and helped is so great that it may overwhelm the patient and discourage him from continuing the experiment. In this lies the art of rehabilitation: to confront the patient with others with similar handicaps who have already progressed in their experiments and perhaps come to terms with their bodies. For this reason rehabilitation should be attempted at a center where other handicapped people are present.

The sense of experiment we are using here is not devoted exclusively to testing physical possibilities and improving diminished functions through exercise. It also entails establishing a renewed trust in one's body. Only in this way can the body become, once again, one's own, once again a component of the self.

Before this new integration over the course of time can be achieved, *subjection* of the body must again become possible. Subjection is meant in the sense that the body can be used and managed; that one is again master of oneself. Until one can speak of this kind of control, a more honest portrayal would be that the body is the ruler of the person, and the self is, to a great extent, defined by its physical functions. In this case there is a kind of inverted subjection of self to body, which throws up great barriers to the process of establishing a new identity. A renewed integration is likely only when persons have become to some degree rulers of the "new" body. A new sense of identity is then not far behind.

For some patients such command over their disabled body is not only remote but in fact impossible. However, a number of them, because of the bitterness of their struggle with the body, can reach a renewed validation of their own self simply by the power of their spirit. In a manner of speaking, the body as object and the self become two separated entities, functioning somewhat independently of each other. The dissolution attendant on this struggle is then permanent, but does not essentially hinder the growth of the self. Of course, the body and the self can never be totally separated. The self in these cases is given definition by its very struggle with the body.

B. CHRONIC ILLNESS

What does it mean to be chronically ill, to be sick without any hope of recovery? We really know so little about this. Chronically ill patients are an almost neglected group. They certainly exist, but they exist outside the normal preoccupations that absorb the lives of those around them.

For one patient, chronic illness may present the possibility of distancing perception, a chance to gain a measure of wisdom and relativity. For another, it leads to distancing *action,* isolating himself from all that has happened to him and forlornly hoping that it will not last much longer. For him existence is something less and less meaningful: an abrasive emptiness. And how threatening, how terrifying, such emptiness must be. As Paul Tillich (1952) observes, the anxiety of meaninglessness is perhaps the most profound anxiety of all, because it means that a person has lost an ultimate concern, which, for Tillich, is the meaning that gives meaning to all other meanings (p. 47).

The chronically bedridden patient who feels his or her bonds with the surrounding slipping away watches in horror as the emptiness, the not-being, approaches. It fills these patients with anxiety, a permanent and expanding terror, because the void they see before them only comes closer and closer.

If at first the patient finds meaning in the question of his existence, he is only to discover later that this question can lead nowhere. This, too, fills him with dread. Thus a man of twenty-one immobilized up to his neck vertebrae said: "Don't ask me about my future plans, I live from moment to moment. If I have to think about things I go really crazy. I can't do that anymore."

Again, this situation is not true for all chronically ill patients. There are some who derive some content from their surroundings for the meaning of their existence. They can give meaning to their own life and those around them. For them, the question of their existence elicits a positive response. Often they find some meaning in their suffering either on human or religious grounds. Our discussion will leave these patients aside.

For those who have little or no capacity left, or are not considered capable by others, can some meaning be discovered for their existence? A nursing-home doctor once sighed: "If you want to know how powerless I feel, I see people vegetating, clinging to life, and I want to help them or do something for them, but God knows, I don't know what I could do." The void of continued existence in a chronically ill state is an anxiety-provoking condition, one that produces dread no matter which way one turns. But it is so not only for patients. Those responsible for their care find it exceedingly difficult to offer anything but purely bodily comfort or palliative measures. Only one question predominates even while the patient continues to survive: his or her death.

Discussion of the past places the patient in the context of a prior existence, when life had meaning. Sometimes this has a salutary effect, because meaning for current existence can be bound up in earlier achievements and memories. In this sense there is still a world of meaning, a dream world perhaps, but a world nonetheless in which life was experienced as having value. Sometimes light comes back into dimmed eyes; stirring can occur. The void, the angst, vanishes for a while.

1. Time

Time plays a central role for every patient. It is even more the case for the chronically ill patient. Since space has lost its significance, owing to the patient's immobility, it seems that the meaning attached to time grows out of proportion to that found when one is functioning in society. The experience of time is now measured against routines such as being bathed and fed, but the void between these events seems endless. As a result, an inordinate concentration on the routines arises, because they provide the only structure in the patients' lives. Sometimes this situation seems to be exploited. Patients complain about the bath, about eating; they play with their food—they seem to complain about the very moments when human contact occurs, when their anxiety is replaced by the here and now. But these complaints serve to prolong the brief respite, making time stand still as long as possible—the void, the meaninglessness, the threatening emptiness, is put off for a while. No matter that the anxiety must return shortly, the patients are currently freed from it while the smallest event is taking place.

Often we see patients with tendencies to escape from real time in their need for a great deal of sleep, to dream away their impending death. Officially they are regarded as "disoriented as to time."

W. Zwannikken (1975) rightly notes that there is a question here of genuine disturbance or simply behaviors negatively valued by surrounding persons and institutions. The patient no longer enjoys the organization of time now or projected into the future; that is, the organization of time around events occurring in their environment afforded fully healthy human beings. In fact, the usual ordering of time is almost completely abandoned. A period of ten years or seven years makes no difference to the patient. He can talk as if it were yesterday. Similarly, it is impossible to project into the future, given the patient's chronic status. Often this observation is bound up with the judgment that the patient has begun to decline, that the patient has become totally disoriented with respect to time. While it is true that dementia is accompanied by disturbances in perception of time, this does not prove that the reverse is always true. For most patients—about whom we are now speaking—there is in fact a chronic deprivation of temporal perception. Just as one can say that time seems endless to these patients, so one can say that time, as experienced by healthy persons, no longer exists. Because time ceases to exist, becomes a void, and because any void is a frightening experience, patients try to escape from real time. Time has significance, perhaps, only inasmuch as it is related to a meaningful death. It has only one meaning: it can lead only to death. There is no other future for the chronically ill.

2. The Quality of Life

A. L. Strauss (1975) appeals to the "quality of life" whenever he speaks of excessive concentration on disease by patients and their environment. His is a different sense of the phrase from the one normally used in bioethics debates, in which the term refers to the status by which one judges the merit of continuous intervention in a downhill disease process. Strauss's use is this. On the one hand, the chronically ill are constantly denied a miracle cure for their disease, while being told "Doctors today are crackerjacks! They will certainly find something soon to help you out." On the other hand, the patient constantly monitors himself to see if any new symptoms have emerged. In this way, preoccupation with disease overwhelms all other values. It is not the patient but the disease process that determines the quality of life. Strauss suggests, therefore, that this preoccupation must certainly have its effect on the identity of the person who is ill. Most saliently, the consequent risk of social deprivation for these patients is especially great. Gradually those around withdraw, almost imperceptibly, offering no answers to the questions posed, no longer discussing the realities so visibly presented by the patient. The process of "stigmatization" slowly but surely appears. The result can only be that the patient, too, withdraws from himself, so that his disease begins to predominate (especially as it is responsible for his condition). Finally the patient has only to wait until that moment when the disease, at least, conquers him.

It is hard to imagine any less dignified or less supportive situation than this withdrawal. It has been called, with respect to the dying, a "conspiracy of silence." No less painful and damaging to the personhood of the chronically ill, social deprivation can be overcome only by the consistent desire to communicate with patients about what really matters to them.

CONCLUSION

J. T. Schröder once said in a lecture: "The chronically ill constantly remind us of the frailty and grimness of life." This is the reason, he suggests, that the chronically ill "always invoke our aggression." This aggression primarily appears as outlandish complaints," because one is tempted to ascribe responsibility for disease to the patient himself. The temptation is most obvious for doctors who typically complain, "The patient is not cooperating." Note here also the impotence of the doctor mentioned earlier; he or she has reached the limits of the craft. But often there is a reluctance to admit these limits. Technology has given doctors a feeling of power, but suddenly the power evaporates. The power of craft and technology is reduced to piddling dimensions. P. Sporken describes the power this way: each day we gain new controls over the body and death such that we are in danger of sinning against human life.

The new techniques are what possess the power. By comparison, the average person is impotent and ignorant. Therein lies the danger for both doctor and patient. As long as human beings do not maintain control over the use and direction of technologies, we will be faced with the enormous questions medical technology poses for the quality of life of the chronically ill.

Both good and bad can result from the use of technical power. For some patients, medical intervention permits a degree of decent quality of life, the chance to maintain human dignity in the midst of a chronic and deteriorating condition. Other patients, however, are more nearly victims of technologies whose iatrogenic effects live on while normal human life has essentially vanished; in these cases death seems more humane than prolonged life. Thus, ethical questions about death are really questions about life, about the meaning of "quality of life," about the moment when life ceases to have value.

In a personal communication, R. Duff (1976) noted that a certain hierarchy of quality has functioned for some time in medicine (he later applied this idea to criteria for treatment of defective newborns). Life has been divided into "health and well-being," followed by "mildly handicapped," "severely handicapped," and "dead." He stated that the time has come, perhaps, to alter this hierarchy such that "dead" would come to stand for "severely handicapped." There are so many forms of destroyed life artificially preserved that on ethical and humanitarian grounds one must question, he suggested, our attempts to maintain such minimal life. Yet the question "Will the quality of life be better after treatment?" is rarely asked from the medical standpoint.

"This fact has often been overlooked in the discussions of palliation and care in patients with disease," J. Oldhoff and E. F. M. Veldhuis say in an article about dealing with patients with cancer of the esophagus or cardia (1976, p. 79). While an operation alone merely offers a minor improvement in statistical survival over the long term, an operation combined with radiation and chemotherapy carries with it negative side effects.

With some note of bitterness the authors state: "In the literature no data concerning this aspect are available, but numerous articles have been written telling us how successful several therapies were. In most articles the length of survival is nearly the only measure of success. However, we do not know how we are changing the quality of life by operation and/or radiotherapy" (p. 80). They arrive at this conclusion: Sometimes it is better to forego surgery and allow the natural process of the disease to take its course. In this regard the author's most perplexing problem is that "more data should be collected regarding the natural course of the disease, especially in comparison with the results after palliative surgery or radiotherapy" (p. 81). It seems almost ironic that because medical technological advances are so actively employed, one no longer possesses an accurate description of the natural course of a disease, by which to draw comparisons relative to the quality of life for the patient.

Warning about this tendency as early as 1965, van den Berg wrote: "The patient is subjected to medical techniques; what is essentially human no longer has a role to play!" (p. 30)

As we made clear, not every chronically ill patient is a negative product of medical technology. Thanks to that same technology, many persons who are chronically ill do obtain some measure of forbearance and perseverance. It is because of this fact that decisions about employing available life-prolonging techniques and drugs become heart-rendingly difficult.

The recent appearance of the quality-of-life question suggests that technology in medicine might have reached its limits, even though the question is infrequently raised at the critical moments it should be. Consequently, health professionals and lay persons alike are not yet on sure footing, from the standpoint of the quality of life, regarding the effects of intervention versus withholding treatment.

8. Dying

In general it is not true that persons are afraid to die. Nor is it in general true that persons are not afraid to die. Generalizations are out of place in every case, because it is impossible to describe adequately preparation for and suffering of death. Just as undergoing sickness is a personal event, so is dying. In fact, it is even more personal and individual. Knowing that one is going to die and fearing dying are highly personal challenges. Nevertheless, some general observations are possible, in spite of the personal accent brought to the dying process.

A. ENVIRONMENT

For centuries dying was regarded a family affair, a ritual carried out amidst relatives and friends. Today it is less so. In fact, eighty percent of deaths today occur in hospitals. The aged are bound to nursing homes; seriously ill patients are almost always brought to the hospital. Persons now die among strangers, who have become routinely accustomed to death. Families are relegated to the status of observers; they are no longer part of the ritual. Patients are supported by medical power rather than the compassion of spouse and relations.

Life as passed on from generation to generation and care in which what is humane is done have both been superseded by a new kind of environment for the dying. This environment means that one no longer dies in a familiar and comfortable room at home. Instead, one is brought to die in a sterile white room with no more character than hundreds of hotel rooms. This new environment gives credence to the truism that hospitals are fine for getting well but horrible for dying.

Because of this new development, life and death today are further disjoined than they ever were, odd as this may sound. Death is denied in day-to-day life, no longer an integral part of existence. One dies estranged, between foreign walls, among strangers. Friends are reduced to expressing their support after death, not during the process.

The dying are alone, often inconsolably lonesome. Mourners are even left alone after the death. Some express their regrets. But helping the dying and their family live through this process has been largely absent. Thus, the community support system has little or no effect.

In many cases the dying are old, very old. They have long since been removed from any significant social intercourse. Their dwellings are smaller than before. Special medical and material devices are needed for old age. As a result, the old are surrounded by medical objects in a tiny space, cut off from subsequent generations still in the midst of life. More and more one hears remarks to the effect that death would be a release for Grandpa and Grandma. A release from what? Is it release from loneliness, estrangement, isolation, the huge loss of direct contact with what is happening around them in life? Or is the release actually for the benefit of the survivors, who cannot cope with the situation as it now stands?

Dying is as old as the world. Only the manner in which the Western person dies is new: a total isolation from life. In this respect it does not matter whether one dies in an intensive-care ward, surrounded by gleaming apparatus and task-oriented nurses, or in a tiny room at a nursing home. Both insure that death is no longer part of life; both insure that dying will be efficient and centralized in properly designated locations.

Case XV

Portions of a diary kept by a sixty-year-old patient in an ICU after an automobile accident:

. . . thus I yearned for the time when I could go to sleep. It seemed best. Always best to have slept. My neighbor, a woman, was removed last evening during the TV period. Where I don't know. I didn't ask because of all the misery. Now I think there's a man there but I don't know anything about him. Sipped a glass of tea with a straw and waited for the meal. Wondered what it would be. A bright spot in the misery: the little girl, you know the one hit on the tricycle, went home this morning. That is a cause for celebration, and here too, because she improved so much while she was here. . . .

So that was the beginning. To be a patient, one brought here. So it was here. My outlook is bright, it seems to me, for my pain has just come to a halt. Some organization or another brought us Christmas presents, a candle. Naturally I can't light it here, but maybe later at home. A rotten day. I knew it but I didn't ask because the curtains stayed closed around the child's bed. I came back from

> the hall and a guy was coming out with a big black box and just then the meal arrived—spinach, meat stew and puree with a big peach. But you don't like to sit and eat after that.
> Had a visit. Great. I even cried a bit and laughed a bit. A whole hour alone with my Leontine.

We can add only a little to this account. The centralized death places are peopled with professionals, usually young people, very young people, who have not given death a place in their own life. But in their professional calling they must confront death every day; in fact, this confrontation is so intense that one wonders whether they can integrate death in their own existence. The opportunity exists, but it is no guarantee that the chance will be seized for integration: quite the opposite. Nurses in intensive-care and coronary-care units are faced daily with mangled and weakened bodies kept alive by means of maximum technological capacities. How often is this technology too much? Very. The number of young people who cannot handle these problems for long is great. They are also isolated. With whom, outside such centers, can they discuss their problems about death? They can do so only with their colleagues. But all of them work in an unfamiliar world, where unfamiliar things happen, where people die. The usual norms of living have very little to offer them.

The extent of trauma to professionals who manage dying patients is tragically revealed by an Associated Press release of March 14, 1980. That release reported on a Las Vegas hospital, Sunrise Hospital, making charges against "members of the graveyard shift" who allegedly made bets on how long critically ill patients would live. One nurse was accused of hastening the deaths of patients by turning off their machines, although she was later exonerated. The executive director of the hospital was quoted: "It probably makes me about as sick as anything I can think of. The charges are as serious as any that could be made in the health care profession" (*Memphis Commercial Appeal*, March 14, 1980).

For these reasons, hospices for the dying have grown up to meet the needs not only of the dying, but also of families and those who care for them. The goals of the hospice, as described by K. P. Cohen (1979), include twenty-four-hour care for the dying, support and counseling for the family, and training for the professional caretakers and the volunteer helpers. As hospice care is viewed as an extension of the doctor-patient relationship, its moral basis in that relation is secure (Thomasma, 1980). Patients are not abandoned by their doctor, but nor are they plucked out of their relationship with family and friends.

Nevertheless, much more still needs to be done to counteract the traditional—and particularly American—denial of death.

B. SECRECY

Isolating death and its manifestations from daily life wrenches from life an essential aspect. In its place is left an unrecognized void, presenting a new problem for the professional in health-sciences centers. Is the patient's death a sign of the inability of the doctor, who, at the moment of death, is faced with the doubt that all his craft is useless? There are those who are so bound up with science that they cannot see they are not all-powerful. There are those who take it amiss when patients begin to die, because this reminds them of their limits. These can only with difficulty accept death. Those in the latter category lose interest in patients who are dying.

Is the possibility of death a medical given, or is it rather obvious only to the patient? In earlier times, as the sick and the aged who died at home began to die, everyone around them knew it, as did the dying persons themselves. And why wouldn't they know? Life and death were one whole and death was a no greater secret than life itself. Now, however, dying has become isolated, a secret of the expert, who debates about whether to tell the patient. The expert first "takes away" death from the patient and then asks himself whether he should divulge the secret, his "professional secret," to the patient, whose death, after all, it really is. The expert arrogantly presumes the patients cannot handle the knowledge, without even asking himself if *he* can handle the patient's acknowledgment of the limits of medicine and the fact that we all must die someday. How remarkable that those doctors who over the years have not kept this secret but rather shared it with patients have never come across a patient unable to deal with the information—not one!

Often we find the opposite situation, in which patients have known this supposed secret for sometime, but did not discuss it with their doctor, because the doctor was having so much trouble coping with it. Many patients fight for their life, but they also seem in some mysterious way to know when the fight is over, when battling for their life makes no more sense.

Isolating death leads to many tragicomedies in the hospital, to much dishonesty and injustice. Right at the time patients know their end is near, authenticity is absolutely essential. It is essential because their death will soon lay them to rest in eternal isolation from others. Not to tell the truth at this time—a truth such patients probably already know—leads to premature and unjust separations between the patient, the doctor, the staff, and the family and friends.

C. FEAR

Very few patients actually fear death. As Y. F. Tuan (1980) argues, our fears are subsumed into art, music, literature, poetry, movies. Our fears are enculturated so that we can deal with them. Patients do, however, fear the dying process, which has been invested with secrecy by the hospital comedy and human shadow play. Because this process is unknown, it causes anxiety. As E. Kübler-Ross (1969) notes, patients fear the abandonment that today is so much a part of the dying process.

When anxiety does appear, it is anxiety about the last period before death: fear of inexorable pain and of the ultimate isolation. But whenever the barriers come down and the secret is out, so that the dying person can speak about what is actually taking place, much of this fear vanishes. Only the last step, then, remains to be taken alone. The fear vanishes for two reasons. First, relevant information about pain control, should it become necessary, alleviates anxiety about pain. Secondly, the discovery that the "death secret" can be handled and thereby reduce isolation is a relief. In sum, anxiety arises when the secret rests in the patient's chart, locked there by a fear-ridden doctor.

Thus, fear of the dying process is largely created by excessive secrecy. Although death may possibly be feared this fear is actually much less severe than fears about the dying process. By the time death arrives, patients are usually ready to leave the foolish comedy behind.

There is a fear of death among those who have not worked out their religious feelings about what will happen to them in the hereafter. There is also a fear of death among those with guilt feelings, whether rational or irrational, who have not been able to accept forgiveness or otherwise discount the feelings. Talking about these feelings can help a great deal, because often this discussion is long overdue. But sometimes such discussion is fruitless. Persons then can only powerlessly accept their immeasurable angst in the hope that death will release them as soon as possible from their fears.

D. WAITING FOR DEATH

Perhaps the most tragic situation occurs when patients peacefully await death, having fully prepared the family, set their affairs in order, and said farewell, but death does not come. While the patient is ready to die, sometimes after surmounting many difficulties and profound grief, life continues. Such patients face a period of unfathomable loneliness.

It is an emotional state observers can in no way enter. To them it does not even appear as an emotional state. It is as if the person had passed through an invisible wall, which blocks the observers, the family, the health-care practitioners. The dying person is on "the other side" of an experience we have not begun to enter. Everything to be said has been said; saying anything seems, in fact, trite. The approach of death in this circumstance forms, for both the patient and loved ones, the most essential vigil.

Leaves have been taken and mourning has already begun, but nothing happens. A vast void between the dying and those surrounding opens up, a yawning gulf over which there is no bridge. If existence once had meaning, it has now vanished. No other meaning now exists save waiting.

E. WHAT THE DYING TEACH US

Contact with many dying patients reveals that they can teach us about life. Their need for some hope illustrates that life hangs on fragile threads of promise from one person to another, be the promise as small as arranging for some flowers, telephoning a relative, or changing a diet. Their need for companionship reveals the extent to which we depend on one another for support. While we are healthy or recuperating we can lose sight of that fact—often patients, as well as families and health-care professionals, succumb to the notion that individuals are autonomous substances, without much need for support from friends and acquaintances beyond certain formal and expected niceties (a get-well card, a bunch of flowers, a brief visit, a perfunctory phone call). The dying teach us the opposite.

When someone is dying, and fears about revealing this fact have been conquered, the dying teach us to talk about these fears, our feelings, and our aspirations. Niceties will not do. Something more profound must take their place, something akin to a discussion of the meaning of life. In sum, the dying teach us to pay attention to our own goals. Many patients have told us not to waste time doing things we do not want to do. Their final advice is most often rather simple: Life is precious. Don't waste it. Make it count.

F. QUESTIONS ABOUT DEATH

As a result of the isolation of death from life, death has become the object of discussion. This isolation from day-to-day living has been made possible by medical technology such that lives that formerly would have ended naturally are now extended. In this context, questions about the "value" of human life and its artificial extension are relatively new ones for the human race.

The awareness that one can manipulate the moment of death, that one can calculate what one deems the essence of life, and that these tasks involve loved ones—a child or other person—are indeed new considerations for humankind. The threat emanating from death has been partially replaced by a threat emanating from life: the threat of living in total physical dependency, living on in spiritual nullity. For this reason a clarification of the role of medicine is necessary in that one may not wish medicine to aim at prolonging life under certain conditions. Hospital patients, especially when the success of a treatment is questionable, who very consciously desire their doctor to suspend treatment, are a new phenomenon. The phenomenon often depends on whether those around the patient can deal with the question of suspending treatment or can even raise it should the patient be unable to, or should the responsible parties find it more convenient to ignore the problem.

In cases such as this the value embodied by medical technology—prolonged life—is clearly in conflict with other human values. Perhaps in the question of "prolonging death" (as opposed to prolonging life; see P. Ramsey, (1973), life, value, and medical technology have reached a common limit. Clearly this new situation, in which dying can be "staged," poses enormous problems for doctors and staff, as well as for the patient and family. Decisions in these situations are extremely difficult. Laws called natural-death acts—which permit the execution of living wills regarding the desire for the termination of extraordinary treatment in the case of irreversible conditions—are certainly a step in the right direction, if one values rational control over one's death. A private request of one's physician to manage the dying process, under a "no code" rubric, is also a valuable suggestion (S. Spencer, 1979).

In the past a seriously malformed newborn whose chances in life were slim presented parents with a fact they simply had to accept. They had only the choice of institutionalizing the child or bringing it home. But the modern concept of euthanasia, meant here as consciously letting someone die (passive euthanasia), and its legal implications have added a third possibility to this choice, although the dilemma is made no easier thereby. In a number of newborn centers this option is followed in certain cases. The doctors speak with the parents as soon after the birth of the deformed child as possible, regarding the child's physical and psychosocial outlook; a joint decision is then reached, either on the techniques to employ to maintain the young life, or whether to practice passive euthanasia.

A similar problem occurs when children or young adults suffer a grave accident. Sometimes the damage is so serious that one must question whether medical help makes any sense. In these instances "making sense" is measured against the future outlook: Are the physical consequences so horrible that continued life would bring absolutely no satisfaction? Is brain damage so extensive that there is no possibility of recovering? Would further life mean extreme physical and therefore social defects?

An even more complicated situation arose in the classic legal case that overturned the definition of death as the moment the heart stops beating. The case occurred in Virginia, in 1972, but others like it appear daily around the world. A team of doctors are uncertain about treating an accident victim. If they treat the victim they may prolong a life, albeit of a minimal quality; but meanwhile, another team has prepared a patient to receive an organ from the accident victim—perhaps a kidney—that is desperately needed to save the former's life. In cases like this the moral conflict is even greater than in regular cases of passive euthanasia, because contingent on the accident victim's death is the survival of another patient, who is already "on the way to the operating room," having been matched with the blood type and transplant type of the accident victim. In the aforementioned Virginia case, the jury decided in favor of the transplant team based on a concept of brain-death not yet legally established. The legal definition of death is important to protect physicians and families who must make a difficult moral decision. Thus, although the legal definition of death has changed to the cessation of certain brain functions, because the law varies from state to state and because morality, though supportive of some laws, transcends the law, the burden of decision making about passive euthanasia still falls on the accident victim's family and physicians.

Other similar conflict situations arise every day in the emergency room. Powers of judgment are unbelievably taxed, especially when the cases involve the patient's family. In a very brief time professionals must assess the condition of the patient and the consequences of therapy. It is never possible to be exactly sure of the implications of the technical findings for daily life, which makes it even harder to provide the parents (or other family members) with information on which to base a sound decision. Moreover, relatives are locked in a highly emotional situation, which can impede their good judgment.

Quite possibly no laws could be enacted to cover the vicissitudes of these life-and-death situations. At present we have not yet developed a generalizable and influential ethic covering all such situations, no single line of moral reasoning that can serve as a guide to solving all aspects of the problem. Thus, the decisions made are highly individual, each time involving both the family and the doctor. Independent of the family, should one doctor be in favor of actively ending the suffering, others might argue that their moral obligation to preserve life requires that the most they can do is withhold life-prolonging means.

Medical science has created for itself and the public a tremendous moral problem about death, whose solution has been only partially brought about, by court actions and legal and ethical discussion. It is unclear whether any complete solution will ever emerge.

REVIEW OF THE LITERATURE

J. H. van den Berg (1965) was one of the first of a long line of authors to write books and articles on dying and euthanasia. He points out that much is being written about dying because so little is being said about it. Between 1965 and 1970 the steady stream of volumes and articles might have begun a change in this situation. The stream has not yet abated ten years later. It is therefore not possible to review all the literature. Rather, we have made a selection that highlights the evolution of writings that have a bearing on patient management.

H. L. Kok (1970) published a history of the "last rites," offering an overview of funeral rituals and other practices. It is often fascinating and noteworthy, but sometimes anecdotal and without much scientific basis. P. Aries (1974) did much the same thing with greater success, focusing on the religious and cultural attitudes toward death in Western civilization. Especially important for contemporary attitudes, he argues, was the rise of Romantic individualism and the decline of religious faith.

We have already made clear how dying and death have gradually been hidden from daily life. The dying have been further and further removed from where one lives and more and more assigned to hospitals and then funeral homes, which take care of all the details. The consequences of this veiling of death for health-care institutions are spelled out in an exceptionally fine study by B. G. Glaser and A. I. Strauss (1965). From a sociological perspective, and using sociological methods, they describe the problem of dying in a hospital, noting that real communication with and about the patient appears only spasmodically.

In studying the relation between the dying and the care givers (doctors, nurses, and family members) Glaser and Strauss reveal how little professionals are willing to answer patients' questions, and patients are too often prepared to endure the resulting "comedy" of lies and evasions. Hence, no one deals directly with the central subject. Appealing to a number of standard models of interaction, the authors demonstrate the extent to which death remains a taboo, despite all efforts to overcome evasion in the hospital setting—it is rarely discussed there.

S. Simmons and B. Givens (1972) conclude that more than half of dying patients suffer serious feelings of isolation. This conclusion stems from a large number of interviews. It is supported by J. C. Quint in an earlier study (1966), who analyzed the behavior leading to the blocking of any confrontation with death. It is another form of research from that of H. Le Shan (1969), but it led to the same conclusion. Le Shan's study might well be a classic in this field. He "simply" measured the time between the moment the patient summoned a nurse and the moment the nurse arrived, finding that this time greatly increases as death approached. In addition, the time spent with the patient who is dying was found to be significantly shorter than that with other patients.

On the basis of his own research, B. G. Glaser (1965) proposed the different phases in the terminal process, which he arranged as follows:

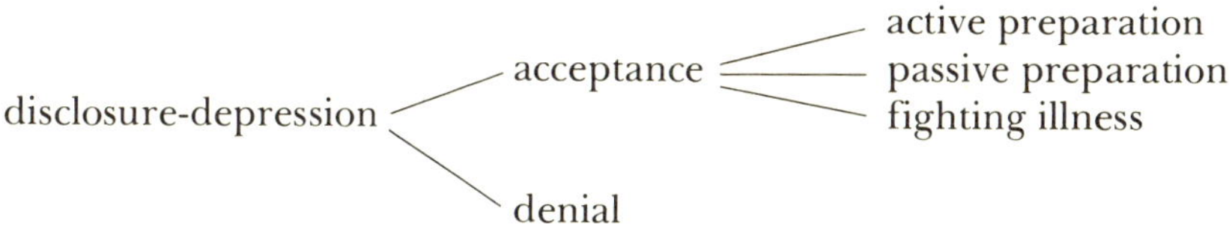

If the patient does not arrive at a radical denial, a form of acceptance is possible, which can lead to active preparation, passive preparation, or a battle with the disease itself. In each of these phases Glaser studied the doctor's behavior, coming to the conclusion that death is a significant problem for doctors but not for patients. Isolation, however, is a problem endemic to the entire situation, not just for the patient. Glaser calls this "reciprocal isolation": the patient seems to experience how his or her death presents a problem for the caregivers and isolates them, just as they isolate the patient. On this basis Glaser then developed models with Strauss (Glaser and Strauss, 1965) that describe different degrees of awareness, from "each denies all" to "each understands all." Quint's contribution lies in the serviceable models between these extremes, models of interaction such as "the patient thinks that the doctor thinks" and "the doctor thinks that the patient no longer thinks." These interactions reveal how caregivers, grasping at rationalization about their roles and hospital policy, continually avoid meaningful contact with the dying, by reducing the time spent with them to a bare minimum.

This holds true particularly in situations where one has little experience of patients as human beings, such as the intensive-care unit. With respect to this service, it would be good to mention again D. Hay and D. Oken's study (1972). Although a somewhat emotional article, it nonetheless offers a very good description of the stress situations encountered in the ICU by nurses—stress produced by the preponderance of unconscious patients needing care. The problem is found in the emergency room as well, but to a lesser extent. In any case, very little of substance has been written on the problems of death denial in either service.

An exception to this rule is the article by M. Snijder, R. Gertler, and E. Ferneau (1973), who developed a system to integrate the death problem in introductory and training sessions for nurses. Similar in scope is the work done by the Dutch physicians A. Sikkel and C. M. Hofman (1973), who created an interdisciplinary team specially oriented to terminal care in the critical services.

By the early 1970s the concept of terminal guidance was being developed, and since then a great deal has been written on this subject. Indeed, there are journals, such as the *Journal of Thanatology,* that are devoted to the topic. We must therefore limit ourselves to a few observations. The terms *psychotherapy* and *guidance* are used constantly in diverse articles, especially case studies. *Psychotherapy* usually denotes a method of altering behavior by the systematic use of psychological techniques. It really does not fit the death situation. We much prefer the term *guidance,* meant as assisting patients in accepting certain inevitable realities (Bergsma, 1975). We see this guidance, on the part of the psychologist at least, not as a lecture to the patient about comforting values, but rather as a form of contact with the patient, in which the latter's isolation is broken down and the problem as the patient sees it is given a chance to be voiced or perhaps even shared.

The patient must be given the opportunity, using his or her own tools, to make a decision for acceptance (or denial). The counselor's role is to facilitate the process within the context of the "usual" (not psychotechnological) human measure of carrying on a conversation. A good guide learns more from his or her patient in crisis situations than does the patient.

With respect to this guidance, Kübler-Ross's standard work of 1969 cannot be forgotten. It is a standard in the sense that it set forth the ideal that many others now follow or emulate. It is also the single most important work contributing to widespread discussion and openness about the problems of death and dying. The more popularized aspects of the book, especially the delineation of stages in the dying process (shock, denial, anger, depression, and acceptance), are helpful as an orientation. As with many other professionals, however, we prefer Glaser's schema, given above, because it is better delineated and rests on psychological research. It is no easy task to base the stages proposed by Kübler-Ross on empirical and experimental research such that personal differences in character among patients are taken into account.

The real danger in using either schema lies in their inherent suggestion that one must follow the stages in a rigid step-by-step fashion, even though both authors take pains to deny this. Rather, the stages as given are descriptive, not normative: descriptive of certain behaviors and attitudes one encounters in preparing for death. Today's "accepting" patient may be tomorrow's total denier. Terminal patients can be drastically influenced by internal and external events, causing great swings in their outlook. Often one can speak of the process as that of a patient learning to cope with life's ups and downs, the more so as the patient adapts to a hospital environment, in which the "natural" course of events quite possibly will be impeded. As a result, one might very well question whether the stages proposed by Kübler-Ross and Glaser are products of patient adaptation to the new situation rather than part of a basic progression all dying persons must make. In this respect, Sikkel and Hofman say something quite perceptive: "That one can actually improve even as the body disintegrates is a concept wholly foreign to a hospital" (1973, p. 1169). The guide, therefore, must aid this healing process in the dying without demanding that the dying artificially go through certain steps to reach it. Death, after all, is a personal and not a systematic event.

CONCLUSION

The great volumes of literature on death and dying in recent years reveal, somewhat ironically, the preoccupation with death in our society without its having penetrated daily life. Death threatens to become a totally misunderstood aspect of life, even though attitudes about it inform virtually every major policy decision about war, crime, violence, the death penalty, aging, and funeral practices (Thomasma, 1979). We shield ourselves from death in order to assure ourselves that we are still living. Artificial grass covers the new grave to create the illusion that nothing is really buried there.

Kübler-Ross, in a recent book (1975), helped parents "choose" between a "hard-and-fast" therapy after the death of their child and a more difficult and tragic one. The hard-and-fast therapy included preparing the child's body for burial, staying with the body, taking the coffin to the grave themselves, and shoveling the dirt on the grave. This seems quite astonishing to anyone familiar with modern burial practices in the West, even though Kok (1973) points out that such was the practice in earlier times. The modern reduction of ritual surrounding death has led to greater survivor problems with the grief process than were formerly experienced. Rituals such as final procession around the churchyard before burial and breaking of the bread together, with its familiar sounds, not only stamp grief with some certitude; they accent the social and communal nature of human life. Today's crematoria offer the image, instead, of an appointment at an office. The family is reduced to the role of observer in these proceedings. Saying good-bye to the body in a sterile hospital environment is hardly better than the crematorium, and is usually not even allowed by the efficient ambulance staff that has come to prepare the body for its move.

The mourners stand alone in their grief, supported most often by Valium. It is quite possible that they are no longer expected to accept their grief. The void they feel on the passing of a loved one is filled by psychopharmacological means. Chemicals are capable of evaporating the most authentic feelings, tied to the most essential aspects of our existence. The mourners are left with estrangement in a technological society.

9. The Other Side of Medicine

This book has been a study of the person, a study of the body and the self. It is a study of the interactions of body and self, not as specific entities but as aspects of the one reality that provokes different attention depending on the circumstances. We dwelt especially on occasions when disruptions occur in these interactions, whether the disruptions stemmed from biological, mechanical, artificial, or normative conditions. However, the basis of all our observations is the person as a unity, whole in direct interchange with his or her environment.

The concept of personal wholeness is based on the unifying experience of being human, and on the striving for reconstituted selfhood that occurs almost automatically in cases of disruption. In these cases, the body functions as a necessary condition and means for such wholeness, such reconstitution. In fact, in the most literal sense the body is the very structure, or gestalt, of such unity. However, other factors also intrude, which we have noted. The most important are the experiences a person has of the self and the body. These are also conditions for reconstitution, and simultaneously the means whereby personal integrity can exist and be reestablished.

In the preceding chapters we discussed the development history of personal integrity and the ways this wholeness is threatened or dissolved. The problem was approached through concrete case instances, as well as different psychological perspectives. We will now recapitulate the main points of the book, with a view to not only a theoretical summary, but also a practical framework for patient management.

1. Bodily Functions

In chapter one we set down the ways integration is gradually achieved through discovery of and experiment with the potentialities of the body. We discussed this integration, the relation between body-image and self-acceptance, and the ways human beings establish their own possibilities and those of the environment by testing one against the other. Our discussion was comparable to the ways Lazarus has described these themes in conceptualizing his stress theories.

In that discussion we underlined the "experience" the body obtains, as well as the self. Both cognitive and emotional experiences lead to identity, which itself is a condition of and means for continuity in space and time.

Having made this point, we then distinguished a number of bodily functions in more or less hierarchical order, from the most basic to the most complex: the machine function, maintenance function, instrumental function, reproductive function, signal function, expression function, communication function, and mediatorship function. Learning, consciousness, and creativity were not singled out as specific corporeal functions. Rather, they occur in a constellation of other functions. There should be no misunderstanding on this point: do not imagine a form of dualism in the Cartesian sense sneaking in through the back door; dualism is simply not the case here. Without the body there can be no consciousness, no creativity, no learning. These higher levels of corporeal potentiality occur in the ways condition and means relate to each other, change places and order, and otherwise guarantee continuity in space and time.

To have consciousness and learning, bodily existence is a necessary condition, but in a very specific sense, that of an almost imperceptible, no-longer-motor condition. On the other hand, consciousness and creativity hardly are necessary conditions for the machine function. In this case, condition and means are virtually indistinguishable.

This point is important, for we can also speak of a subtle interplay among underlying conditions and means that first determine being human as such, then determine the specific identity of a single person and that person's experiences, and finally are concerned with the direct interaction of this identity with its environment and individual circumstances.

Consciousness, creativity, self-consciousness, and thought are conditions whereby the self experiences itself as a self. They are also necessary conditions for the subject to experience oneness with itself. In a word, they are necessary conditions for the experience of identity between experiences and the self. The conditions, however, are also the means whereby self and/or body can be made into an object, or thing, so that rational analysis can be directed to them. Thus, the gymnast must consciously make her body into an object in order rationally to calculate how to place her hands and feet to execute a handspring. A handicapped man must consciously—that is, rationally—make his body an object in order to manipulate it around what, because of his handicap, can constitute a trap: in order to subject his body he must distance himself from it, make it an object, even though complete integration and personal identity are hinged on the body's ability to be an experiencing subject. Consciousness, thought, and creativity are conditions necessary to objectify oneself: sometimes they can be used to objectify the self; at other times they can even be used to objectify themselves.

This ability to make the body by turn an object and a subject is something that can be learned. In fact, it *must* be learned in order to optimize, for example, the conditions for the mediatorship function. As such, this learning is absolutely necessary for certain rehabilitation patients. The degree of consciousness necessary to execute and handle these shifts in emphasis and experience of the body and self is totally dependent on the demands individuals make on themselves and those the environment in which they exist makes on them.

These activities require the machine function, of course. But they also require other motor activities, especially the use of specific musculature. These functions can be exercised almost passively, with hardly any conscious awareness, but they can also be consciously optimized and intensified.

Consciousness and creativity are thus necessary conditions for almost all of the possibilities called forth by the body. It takes mutual conditioning. And this interactive conditioning contributes to the specifics of human identity, for it is conditional for its own means; it is a means for its own condition. In this sense, it is a totality, a whole, a unity in and of itself.

2. Body and Self

Conscious distancing from the body that simultaneously makes the body an object is oriented to a goal, better control, the ability to subject the body to a higher level of integration and unity. But at the same time whole or partial distancing leads to an experience of disjunction between body and self.

One could say that self-experience is itself a condition for partial objectifying, even though this means that simultaneously something of oneself is lost. One could even argue further that in just such a process of objectifying the body the experience of self simultaneously is enhanced—indeed, is intensified in every case. It is intensified in the expectation of an eventually enhanced identity.

Put another way, one is prepared to experience temporarily a duality between the self and the body in the positive expectation of a strengthened identity as the outcome. In fact, one consciously manipulates one's conditions and means in conjunction with an affirmative expectation formula: the duality is wished and created in order to obtain a "better" unity. It is therefore acceptable, just as dissonance in music is acceptable and desirable when it leads to an enhanced harmonic resolution: the duality created along the way brings tension, but this is also acceptable because it is willfully induced in anticipation of the positive outcome.

Thus, practicing a difficult passage of a piano sonata is in itself not very pleasurable, but it is acceptable in anticipation of one's command of the passage, which will lead to the pleasure of heightened identity as body—left and right hands—and the self complete each other in a new unity.

Temporary tension is like an investment one wants to make for a positive outcome. Note well that the investment itself is consciously chosen, freely taken on, inaugurated on one's own initiative, in order to reach a self-selected goal; one does not just choose the goal and put up with the means. These means, as well, are chosen. The more important the goal—that is, the more directly it will strengthen one's identity—the more tension one will choose to undergo, the more one is prepared to invest; indeed, the more one will endure the tension no matter how long that tension may last.

We have emphasized the distancing one chooses with a view to an end, in contrast to that which is not chosen but inflicted. How different the second duality is from the first! This duality is a result of an undesired disruption. The purpose is not visible. The time span is not clear. We described disruptions and dis-ease in chapters two and four. In what follows we treat them as an overarching whole within duality.

3. Duality of Self and Body as a Result of Disruption

Disruptions of unknown origin, as we described in those earlier chapters, almost always lead to a certain degree of dissolution between body and self. The word *alienation* would be good to describe this effect were it not that it carries unwanted rich and varied connotations from its use in so many other contexts. But the dissolution is there, in the threefold unity of body-self-environment.

This dissolution can be described by a number of behavioral characteristics that apply for the most part to every person faced with such disruption. We will summarize these behavioral consequences in the following subsets as behavioral dimensions of those who are sick, whether that sickness is a result of functional, structural, or even normative disruption. We are of the opinion that these behavioral dimensions are largely independent of higher culture, although the way they are expressed and embodied may be culturally dependent.

(a) *Increased Dependency*—The most basic behavioral dimension of the sick—*sick* now understood in the collective sense noted above—is observed to be increased dependency. One can therefore speak of a physical dysfunction that implies the sick must call upon others to compensate for their physical shortcomings.

This dependency finds direct expression in the world of the patient. Such physical dependency includes the need for help in performing those activities the body can no longer exercise on its own. The maintenance and instrumental functions in cases of serious disruption are the ones primarily at risk and in need of compensation. The higher body functions—signaling, expressing, communicating—are often less at risk, unless one has a very special illness (as in serious neurological disorders).

The dependency now under discussion is the physical kind that calls for (expert) help for restoration and treatment of the causes in order for the patient to continue to live. Implied in the patient's plight is, in fact, a twofold dependency. First, a dependency arises with the need for help to compensate for all or part of nonfunctioning life's essential conditions and activities. Second, dependency comes from the need to rely on experts to remove the first dependency. Life-and-breath existence can continue only on condition that others are prepared to assume activities in behalf of the sick. The sick person is therefore oriented to a great extent to others in that she or he must project dependency on fellow human beings. The person is thus placed in the hands of others. And this holds true as much for compensation for present shortcomings as for healing.

With respect to one's perception of relations with others, then, one's existence is characterized by hope, expectation, and trust, or else by despair and mistrust. The world is judged by the degree of care the other wishes and is able to extend.

In addition, the degree of sickness determines the degree of help offered by others: care is measured by the seriousness of the illness. Thus the patient also discovers dependency in the way in which both he or she and the environment perceive the illness. The greater the discrepancy between the two perceptions, the greater the chance for patient despair. This situation easily arises when a person from one cultural system gets sick in another (e.g., Moroccan laborers in Europe, Americans in Saudi Arabia).

This kind of existential dependency requires more than usual orientation to others, which simultaneously produces passivity with respect to oneself. Existing and survival are now at least partially delineated by others and not by the self, which heretofore has always been one and the same as existence. The sick person is thus directed to the existence of the other, the other's existence becoming essential for his or her own life. One's existence in this way becomes relativized. If existences were now ranked, the existence of others would take precedence over one's own—dependency means that the existence of others is more important than my own. If others should disappear, my own existence would be threatened, because it is so completely reliant on others. Of course, to continue to exist is still my ultimate goal. But if the means—the others—should vanish, my goal can no longer be achieved. It depends on the enduring presence of others.

What this means is that the sick person hands over to another's care an integral part of her or himself, which has now become disengaged. There is no alternative. It is unavoidable.

This is an important point for professionals to remember. In giving "custody" of all or part of one's body to the health professionals, the patient also gives an essential part of the self, the conditions for continued life.

Thus, in the tension field set up between self and body—a duality that is itself unchosen but rather imposed on the sick person—the health professional plays an essential role. A (reputed) increase in bodily dysfunction means for the patient an increase in this tension, and therefore an increased threat to, if not dissolution of, existence.

Most often such tension and dissolution necessarily elicit patient anxiety. Anxiety occurs with the very real radical encroachment on function. But it can also occur when the health professional attempts to set the patient's mind at ease by saying that the dysfunction is not to be taken seriously. The patient may then worry about reproach or certain directives, no matter now insignificant these may appear to the professional. Fears emerge such as "The doctor says not to worry. He doesn't really believe I'm sick!"

Most important of all to the sick person is the presence of *someone.* This presence does not mean just the living reality of another, but rather the unconditional readiness to help on the part of those to whom one has given custody of one's body. When there is a perceived disinclination to help on the part of the health professional, it is often ascribed by the patient to his or her body's unacceptability. This can be the most fearsome element of dissolution.

(b) *Increased Concern for the Body*—Almost as fundamental as the first dimension is the second, the increased concern for the body. The signaling function of the body is concerned with attention to modifications or changes in the body's functions. In small or great numbers, signals focus attention on the body. In essence this means that attention is directed to the body in two ways: first, on the basis of the signals emanating from the body; second, on the basis of the interpretation the possessor of the body gives to these signals and the consequences they portend.

The dependency of the self is at once chained to the dependency of the body, because the body is a condition for recovery and continuation of identity. It is also a condition for the manner in which such continuation will be carried out. With this process of ascribing meaning, the signals are endured and interpreted. We described earlier the situation in which the body is experienced as an unfaithful ally in whom one can no longer trust.

Signals (pain, tiredness, itching) call direct attention to the body. However, the attention itself is laden with meanings, depending on the signals. When the signals are unclear, it is more difficult to interpret them. The more suspicious the interpretation, the more uncertain and consequently anxious the patient becomes.

Uncertainty is the reason for the crucial importance of information. Discerning and interpreting the meaning of signals is especially dependent on interpretative skill and recognition. Not knowing, not recognizing, only strengthens distrust, fear of the unknown, the threat of what cannot be classified. The ability to recognize meanings, affective as well as cognitive, brings peace of mind. As we described it much earlier in the text, certainty brings relief, even if the certainty embodies negative news.

The literature offers many examples underscoring the importance of information for the patient. Lindeman and van Aernham and Lindeman and Stetzer give examples of the good effects of giving surgery patients information before their operation on the signals they should expect postoperatively: the postoperative period was remarkably more restful for these patients than for those without the information.

The almost classic study by Skipper and Leonard demonstrates how indirect information given by parents to children has a beneficial effect. Too often "informed consent" is viewed in the United States as a strictly juridical obligation, which plays down the necessity of information for the patient to understand his or her own signals. A study done by Willner both reveals and clarifies this point. Familiarity with signals—their meaning and especially the kinds to be expected (e.g., after exploratory or radical surgery)—strengthens not only patients' trust in their own bodies, whose condition, because predicted, progresses along "normal" lines, but also trust in the professional who predicted the effects. It also serves to strengthen the sense of professional availability. A result is that dependency does not predominate in the patient. Trust is one's body, however slight its normal function, is not further undermined such that dissolution appears; the tension between body and self is not needlessly heightened. As a result, the chances for recovery and reintegration are significantly bettered.

(c) *Increased Egocentrism*—At first blush it seems odd to insist that the sick suddenly are forced into other dependency while simultaneously experiencing increased egocentrism. But the oddity is real: it illustrates the special position of the sick. Yet orientation to the other and increased egocentrism are not essentially contradictory. In order to develop this point it is necessary to encapsulate our earlier discussion of the concept of the ego. There are two reasons for this. The first is to ward off the usual fuzzy use of the word *ego.* The second is that it is not possible at this point to detail the many culturally determined meanings that can be given to the terms *ego* and *self.* For our purposes we can understand by ego the Identity as a unity of past, present, and future, through which the individual is experienced as a "self."

Based on this understanding, then—whenever and in whatever the circumstances a threat to the existence of the self appears—attention is immediately focused on the ego. This concrete life of mine, my existence, is to a certain degree at risk. The goal of most patients is to continue to exist. Past and future are subsumed into the present. The unity of the self, the identity, is the subject of concern: it must be maintained and completed. The concrete physical dependency discussed under "Increased Dependency" does not entail a sloughing off of attention to the ego. Rather, such dependency puts the ego in relief; it entails a clarification, an increased consciousness of the self. Dependency and threat create attention. At the precise moment of illness or crisis the menace of a break between history and future intensifies and calls attention to the self, the very self that represents a bundle of experiences in the past and present through which one maintains a unity in time. The place of one's existence in the hierarchy of many existences means nothing more than this: the self is so much in need, particularly with respect to its existential continuity, that it is prepared to assume a temporary but profound dependency relation with its environment—others or a significant other. To continue to exist is a goal. To carry the ego to fruition in time is a goal. In fact, the affirmation of the existence of others is also a goal, in the manner already argued; namely, that the other is primarily a means to one's own recovery. The other(s) must continue to exist in order to assist and guarantee my own existence.

Thus, the apparent conflict between dependency and egocentrism is less than may at first appear. This is not to say that the twin dimensions cannot create extremely ambivalent relations and situations. The reason is that the other-directedness of the sick is really a means-directedness, a means that is simultaneously a necessary guarantee of one's own continuation. For that is the primary goal: to endure.

Problems occur if the patient's interpretation of his continuation is not reconciled with the interpretation of change in the way the means are viewed. Among the goals of the patient, the ego, are demands that health care professionals can see only as unreal. Complaints then appear: recovery is not quick enough, the technologies used are inadequate or ineffective, and so on.

It is quite often difficult for the health professional to function as a means for patient recovery, because being so categorized gives such short shrift to his or her own identity. We offered the example of the surgeon and the accident victim. In addition, the egocentrism of the patient and its manifestations are very difficult to accept, because the demands so often exceed professional capabilities.

Mutual role expectations and recognitions appear in all the areas discussed: bodily dependency, real and symbolic offers of help, body orientation, information exchange. The professional who is uncomfortable with his or her function as a means for patient recovery can easily come into conflict with that patient. The patient who desires a relationship with the health professional—particularly during lengthy recoveries—that transcends the usual relationship with means will also create conflicts. Such conflicts are related to the personal egocentric goals of the professional. Conflicts arise because the patient wants to place the professional within his or her personal, egocentric goals. In such instances a clash of wills, of egos, is bound to arise.

(d) *Increased Consciousness of Existence*—The ideas so far discussed can be summarized in the following schema:

Dependency → Increased orientation to the body
Dependency → Increased egocentrism

This schema is not complete, however. A fourth dimension should also be included. On the one hand this dimension seems to be a consequence of the other three primary dimensions: but on the other, the fourth dimension can be viewed as a separate aspect of being sick, a more abstract aspect than the other three. We call this dimension consciousness of existence.

As we employ the term, it means increased consciousness with respect to the meaning of existence for this individual, the "being there" of the individual, within the relations that to a greater or lesser extent define the life of that individual—familial relations, social relations, relations to the powers that be above and beyond the earth.

As a threat to existence, illness not only alters the relation to others, in the sense of increased dependency, and the relation to oneself, in the sense of heightened consciousness of body and/or the self, but it also alters the relation to the concrete and abstract world that circumscribes one's life. Such alteration can be described as a change in imputed meaning for that which lies outside the sick person. Just as changes in the body signal attention to that body, so too do changes in the meaning of the surrounding world signal attention to that world.

Conscious and considered alterations in meaning on the part of the patient are hardly detectable; new meanings do not tumble out of a rational approach to surroundings. Rather, the significance of altered relations in the environment issues from the patient's situation as ill. It is a more crisis-attentive form of being, one in which the continuity of existence is menaced. It changes the significance of objects and abstractions seemingly independent of the patient's wishes. The new meanings sometimes threaten and upset the patient, especially since the patient seldom realizes that he or she is in fact the author of the changing significance of things, because of his/her impaired state of being. The changes demand attention and result in greater consciousness of existence. As a consequence, a new conglomerate of relations and values is constituted. The sick frame a new world (van den Berg). The meaning a patient ascribes to his or her life undergoes a renewal.

As a result of these reflections, the schema can be completed thus:

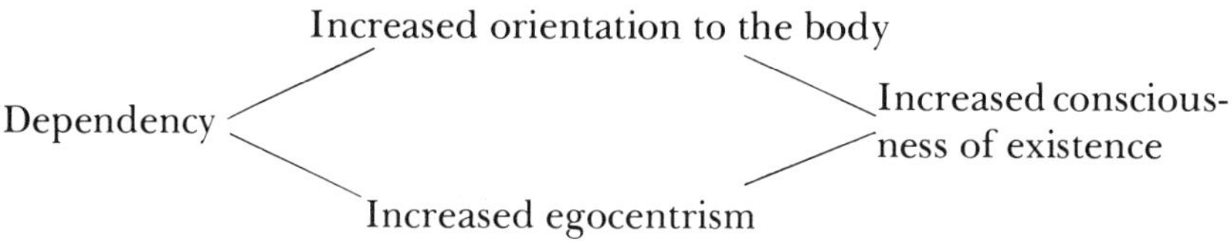

Note again that we are dealing with a four-way system of independent, or primary, disease characteristics. In different cultural systems different content can be ascribed to each dimension, thus altering the accent on their interaction. None of the characteristics is divorced from the others. Together they describe a total experience sick persons must face. Understanding this experience can help us fathom what it means to be ill.

Environmental changes in the perception of the patient can be observed in respect to physical objects, the objective aspects of space, as well as more abstract aspects, as we described in chapters six and seven. Examples of concrete aspects include grasping and walking, but also the perceptibility of things and persons. Examples of more abstract aspects affected by illness include the values persons attach to perceptions, events, and relations.

Both teasing and compassionate remarks, not a problem for the healthy person, can suddenly change their character when one becomes sick, because of the altered perception of the patient. They are laden with a different meaning now. A remark aimed at conveying compassion can take on an unintended content for the patient, such as that the other is losing effectiveness as a means, that reintegration through the other can no longer be anticipated, and that there is a refusal by the identity to remain in the background.

The same process is more evident with relation to the values and norms regulating the human environment, as well as the values and norms brought to bear on the situation by the patient. Sometimes these deviate greatly from customary interpretations, so that both the patient and those caring for the patient can become extremely frustrated.

4. Interrelation of the Dimensions

As has been made clear in the foregoing discussion, the four dimensions of illness are not independent of one another. They interact, mutually influencing one another, giving each color and content. Thus, the patient confined to bed with a serious structural disorder will give an entirely different content to changes in perception of the environment from the patient who, following an operation on the stomach, can quickly regain mobility. A patient whose profession is intellectual will interpret his or her signals from a broken leg quite differently from a sports figure whose professional future depends on the leg's mending.

Our description of different disruptions has made it clear, we hope, that no single set of givens can be ascribed to the characteristics of dis-ease behavior. The underlying significance depends largely on the kinds of disruption occurring and the particular patient. Most important, the patient determines the content and interaction by the ways in which she or he undergoes the disruption at this moment in life, as Safilos Rothschild writes. A child, still on the path of discovering an identity, will derive different meaning from a permanent handicap from an adult, whose identity has crystallized. The latter's identity is less dependent on the body's activities for a future meaningful life.

In this sense, then, it is wrong to think that a single schema can be developed so that one can plug in a patient or emotion and receive a classificatory printout. Certainly in a psychological sense there is no standard patient, nor, hence, standard behavior, patient desires, or ways that desires will be expressed.

What is important is that a number of dimensions are discerned in the behavior of patients. Their presence is an absolute, while their content is relative. The need for someone nearby or rules for getting help is always present, but not for all in the same degree. The necessity of gaining information in order to interpret signals is always there, but not for all to the same extent. The patient-health-care-professional relation always occurs according to the goal-means condition, but it takes many different forms. Finally, the patient always reinterprets the environment from the new perspective of illness, but sometimes the perspective is radical and sometimes it is barely noticeable.

The doctor-patient relation cannot be replaced by computers. It is essential that the health professional build a relationship with the patient in order to help the patient restore identity, as well as cure the disease. The relationship makes possible the recognition and handling of the unique dis-ease suffered by the specific patient according to the behavioral dimensions or disease characteristics discussed. Without attention to the content and configuration that these dimensions assume, the health professional cannot help diminish the personal disruption experienced by the patient.

5. Cross-cultural Aspects

Given that the underlying configuration and interpretation of the four dimensions differs from individual to individual, dramatic differences among individuals can be attributed to the influence of cultural values.

First of all, the body-self relation is strongly affected by and dependent on cultural norms. The degree to which one can speak of a culture as ego-externalized or ego-internalized (D. Riesman, M. Wober, P. Farb, E. Fromm) and the degree of involvement in or alienation from the support group determine the range of body-self relations and, therefore, the possibilities for objectifying and distancing from the body. It is a rule that in developing cultures (Wober) one is a body and the mutual support and involvement of others stand in the foreground, while in technological cultures (J. Ellul, J. Brew, C. Geertz) alienation from the body and from others is the rule. The disruption of the unity we call identity into a temporary duality of body and self is much influenced by these cultural differences and their implications.

This becomes very clear, for example, by looking at the importance of time. In less developed cultures the important dimension is space, because space is needed to survive. For Westerners, however, time is essential for survival, while space is far less so (P. Farb, H. Fortmann). Westerners mark time with planned events. Thus, recovery from illness and its tempo, the restoration of unity, is marked by a future perspective not found in less developed cultures. Recovery has a different meaning for a person who, on becoming sick, suffers a real assault on his life and for whom the future is of little concern or is hardly a conscious goal, because tradition has already mapped it out.

Thus, the body-self relation is distinct against the backdrop of cultural values about time and space. There are also other differences.

Pain signal, fatigue, and functional or structural changes are pretty much the same the world over. However, the implications and interpretation of the signals diverge widely in different cultures. In the West, measles are a childhood disease taken in stride; but in 1979 hundreds of Pygmy children died of the measles. While the signals and symptoms are the same, their meaning is as distinct as life from death, depending on one's culture. Whereas diarrhea is a nuisance to those in a Western culture, it is very serious in African countries: it signals the start of a gradual decrease in the powers necessary to keep oneself alive, to remain competitive.

We have room here only to mention the differences resulting from ritual systems of meaning, and the social significance of certain signals. A good example is epilepsy. For Westerners epilepsy represents a cerebral storm, a breakdown in the regulation of synapses. But for some non-Westerners it represents a special state of heightened consciousness in a chosen seer. The former treat it with drugs; the latter do not interfere with it, indeed look forward to it.

In small, threatened tribal groups the fertility of a woman is of the highest value, because it represents the security in old age of children to care for one. In the West, fertility is something largely to be checked.

Misunderstandings caused by such cultural differences occur at the junction between a dominant culture and certain subcultures. Medicine and nursing have advanced in the Western tradition. Western medicine can easily conflict with traditions of a different stamp.

6. Values and Norms

More specific than cultural influences on health care are those collected under the rubric "values and norms." These are the more or less expressed rules governing behavior and its judgment.

With R. Duff a model was proposed by J. Bergsma in which one could rank these norms and their interaction (1980). We have discussed therein three levels of values—the macro, meso, and individual—that represent the degree of an individual's identification with certain values.

Values on the macro level are those governing conduct on the most general and long-term plateau. Examples are those fostered by a religion, a society, or a large organization. For adherents, these values are perceived as absolute.

On the meso level are values promoted by a smaller group—a club or family, for instance. These values have been developed and maintained through daily confrontation with the realities of life. They are much more short-term than macro levels, given that they arise in particular circumstances.

Values on the personal level are those which arise through individual confrontation with stress and crises.

Although it is possible for values on all three levels to be congruent or easily reconciled, this condition rarely occurs. More often than not, depending on an individual's identification with values on the different levels, discongruity and conflicts arise. For example, macro values may forbid sterilization and abortion, as is the case in many religions. But this negative command does not mean that certain families will follow it absolutely, or that a single person will choose to be guided by either this command or his or her family's acceptance of the values it embodies.

Just as these values obtain for every individual, so too the hierarchy of values within a culture have specific applications to health professionals. Medical professionalism by definition includes the development of an ethical code on the macro level, a code that contains directives regarding professional conduct.

On the meso level, too, institutions and professional associations develop directives governing individual professional conduct. And, of course, individual health professionals develop their own values, both personal and professional, in conjunction, one hopes, with those on the macro and meso levels. Sometimes, however, these personal professional values are only partially congruent with those on other levels, leading to the possibility of discongruity and conflict.

On the basis of macro norms, a physician may not be permitted to perform an abortion; the hospital may permit abortions only in cases of medical indication. But the doctor might interpret a social indication (too many children in the family already) as a medical one.

In the model developed with Duff, not only the conflicts among vertical levels are important, but also those that occur horizontally. For example, political considerations on a social macro level may not conform to professional codes on the macro level, as happened in Germany when the Nazis were in power, or as is the case in many repressive nations today. Physicians are asked to violate their code by assisting in the torture or confinement of political prisoners.

On the meso level industrial health care is a good example of where conflict can occur. The question here is whether the physician will serve the profit-making goals of the corporation or the needs of individual laborers. The Karen Quinlan case also represents a conflict on the meso level, between the hospital directives, the law in New Jersey, and professional values. However, it is the personal level that is becoming more and more the locus of conflict between patients and attending physicians responsible for their care, a point to which we now turn.

7. The Health-Professional–Patient Relationship

Many articles appear in the professional and popular literature on the doctor-patient relationship; it is idealized on television. In this section we will cover not only the physician-patient relation, but also the broader relation between the sick person and the one upon whom that person must call for help. Our interest is in the value system of such care, a value system that contributes moral content to the relation and is aimed at the healing of the sick.

In the helper-sick relation one can find, in principle, two value hierarchies. The fundamental relation is governed by the encounter between two value systems, that of the helper and that of the client. A process of events in the fundamental relation based on this encounter of value systems results in a dynamic exchange. The process is a decision-making one. The patient must decide to request help and then decide how to lay out the facts of the complaint. The helper, most often a professional, must thereupon decide how the problem will be approached, what means to employ (both diagnostic and therapeutic). The professional's recommended means are then examined by the patient, who makes a decision about their acceptability in terms of that person's value system. Ideally, one could speak of this process as a dialectic, wherein both patient and professional contribute to a joint decision (E. Pellegrino and D. Thomasma, 1981).

Because of individual variances it is impossible to describe this decision-making process except under a few basic principles. The content of the process naturally depends on the individual circumstances of each case, so that all we may generalize about is that the decision-making process is formed by the value systems both patient and professional bring to the relation of care. In chapter three we discussed aspects of this process that form the lore of care; in this chapter we have drawn attention to a few behavioral dimensions that govern all patients. The *content* of the dimensions, however, is derived from the particularities of person, culture, and value systems. Moreover, the health professional is similarly governed by individual differences, cultural distinctions, and professional value systems.

Having said that, we can now address the moment when the patient and the professional meet: the patient with her/his request for help, the professional with her/his technological tools. In chapter three we argued that a good clinical decision requires dialogue; that is, the patient and professional must treat each other as partners in the decisions leading to relief of the complaint. The much touted diagnosis by computers should be only a tool in, and not a replacement for, this dialogue, because computers cannot deal with the unique combination of values represented by each individual case.

Our model in the third chapter was based on Western cultural values and should be taken as an ideal toward which to strive. The realities of clinical decision making are well known. R. Kertész (1967) described the situation well when he typed the doctor-patient relation as a classic example of the parent-child interaction. For this and other reasons, Pellegrino and Thomasma (1981) were concerned with the vulnerability of patients in the relation, and therefore formulated an axiom of medical ethics based on the dependency of patients in Western medicine.

In the most primitive tribal groups the doctor-patient relation does not take on the character of parent-child, perhaps because there is not an awesome technological presence, even though the medicine man has as much authority as, if not more than, the Western doctor. Since it is in fact the tribe that is the master of healing, in deriving his authority from the collective ego of the tribe the medicine man includes the sick person in that collective. The patient is continually reminded that she/he is a part of the collective, part of the tribe, for only when the patient is imbued with this unique tribal unity will the power of the evil spirits have no more hold on her/him. Despite his authority, the medicine man is simply the leader of the ceremony, representative of the group; he does not have special powers, knowledge, or gifts (P. Farb, 1969). Group cohesion is maximal. Neither the patient nor the helper stands outside the tribe. In cultures like this, it would not be proper to speak of a decision-making process, for the "decision" has always lain within the values of the collective, viewed as the maximum protection against the evil spirits sent against it by outsiders. In this situation the four characteristics of disease discussed earlier are virtually indistinguishable.

I.

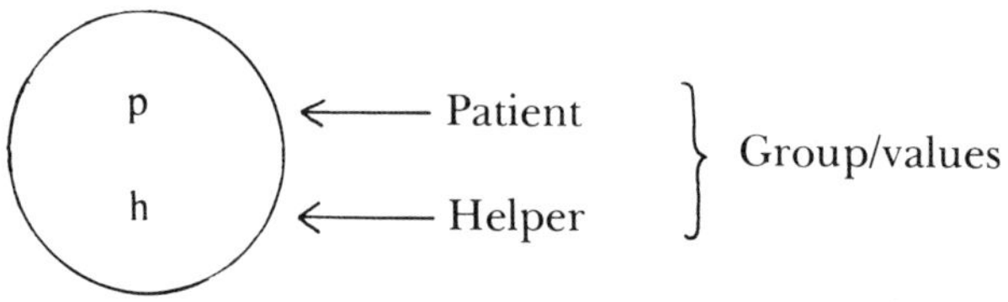

Nevertheless, as important as group cohesion may be, it is probable that the patient and the medicine man hold a more singular position within the group. The patient may obtain this position as a result of accenting one of the basic disease behaviors, most probably that of dependency. The medicine man in larger tribal units than that just discussed may attain a certain status in the group by his knowledge of disease types or by some recognized prowess in influencing evil spirits. To underscore this special position, he no longer lives among the others in his tribe. He erects a hut on the outskirts of the village, where he treats his patients, outside the group (as observed by J. van de Koppel):

II.

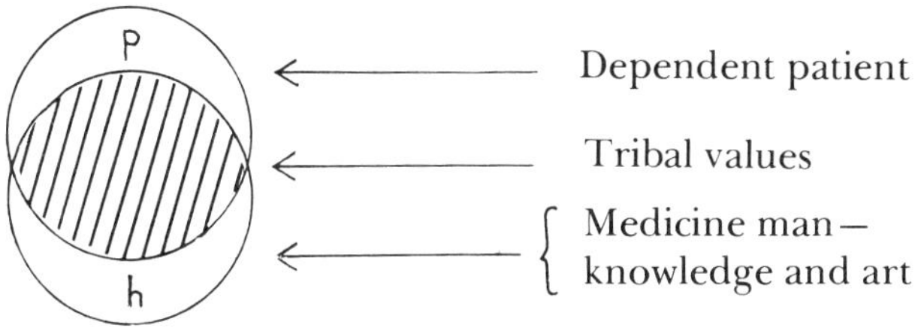

In the first situation (I), the value system of patient and helper is identical; in the somewhat more developed situation (II), there are still many shared values, yet the medicine man is special because of his knowledge—he specializes, an important characteristic of evolution and differentiation. But specialization also contributes to the uncouling of shared values. A good example of this is described by M. Fabrega and P. K. Manning (1973) as an introduction to the description of their stay among an isolated group of Mexicans in the Chiapas highlands, the Ladinos and Mestiros.

Without tracing the whole history of Western culture, it can be said that, in the West, real group cohesion within cultural units still occurs, at best, only sporadically. The development of the process occurring in (II) leads to another end. Abstracting from the currently extreme case, in which the patient rarely knows the specialist, the situation occurs in which although patient and professional represent the same value system, the professional has, over and above the patient, an almost unlimited amount of knowledge and art. This knowledge and its application are subsumed within a special macro value system, the medical code, but are largely exercised through the power they give its possessors.

The professional has the knowledge and the potential to put it in to practice. As a result, the patient becomes dependent. The distance between the degree of knowledge and degree of dependency is the amount of power that can be brought to bear on the relation.

Such power relates directly to the technological superiority of the expert, the professional, and not to the possibility that her or his value system is better than the patient's, in the sense that one value complex cannot be judged better than another. Clearly, the relation is jeopardized by this imbalance of power. The danger that so obviously emerges is that because of the professional's relative superiority of knowledge, decisions are imposed on the dependent partner, the patient. Inevitably, these decisions may conform to the values of the professional but may be discongruent and in conflict with those of the patient. The partners are thus divorced from each other. Power becomes the only binding factor, and it is certain to be resented by the patient:

III.

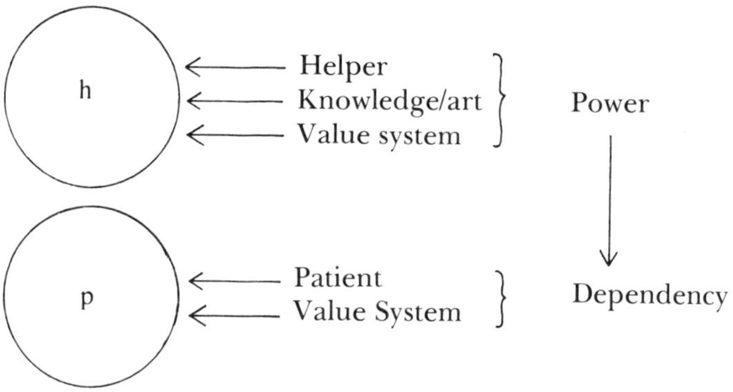

The last step in this unfortunate process seems to be the discovery that the value systems of the dependent patient and of the powerful professional have separated to such an extent that the application of medicine's capacity is no longer adequate to fulfill the goal of healing the patient. For this reason a great deal of attention over the last twenty years has been paid to problems in medical ethics, problems that arise in the heat of conflicting values amidst technological capacities.

8. The Other Side

Health care is inadequate when it no longer attends to the request by the patient for help. Of importance to the patient and his or her dis-ease are the four characteristics of disease: dependency, orientation to the body, egocentrism, and the intensified experience of existence. To be a patient implies dissolution, a history of disruption, and often an anticipation of recovery. We describe recovery as a reintegration of the duality of self and body into a whole, an identity sometimes approximating the unity prior to illness and sometimes constituting a new identity. Health care is healing, the art of making whole again, the art of restoring a broken unity.

However, medicine has become a technology, and the health-care practitioner a technocrat. A technology can function only in the direction of its object. By definition a technology has no place for subjectivity.

Dis-ease means that a distance has occurred between self and body. A part of one's identity has become an object, a very important part indeed. Applying technology to this process of objectifying the body can only strengthen the body as object, because technology deals with objects. By consequence, an unmitigated technologized medicine can no longer reduce dis-ease and rehabilitate the patient's identity. Everything hinges on the health-care professional, who is applying this technology. If he or she is not careful, the dire consequence of loss of identity can result.

Orientation to the body and egocentrism are important behavioral dimensions of the patient and, therefore, important characteristics of the disruption in health. Ths presence of the helper, the professional, is important to overcome the distance between self and body, or at least to arrest its progression. Information is important for interpreting the body's signals, which so often cause uncertainty and fear.

The quality of the presence of the helper and of the information are both highly dependent on cultural background, which also determines the relation among disease characteristics. The helper's presence and the information also depend largely on the interpretation of the value systems in which the characteristics are undergone.

The fourth dimension of illness involves the perceiving of, the giving of meaning to, and the valuing of the human and physical environment. In this dimension what can be more important than individuality, cultural background, and value systems? The assumption of roles within the healing relationship perhaps has hidden this dimension unduly: more attention should be paid to the elements of perception, especially the ways patients interpret events, actions, and their surroundings.

In view of the above remarks it is clear that the health-care practitioner has every potential for bringing the patient to a renewed or new identity, in the sense we have described it. But this can happen only if the practitioner refuses to place technology between him- or her-self and the patient. In effect, the practitioner cannot abandon the *relation* with the patient. Rather, the relation must be recognized and assumed.

The helper, the physician, will be only as adequate as his or her ability to handle medical technology in the context of a personal relation to the patient, a relation with a mutual appreciation of individuality, cultural backgrounds, and value systems. Only if both physician and patient understand the significance of dis-ease and recognize the signals based on an underlying relation can there be a mutual appreciation of their roles and of the place technology can and must assume in the relation. A technology applied without regard to the values placed on it and its results is reduced to an inadequate instrument. The physician who resolutely employs technology in this manner is actually only exercising power. This physician becomes a technocrat, behaving like an objective instrument. Such a practitioner does not mitigate the disruption caused by disease, but serves to enhance it. In the end, the physician does not heal.

Given this possibility, the future development of medicine must retreat from technologization. Replacing it must be new attention paid to the use of technology not to enhance professional power but to be applied *within the world of the patient.* In other words, technology must be balanced against or synthesized within the values of the individual patient. In keeping with prior models, the new direction of medicine should look like this:

IV.

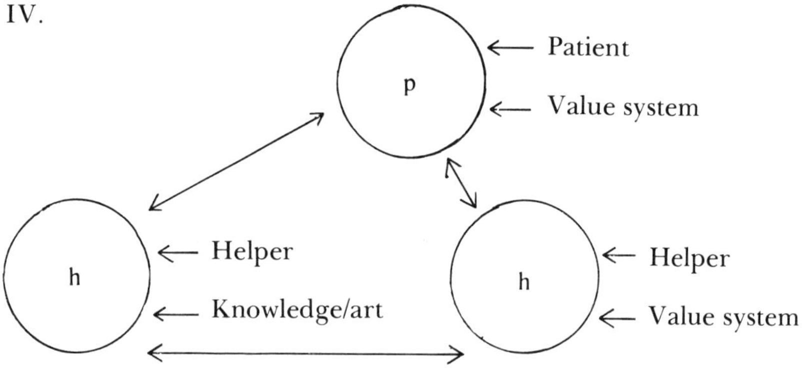

In many diverse places the new direction of medicine is in fact beginning to develop. Obviously, the development cannot occur unless an authentic dialogue takes place between patient and helper. The parent-child characterization of the medical relation can be replaced by the adult-adult relation. Knowledge and technique can then be brought to bear where they belong; namely, within the deliberations of both the physician and the patient and their respective value systems.

In this way medical technology can be included as an element in a human relation between patient and practitioner; it can be applied within the context of their dialogue. It can also be the true means of providing the care that it professes to deliver. If thus applied, it would no longer rest exclusively on the objects of its technologies and on the limited potentialities created by those objects. Instead, it would rest on human values and goals.

CONCLUSION: [*Implications for the Philosophy of Medicine and Medical Ethics*]

The relationship between clinical psychology, medical ethics, and the philosophy of medicine has yet to be worked out in detail. Nevertheless, several ideas that we have explored can enrich both medical ethics and the philosophy of medicine. Some of these ideas fall under the headings 1) "The First Clinical Moment," 2) "Illness and Medical Ethics," and 3) "Vulnerability."

1. The First Clinical Moment

E. Pellegrino (1979) was the first to suggest that the moment a person recognizes something amiss in his or her life—what we have called dis-ease—should be considered the first clinical moment of medicine. As suggested in chapters two and three, a person's surroundings, culture, and even role in life have a great deal to do with the subjective impression of the dis-ease. Consequently, developing a workup of the dis-ease until it matches some scientific category of disease poses difficulties for medical problem solving (P. Cutler, 1979), the epistemological basis of clinical judgment, and current debates about whether clinical judgment can be computerized (K. Schaffner, 1979).

The import of the data proposed regarding dis-ease—the disruption of a person's selfhood and the self's changing relationship to environmental factors—is simply this: Although the process of medical decision making may be computerized in part, such diagnosis cannot begin to respond to the patient's disruption on the existential level. On the one hand, M. Siegler (1980) argues that the first clinical moment is not of clinical medicine. Clinical medicine aims at discovering a clinical entity, whereas in fact the realm of the first clinical moment is actually a reality defined by a much broader context than that of clinical medicine. On the other hand, H. T. Engelhardt, Jr. (1980) considers medicine to embrace a broad response, including the disruption evidenced during the first clinical moment. This view, shared by Pellegrino and Thomasma (1981), holds that a decision regarding the role of the first clinical moment in clinical medicine has a definite bearing on one's conception of the nature and scope of medicine. As we have shown throughout the subsequent chapters, the impact of having a disease or an injury is wholly personal, from communication problems while being bedridden to fear of dying, from temporary disruption of selfhood to permanent impairment and death. At the very least, the first clinical moment should be viewed as essential to clinical medicine because the patient self-selects medicine; that is, the patient decides that the problem he or she faces is a medical rather than other kind of problem—the decision to seek help is precisely that, to seek help with the *problem* now recognized. For the most part, this help is forthcoming in terms of a cure. But even a cure may not address the personal problem raised in the first clinical moment unless it is delivered in the style of personal and professional interchange discussed in chapter three. Siegler would agree with this last view, as he holds that the clinical relationship is mutually determined by the doctor and the patient.

The discussion of dis-ease and the subsequent illumination of the personal problems faced by the patient both serve to underscore the importance of resisting artificial limitations placed on the nature of medicine. Admittedly, medicine has become very technological and specialized and if it is to be circumscribed to this limited extent, as Siegler suggests, then persons will begin looking elsewhere for the wholeness that medicine formerly brought through the doctor-patient relationship. Ultimately, if this trend continues, all that will remain will be a technician-patient relationship. As J. Bergsma (1980) argues, both doctor and patient suffer a curtailment of their power as human beings in such a relationship. Few physicians would want to call this medicine.

2. Illness and Medical Ethics

A great deal of medical-ethics literature is derived solely from ethical norms and metaphysical assertions. While this literature is important, it betrays a view of medical ethics as a derivation from a-priori norms of ethics, with little relation to the disciplines in which the ethical problems arise, their values, patient values, and cultural norms. On the other hand, A. MacIntyre (1980) has shown how fruitless is the search for ethical norms within cultural and social life. We propose that a middle ground between a-priori deductions and cultural relativism can be found in the explorations conducted in this volume (these explorations, of course, only sketch the starting point of such a middle ground).

E. Cassell (1976) has argued that the sick are different from healthy persons. Later (1978) he argued that the difference, from the ethical point of view, lies in sick people's being impaired in autonomy; that is, their authenticity and independence are restricted not only by disease or injury, but also by the inducements of medicine seeking their recovery. This important point has certainly been supported by at least some of the ideas we have proposed: the requirement to heal dis-ease as well as cure disease; the existential and personal disruption caused by injury and disease, as well as the psychosocial impact of surroundings on the recovery, the chronic, and the dying processes, the disturbances of judgment, communication, perception of time, and quality of life all patients undergo.

Seeking application of ethical principles to sick persons *as if they were healthy* is certainly ruled out by our findings. Thus, questions in medical ethics of paternalism, informed consent, and truth–telling all must be rigorously reexamined in light of the disruptions to personhood that are developed in our text. It would be dangerous, for example, to assume that preserving the incipient autonomy of a child and the rights of children developed in normal circumstances should be applied to sick children without modification. (In fact, we tend to err in the wrong direction: we tend to protect child autonomy to a greater extent during illness than during normal life, presumably because of the principle of vulnerability [T. Ackerman, 1979].)

Two other examples might be noteworthy. A chronically ill and aged patient requests no treatment for a urinary-tract infection in the hopes of dying. As we have seen, however, the personal disruption of such patients and the void they face can hardly qualify them for protection of their autonomy on an equal plane with persons who are healthy. The question should not be one of autonomy in these cases, but of beneficience. Would honoring the request, despite what we know about personal disruption, be the most merciful action to take with this patient?

A second example is derived from the problem of truth-telling. While some ethicists argue that the truth must always be told, others agree with A. Buchanan (1978) that if patients are involved in conditions beyond their control, such as chronic depression with suicidal tendencies, then it might be justified to withhold certain information or override informed consent. This is called a "weak paternalism" stance. However, our evidence supports occasions for "strong paternalism" as well (T. Ackerman, 1980); namely, certain states in which patients would be harmed by full disclosure of information and would, thereby, lose their remaining minimal sense of proportion and hope (e.g., at certain stages of disability recovery). Ackerman argues that in such cases, in which evidence exists of possible harm, strong paternalism is justified.

3. Vulnerability

Pellegrino and Thomasma (1981) argue that an axiom of clinical medicine is the patient's vulnerability. That is, in order not to violate the value of healing that medicine professes, practitioners must protect against the vulnerability of the patient. This vulnerability is seen to stem from the unbalanced relation between expert and lay-person in the healing interaction. Later in Pellegrino and Thomasma's work a new code of professional ethics is developed based on this axiom.

The presentations in the general theory of disease found in the first part of this chapter can serve as a psychological basis for this axiom. If, as we suggested, the foremost primary characteristic of disease is dependency, then the obligation of health-care professionals must be not only to elevate the diminished autonomy of the patient in the relationship of healing, but also to attend to the imbalance of the healing relationship itself.

As a consequence, those elements of dependency that help compliance and restoration ought to be reinforced, while those that impede healing ought to be eliminated. If the latter include such things as broken communication, lassitude, time warps, abandonment by families, and so on—as suggested in the section devoted to secondary characteristics of disease—the obligation to remove these impediments to healing and restoration of personhood rests primarily on the health-care professionals in charge of patient management. It should not be left to hospital officials and the government, for the obligation is at root, a moral one, stemming from the nature of the healing relationship itself.

Our discussion of these implications is meant to suggest the importance of including clinical psychology among the disciplines involved in the dialogue on medicine. Because medicine deals with the whole human person, and the whole human person is intimately related to others, society, culture, and nature, medicine opens an enormous window on the human experience. It will not do to reduce that window to a peephole.

Suggestions for Further Reading

METHODOLOGICAL CONSIDERATIONS

Andreski, S. 1974. *Social Sciences as Sorcery:* Baltimore: Penguin.

Bergsma, J., and Rullmann Schadee, G. R. 1975. *Een bijdrage van de psychologie aan het ziekenhuis klimaat:* Utrecht: Nationale Ziekenhuis Raad.

Festinger, L., and Katz, D. (ed.). 1953. *Research Methods in the Behavioral Sciences.* New York: Dryden.

Kimball, C. P. August 1970. Conceptual Developments in Psychosomatic Medicine, 1939-1969. *Annals of Internal Medicine* 73: part 1, 307-316.

Querido, A. 1955. *Inleiding tot een integrale geneeskunde.* Leiden: H. E. Stenfert Kroeze N.V. Reprinted by Lochem: De Tijdstroom, 1973.

Richardson, H. B. 1948. *Patients Have Families.* New York: The Commonwealth Fund.

Society for Health and Human Values. 1978. *Human Values in the Health Care of the Elderly.* Philadelphia: Society for Health and Human Values.

CHAPTER 1:THE BODY AND THE SELF

Bladergroen, W. J. 1971. *De lichamelijke en geestelijke ontwikkeling van het kind.* Amsterdam: Wetenschappelijke Uitg.

Buytendijk, F. J. 1948. *Algemene theorie der menselijke houdingen en bewegingen.* Utrecht: Spectrum.

Cratty, B. J. 1970. *Perceptual and Motor Development in Infants and Children.* London: Macmillan.

Des Pres, T. 1976. *The Survivor: An Anatomy of Life in the Death Camps.* New York: Oxford University Press.

Erikson, E. 1968. *Youth and Identity.* New York: Norton.

Fisher, S. 1970. *Body Experience in Fantasy and Behavior.* New York: Meredith.

Fredericks, J. A. M. 1966. *Het lichaamsschema* (diss.). Amsterdam: Van Rossum.

Gertsmann, J. June 1958. Psychological and Phenomenological Aspects of Disorders of the Body-Image. *Journal of Nervous and Mental Disease* 126: 499-512.

Gusdorf, G. 1948. *La découverte de soi.* Paris: R. U. F.

Jourard, S. M., and Secord, P. F. 1954. Body Size and Body Cathexis. *Journal Consult. Psych.* 18: 184.

Kwant, R. C. 1968. *De wijsbegeerte van Merleau-Ponty.* Utrecht: Aula.

La Mettrie, J. O. de. 1774. *Oeuvres philosophiques.* Amsterdam: Les editions d'Amsterdam.

Laurendeau, M., and Pinard, A. 1970. *The Development of the Concept of Space in the Child.* New York: International University Press.

Marcel, G. 1967. *Man Against Mass Society.* Chicago: Regnery Press. 2 Volumes.

Merleau-Ponty, M. 1945. *Phénoménologie de la perception.* Paris: Gallimard.

Mussen, P. H., and Jones, M. C. 1957. Self-conceptions, Motivations and Interpersonal Attitudes of Late and Early Maturing Boys. *Child Development* 28: number 2, 243-256.

Piaget, J., and Inhelder, J. 1971. *Child's Conception of Space.* London: Routledge.

Rogers, C. 1961. *On Becoming a Person.* London: Constable.

Scheflen, A. F. 1972. *Body Language and the Social Order.* Englewood Cliffs: Prentice-Hall.

Schilder, P. 1923. *Das Körperschema.* Berlin: Springer Verlag.

Spicker, S. 1975. The Lived Body as Catalytic Agent: Reaction at the Interface of Medicine and Philosophy. In *Evaluation and Explanation in the Biomedical Sciences,* H. T. Engelhardt, Jr., and S. Spicker, (eds.), pp. 181-204. Dordrecht and Boston: D. Reidel.

Spiegel, J. P., and Machotka, P. 1974. *Messages of the Body.* New York: The Free Press.

Thomasma, D. 1972. *A Critical Examination of Pre-conceptual Knowledge* (diss.). Ann Arbor: University of Michigan Microfilms.

Van den Berg, J. H. 1962. *Het menselijk lichaam* (I). 4th Edition. Nijkerk: Callenbach (Flourens P. *Histoire de la circulation du sang.* Paris: 1854).

Van Meel, J. M. 1973. *Kinderen in beweging.* Meppel: Boom.

Von Uexkull, T. 1970. The Problem of a Psychosomatic Theory and the Mind-Body Unit Model. In *Recent Research in Psychosomatics.* Basel: Karger.

Wachs, H. and Zaks, M. S. 1960. Studies of Body Image in Men with Spinal Cord Injury. *Journal of Nervous and Mental Disease* 131: 121-126.

Witte, A. J. J. de. 1948. *De betekeniswereld van het lichaam.* Utrecht: Spectrum.

Wylie, R. 1967. *The Self-concept.* Lincoln: University of Nebraska Press.

CHAPTER 2: DIS-EASE

Asken, M. J. January 1, 1975. Psychoemotional Aspects of Mastectomy: A Review of Recent Literature. *American Journal of Psychiatry* 132: 56-59.

Bernstein, N. R. 1976. *Emotional Care of the Facially Burned and Disfigured.* Boston: Little, Brown.

Canguilhem, G. 1978. *On the Normal and the Pathological.* Dordrecht and Boston: D. Reidel.

Cassell, E. March-April 1976. Disease as an It. *Social Science in Medicine* 10: 43-46.

Chilvers, A. S. November 1971. The Social Fate of the Amputee. *The Lancet* 27: 1192-93.

Duff, R. S., and Hollingshead, B. 1968. *Sickness and Society.* New York: Harper & Row.

Fabre, M. 1967. *Geschiedenis van de mode.* Amsterdam: Scheltema.

Fiedler, L. 1978. *Freaks: Myths and Images of the Secret Self.* Los Angeles: S. & S. Enterprises.

Foulds, G. A. 1976. *The Hierarchical Nature of Personal Illness.* London: Academic Press.

Gartley, J. E. 1958. *Patients, Physicians and Illness.* New York: The Free Press.
Harris, P. L., Read, F., Eardley, A., Charlesworth, D., Wakefield, J., and Sellwood, R.A. 1974. The Fate of Elderly Amputees. *British Journal of Surgery* 61: 665-68.
Kaiser, B. L., and Kaiser, J. H. November 1, 1974. The Challenge of the Women's Movement to American Gynaecology. *American Journal Obst. and* Gynaec. 652-65.
Levinson, D., Darrow, N., Klein, E., Levinson, M., and McKee, B. 1978. *The Seasons of a Man's Life.* New York: Knopf.
Mattson, E. J. 1975. Psychological Aspects of Severe Physical Injury and Its Treatment. *Journal of Trauma* 15: no. 3, 217-34.
Monat, A., and Lazarus, R. 1979. *Stress and Coping.* New York: Columbia University Press.
Pellegrino, E. D. 1979. *Humanism and the Physician.* Knoxville: University of Tennessee Press.
Prichard, E., et al., (eds.). 1979. *Home Care: Living with Dying.* New York: Columbia University Press.
Querido, A. See Chapter One.
Schnaper, N. 1961. Postanaesthetic (Postoperative) Emotional Responses. *Anaesthesiology* 22: 674-81.
Schnaper, N. 1975. The Psychological Implications of Severe Trauma. *Journal of Trauma* 15: no. 2, 94-98.
Titschener, J. L. 1970. Management and Study of Psychological Response to Trauma. *Journal of Trauma* 10: no. 11, 974-80.
Tubesing, D. 1979. *Holistic Health Care.* New York: Human Sciences Press.

CHAPTER 3: CLINICAL DETERMINATION

Admiraal, P. H. 1976. *Besluitvorming in het consumptieproces* (diss.). Leiden: Stenfert Kroese.
Crisp, A. H. 1970. Therapeutic Aspects of the Doctor/Patient Relationship (Review of the Literature). In *Recent Research in Psychosomatics.* Basel: Karger.
Davis, G. A. 1973. *The Psychology of Problem Solving.* New York: Basic Books.
Hansen, F. 1972. *Consumer Choice Behavior.* New York: The Free Press.
Kertész, R. 1970. Research on Doctor-Patient Relationships in a General Hospital Setting. In *Recent Research in Psychosomatics.* Basel: Karger.
Lindeman, C. A., and van Aernham, B. 1971. Nursing Intervention with the Presurgical Patient. *Nursing Research* 20: no. 4, 319-32.
Menting, C. L. 1976. . . . *hij is in vergadering* (diss.). Deventer: Kluwer.
Mulder, M. 1958. *Groepsstructuur, motivatie en prestatie.* Den Haag: COP.
Simon, H. A. 1960. *The New Science of Management Decision.* New York: Harper & Brothers.
Skipper, J., and Leonard, R. C. 1968. Children, Stress and Hospitalization. *J. Health and Social Behaviour* 9: no. 4, 275-87.
Spicker, S. and Engelhardt, H. T., Jr., (eds.). 1979. *Clinical Judgment.* Dordrecht and Boston: D. Reidel.
Thibaut, J. W., and Kelly, H. H. 1959. *The Social Psychology of Groups.* New York: Wiley.
Tyson, P. A., and Leonard, R. C. 1966. A Clinical Test of Patient-Centered Nursing. *J. Health and Human Behaviour* 7: 183-92.

CHAPTER 4: DIS-EASE WORKUP

Boswell, D. M., and Wingrove, J. M., (eds.). 1974. *The Handicapped Person in the Community.* London: Tavistock Publications.
Campbell, J. D. 1974. Attribution of Illness: Another Double Standard. *J. Health and Social Behaviour* 15: 114-26.
Canter, D. 1977. *The Psychology of Place.* London: Architectural Press.
Cole, T. M., Children, R., and Rosenberg, P. 1973. A New Program of Sex Education and Counseling for Spinal Cord Injured Adults and Health Care Professionals. *Paraplegia* 11: 111-24.
Comer, R. C., and Piliavin, J. A. 1974. The Effects of Physical Deviance upon Face to Face Interaction: The Other Side. In *The Handicapped Person in the Community.* Ed. by Boswell and Wingrove, pp. 100-108.
——. July 1975. As Others See Us. *Rehabilitation Literature* 36: no. 7, 206-22.
Dembo, T., Leviton, G. L., and Wright, B.A. 1970. Adjustment to Misfortune: A Problem of Social Psychological Rehabilitation. In *Selected Articles from Artificial Limbs.* Huntington, N.Y.: Krieger.
Deno, E. 1953. Self-identification Among Adolescent Boys. *Child Development* 24: 269-73.
Dresen, J. 1976. *Op bezoek.* Lochem: De Tijdstroom.
Elledge, C. H. 1948. *The Rehabilitation of the Patient.* London: Lippincott.
Farina, A., Allen, J. G., and Sauld, B. B. B. 1968. The Role of the Stigmatized Person in Affecting Social Relationships. *J. Personality* 36: no. 2, 169-82.
Field, M. 1967. *Patients are People.* New York: Columbia University Press.
Fieret, G., and Bergsma, J. 1980. Enkele bouwstenen voor het therapeutisch klimaat. Report of the Psychology Faculty, Tilburg: Tilburg University.
Fisher, S. 1970. *Body Experience in Fantasy and Behavior.* New York: Meredith.
——. 1973. *Body Consciousness: You are What You Feel.* Englewood Cliffs: Prentice-Hall.
Goffman, E. 1963. *Stigma.* Englewood Cliffs: Prentice-Hall.
——. 1974. Stigma and Social Identity. In *The Handicapped Person in the Community.* See Boswell and Wingrove, pp. 79-93.
Hesseling, K., and Verkuyl, A. 1972. *Wij zijn niet van steen.* Leiden: Stafleu.
Janse de Jonge, A. L. 1956. *De mens in zijn verhoudingen.* Utrecht: Bijleveld.
Jarwis, J. H. 1967. Post Mastectomy Breast Phantoms. *J. Nervous and Mental Disease* 144: 266-72.
Kolb, I. C. 1959. Disturbance of the Body Image. In *American Handbook of Psychiatry.* New York: Basic Books.
Mahrebian, A., and Russel, J. A. 1974. *An Approach to Environmental Psychology.* Cambridge: MIT Press.
Marcel, G. 1967. *Man Against Mass Society.* See Chapter One
Menzies, J. E. P. 1960. A Case Study in the Functioning of Social Systems as a Defense Against Anxiety. *Human Relations* 13: 771-77.
——. 1974. Nurses under Stress: A Social System Functioning as a Defense Against Anxiety. In *The Handicapped Person.* See Boswell and Wingrove, pp. 425-32.
Merleau-Ponty, M. See Chapter One
Moulyn, D. C., and Keizer, R. (eds.). 1965. *Revalidatie.* Haarlem: De Toorts.
Naylor, V. M., and Michaels, D. 1961. *The Suffering of the Cancer Patient.* London: Hutchinson.
Proshansky, M., Ittelson, W. H., and Rivlin, G. L. 1969. *Environmental Psychology.* New York: Holt, Rinehart and Winston.

Richardson, S., Hastorf, A. H., and Dornbusch, S. 1964. Effects of Physical Disability on a Child's Description of Himself. *Child Development* 35: 893-907.

Rogers, C. R. 1961. *On Becoming a Person.* London: Constable.

Rumke, H. C. 1954. *Psychiatrie,* vols. 1 and 2. Amsterdam: Scheltema en Holkema.

Safilos-Rotschild, C. 1970. *The Sociology and Social Psychology of Disability and Rehabilitation.* New York: Random House.

Scheff, T. J. 1967. *Mental Illness and Social Processes.* New York: Harper & Row.

Scott, R. A. 1974. The Construction of Conceptions of Stigma by Professional Experts. In *The Handicapped Person.* See Boswell and Wingrove, pp. 108-20.

Skipper, J. K., et al. 1964. Some Possible Consequences of Limited Communication Between Patients and Hospital Functionaries. *J. Health and Human Behaviour* 15: 34-39.

Szasz, T. S. 1961. *The Myth of Mental Illness.* New York: Harper.

——. 1968. The Psychology of Persistent Pain. In *Pain.* Ed. by Soulairac, A., Cahn, J., and Charpentier, J. London: Academic Press, p. 93.

Traub, A. C. and Orbach, J. 1964. Psychophysical Studies of Body Image, Part One: The Adjustable Body Distorting Mirror. *Archives of General Psychiatry* 11: 53-66.

Vroon, P. A. 1975. Psychosomatiek en cognitieve processen. *Tijdschrift voor psychotherapie* 1: no. 5, 195-210.

Weiss, S. A. 1958. The Body Image as Related to Phantom Sensations: A Hypothetical Conceptualization of Seemingly Isolated Findings. *Annals of the New York Academy of Medicine* 74: 25-29.

Wilson, L. M. 1972. Intensive Care Delirium. *Archives of Internal Medicine* 130: 225-26.

Wolff, H. G. 1950. *Life Stress and Bodily Disease.* Baltimore: Williams and Wilkins.

CHAPTER 5: PAIN

Bandler, R. J., Mandaras, G. R., and Bern, D. J. 1968. Self-observation Over Source of Pain Perception. *J. Personality and Social Psychology* 3: 205-209.

Barber, T. X. 1969. *Hypnosis: A Scientific Approach.* New York: Van Nostrand.

Beecher, H. K. 1959. *Measurement of Subjective Responses.* New York: Oxford University Press.

Beek, H. H. 1974. *Waanzin in de Middeleeuwen.* Haarlem: De Toorts.

Bond, M. 1975. Post-operative Pain: Its Relation to Analgesic administration and Personality Structure. London: The Society for Psychosomatic Research, 19th Annual Conference.

Breughel, M. A. 1971. Relationship of Preoperative Anxiety to Perception of Postoperative Pain. *Nursing Research* 20; no. 1, 26-31.

Buytendijk, F. J. 1957. *Over de pijn.* Utrecht: Aula.

Callens, M. 1972. *Leerboek der neuropsychologie.* Lochem: De Tijdstroom/Arco.

Conroy, R. T. W. L., and Mills, J. N. 1970. *Human Circadian Rhythms.* London: Churchill.

Copp, L. A. 1974. The Spectrum of Suffering. *American J. Nursing* 74: no. 3, 491-95.

Dallenbach, K. M. 1939. Pain: History and Present Status. *American J. Psychiatry* 52: 331-47.

Fordyce, W. E., Fowler, R. S., Lehmann, J. F., Lateur, B. J., de, Sand, P. L., and Frischmann, R. B. 1973. Operant Conditioning in the Treatment of Chronic Pain. *Archives of Physical Medicine and Rehabilitation* 54: 399-408.

Geldard, F. A. 1972. *The Human Senses.* New York: John Wiley & Sons.

Glynn, C. J., and Folkard, S. 1975. The Diurnal Variation of Pain Perception. London: The Society for Psychosomatic Research, 19th Annual Conference.

Hardy, J. D., Stolwijk, J. A., Hammel, H. T. and Murgatroyd, D. 1963. Skin Temperature and Cutaneous Pain During Warm Water Immersion. *J. Applied Physiology* 20: 1014-21.

Hardy, J. D., Stolwijk, J. A., and Hoffmann, D. 1968. Pain Following Step Increase in Skin Temperature. In *The Skin Senses.* Ed. by D. R. Kensalo. Springfield: Thomas.

Illich, I. 1975. *Medical Nemesis.* New York: Pantheon.

Kossman, A. 1973. *Laatst ging ik spelevaren.* Amsterdam: Querido.

Kübler-Ross, E. 1969. *Lessen voor levenden.* Bilthoven: Ambo.

Lersch, P. 1960. *Algemene psychologie.* Utrecht: Spectrum.

Lindeman, C. A., and van Aernham, B. 1971. Nursing Intervention with the Preoperative Teaching. *Nursing Research* 20: no. r, 319-32.

Melzack, W. R., and Wall, P. D. 1968. Gate Control Theory of Pain. In *Pain.* Ed. by Soulairac, A., Cahn, I., Charpentier, J. London: Academic Press, pp. 11-33.

Melzack, R. 1975. *Het raadsel pijn.* Utrecht: Aula.

Metz. W. 1964. *Het verschijnsel pijn* (diss.). Haarlem.

——. 1975. *Pijn, een teer punt.* Nijkerk: Callenbach.

Nisbett, R. E., and Schachter, S. 1966. Cognitive Manipulation of Pain. *J. Experiments in Social Psychology* 2: 227-36.

Putt, A. M. 1970. One Experiment in Nursing Adults with Peptic Ulcers. *Nursing Research* 19: no. 6, 484-94.

Schmitt, F. E., and Wooldridge, P. J. 1973. Psychological Preparation of Surgical Patients. *Nursing Research* 22: no. 2, 108-16.

Siegele, D. 1974. The Gate Control Theory. *American J. Nursing* 74: no. 3, 48-502.

Sternbach, R. A. 1974. *Pain Patients: Traits and Treatments.* New York: Academic Press.

Szasz, T. S. 1968. *The Psychology of Persistent Pain.* See Chapter Four.

——. 1975. *Pain and Pleasure.* New York: Basic Books.

Van den Berg, J. H. 1960. *Metabletica.* Nijkerk: Callenbach.

Van Eps, L. W. S. 1954. *Over de baringspijn* (diss.). Amsterdam: Paris.

Van Woodrow, M., Friedman, G., Siegelaub, A. B., and Collen, M. E. 1972. Pain Tolerance: Differences According to Age, Sex and Race. *Psychosomatic Medicine* 34: no. 6, 548-56.

Von Frey, M. 1899. Über Die Funktion Des Tastkörperchen. *Zeitschrift der Physiologie* 20: 126-63.

——. 1922. Versuche Über Schmerzerreigende Reize. *Zeitschrift der Biologie* 76: no. 1, 24.

Weddel, G., Sinclair, D. C., and Feindel, W. H. 1948. An Anatomical Basis for Alterations in Quality of Pain Sensibility. *J. Neurophysiology* 11: 99-109.

Weisenberg, M., Kreidler, M. L., Schacht, R., and Werboff, J. 1975. Pain Anxiety and Attitudes in Black, White and Puerto Rican Patients. *Psychosomatic Medicine* 37: no. 2, 123-35.

Winsberg, B., and Greenlich, J. 1967. Pain Response in Negro and White Obstetrical Patients. *J. Health and Social Behaviour* 8: 222-27.
Zborowski, M. 1952. Cultural Components in Responses to Pain. *J. Sociology*: 16 ff.

CHAPTER 6: OTHER ASPECTS OF ILLNESS

Bartley, S. H. 1965. *Fatigue.* Springfield: Charles Thomas.
Bartley, S. H., and Chute, E. 1945. A Preliminary Classification of the Concept of Fatigue. *Psychological Review* 52: 169-74.
Blitz, P. S., and van Moorst, A. 1976. Vermoeidheid: toestand of waarneming? *Gedrag*: 160-84.
Bremer, J. C. B. 1972. *De ziekenhuispatiënt.* Nijmegen: Dekker en van de Vegt.
Buytendijk, F. J. 1948. *Algemene theorie der menselijke houding en beweging.* Utrecht: Spectrum.
——. 1974. *Prolegomena to an Anthropological Physiology.* Pittsburgh: Duquesne University Press.
Chauchard, P. 1966. *De vermoeidheid.* Amsterdam: Spectrum.
Dresen, F. 1975. *Op bezoek.* Lochem: De Tijdstroom.
Foster, S. B. 1974. An Adrenal Measure for Evaluating Nursing Effectiveness. *Nursing Research* 23: no. 2, 118-24.
Gross, I. H., and Bartley, S. H. 1951. Fatigue in House Care. *J. Applied Psychology* 35: 205-7.
Kwant, R. C. 1968. *De wijsbegeerte van Merleau-Ponty.* See Chapter One.
Luypen, W. 1951. *De psychologie van de verveling.* Amsterdam: Paris.
Merleau-Ponty, M. 1945. *Phénoménologie de la perception.* See Chapter One.
Pride, L. F. 1968. An Adrenal Stress Index as a Criterion Measure for Nursing. *Nursing Research* 17: no. 4, 292-303.
Puyol, R. 1962. Réflexions sur la fatigue et ses aspects psychologiques. *Annales medico-psychologiques* 125: 1, 23-25.
Simenon, G. 1963. *De klokken van Bicètre.* Utrecht: Bruna.
Simonson, E. (ed.). 1971. Physiology of Work Capacity and Fatigue. Springfield: Charles Thomas.
Van den Berg, J. H. 1966. *Psychology of the Sickbed.* Pittsburgh: Duquesne University Press.

CHAPTER 7: PERMANENT HANDICAP AND CHRONIC ILLNESS

Buytendijk, F. J. 1974. *Prolegomena.* See Chapter Six.
Duff, R. 1976. Personal Communication.
Erikson, E. 1968. *Youth and Identity.* New York: Norton.
Kübler-Ross, E. 1969. *Lessen voor levenden.* See Chapter Five.
Naylor, V. H., and Michaels, D. 1961. *The Suffering of the Cancer Patient.* See Chapter Four.
Oldhoff, J., and Veldhuis, E. F. M. 1976. Some Thoughts About the Treatment of Patients Suffering from Cancer of the Esophagus or Cardia. *Archivum chirurgicum Neerlandicum* 28: no. 11, 79-84.
Piaget, J., and Inhelder, J. 1971. *The Child's Conception of Space.* London: Routledge.
Schröder, J. T. R., Rang, J. F., and Sporken, P. 1972. *Leven tot (w)elke prijs?* Lochem: De Tijdstroom.

Strauss, A. L. 1975. *Chronic Illness and the Quality of Life.* St. Louis: C. V. Mosby.
Tillich. P. 1952. *The Courage to Be.* New Haven: Yale University Press.
Van den Berg, J. H. 1963. *Psychology of the Sickbed.* See Chapter Six.
——. 1965. *Medische macht en medische ethiek.* Nijkerk: Callenbach.
Zwannikken, W. 1975. *Tijdsbeleving en ouderdom.* Deventer: Van Loghum Slaterus.

CHAPTER 8: DYING

Aries, P. 1974. *Western Attitudes Towards Death: From the Middle Ages to the Present.* Tr. by P. Ranum. Baltimore: Johns Hopkins University Press.
Bergsma, J. 1975. Begeleiding van patiënten: enige consequenties. *Tijdschrift sociale geneeskunde* 53: 337 ff.
Cohen, K. P. 1979. *Hospice: Prescription for Terminal Care.* Germantown, Md.: Aspen Systems Corporation.
Glaser, B. G. 1965. Disclosure of Terminal Illness. *J. Health and Human Behaviour* 6: 83-91.
Glaser, B. G., and Strauss, A. I. 1965. *Awareness of Dying.* Chicago: Aldine Publishing Company.
Hay, D., and Oken, D. 1972. The Psychological Stress of ICU Nursing. *Psychosomatic Medicine* 34: 2.
Kok, H. L. 1970. *Geschiedenis van de laatste eer in Nederland.* Lochem: De Tijdstroom.
Kübler-Ross, E. 1969. *On Death and Dying.* New York: Macmillan.
Kübler-Ross, E. 1975. Death: The Final Stage of Growth. Englewood Cliffs: Prentice-Hall.
Le Shan, H. 1969. Psychotherapy and the Dying Patient. In *Death and Dying.* London: Press of Case Western Reserve University.
Memphis Commercial Appeal. March 14, 1980. Bets on Patient Deaths Revealed. B. 16.
Quint, J. C. 1966. Awareness of Death and the Nurse's Composure. *Nursing Research* 15: no. 1, 49-55.
Ramsey, P. 1973. *The Patient as Person.* New Haven: Yale University Press.
Sikkel, A., and Hoffmann, C. M. 1973. Begeleiding en behandeling van ongeneeslijke patienten in het ziekenhuis. *Tijdschrift voor ziekenverpleging* 26: 1165-70.
Simmons, S. and Givern, B. 1972. Nursing Care of the Terminal Patient. *Omega.* 3: no. e, 217-25.
Snijder, M., Gertler, R., and Ferneau, E. 1973. Changes in Nursing Students' Attitudes Toward Death and Dying. *International J. Social Psychiatry* 19; 294-99.
Spencer, S. 1979. Code or No Code? *New England Journal of Medicine* 300: no. 3, 138-40.
Thomasma, D. C. 1979. *Americans and Death* (Six one-hour TV programs). Produced and directed by Linda Hardwick. Available from WKNO-TV, Memphis, Tn. 38104.
——. 1981. Ethical Considerations in the Care of the Dying and the Hospice Concept. *Linacre Quarterly,* forthcoming.
Tuan, Y.-F. 1980. *Landscapes of Fear.* New York: Pantheon.

CHAPTER 9: THE OTHER SIDE

Ackerman, T. F. November 1979. Justified Strong Paternalism in Clinical Medicine. Delivered at the Tennessee Philosophical Association Annual Meeting, Nashville, Tennessee.
——. December 1979. Fooling Ourselves with Child Autonomy and Assent in Nontherapeutic Clinical Research. *Clinical Research* 27: no. 5, 345-48.
——. August 1980. The Limits of Beneficence: Jehovah's Witnesses and Childhood Cancer. *The Hastings* Center Report 10: no. 4, 13-18.
Ballard, E. G. 1978. *Man and Technology*. Pittsburgh. Duquesne University Press.
Beek, H. H. 1974. *Waanzin in de Middeleeuwen*. Haarlem: De Toorts.
Bergsma, J. November 1979. De arts als verlengstuk van de techniek en de steeds meer afhankelijke patiënt. *Project* 7: 384-91.
Buchanan, A. 1978. Medical Paternalism. *Philosophy and Public Affairs* 7: 370-90.
Cassell, E. 1976. *The Healer's Art*. New York: Lippincott. Pp. 47-83.
——. 1978. What is the Function of Medicine? In *Death and Decision*. Ed. by E. McMullin. Boulder, Colorado: Westview Press for AAAS Selected Symposium, vol. 18, pp. 35-44.
Cutler, P. 1979. *Problem Solving in Clinical Medicine: From Data to Diagnosis*. Baltimore: The Johns Hopkins University Press.
Ellul, J. 1964. *The Technological Society*. New York: Vintage Books.
Engelhardt, H. T., Jr. 1975. The Concepts of Health and Disease. In *Evaluation and Explanation in the Biomedical Sciences*. Ed. by Engelhardt, H. T. Jr., and Spicker, S. Dordrecht and Boston: D. Reidel, pp. 125-42.
Fabrega, M., and Manning, P. K. 1973. An Integrated Theory of Disease. *Psychosomatic Medicine* 35: 223-39.
Farb, P. 1969. *Man's Rise to Civilization*. New York: Discus.
Fortman, H. 1971. *Inleiding tot de cultuurpsychologie*. Bilthoven. Ambo.
Foucault, M. 1972. *Madness and Civilization*. New York: Vintage Books.
Fromm, E. 1963. *Escape from Freedom*. New York: Holt, Rinehart and Winston.
Geertz, C. 1973. *The Interpretation of Cultures*. New York: Basic Books.
Kertész, R. 1967. *Research*. See Chapter Three.
MacIntyre, A. August 1979. Why is the Search for the Foundations of Ethics So Frustrating? *Hastings Center Report* 9: no. 4, 16-22.
Mead, M. 1955. *Cultural Patterns and Technological Change*. New York: Mentor Books.
Nederlandse Huisartsen Instituut. 1974. Vier jaar continue morbiditeits-registratie door middel van pielstations. *Huisarts en wetenschap* 17: 407.
Pellegrino, E. D. 1979. *Humanism and the Physician*. Knoxville: University of Tennessee Press.
Pellegrino, E. D., and Thomasma, D. C. 1981. *A Philosophical Basis of Medical Practice*. New York: Oxford University Press.
Riesman, D. 1973. *The Lonely Crowd*. London: Yale University Press.
Sartre, J. P. 1975. *Le mur*. Paris: Gallimard. Reprint from 1939.
Schaffner, K. Forthcoming. Problems in Computer Diagnosis. In *The Ethics of Diagnosis*. Ed. by H. T. Engelhardt, Jr., and S. Spicker. Dordrecht and Boston: D. Reidel.
Siegler, M. On the Nature and Limits of Clinial Medicine. Conference

on"Changing Values in Medicine." Cornell University, Nov 1979. Unpublished.
Sikkel, A. and Hoffmann, C. M. 1973. Begeleiding. See Chapter Eight.
Van de Koppel, J. 1973-1976. Monthly Correspondence on Pygmies.
Van den Berg, J. H. *Het menselijk lichaam,* vols. 1 and 2. Nijkerk: Callenbach.
——. 1965. *Medische macht.* See Chapter Seven.
——. 1966. *Psychology of the Sickbed.* See Chapter Seven.
Van Hooft, G. 1978. *De maloppodans* (diss.). University of Leiden.
Wober, M. 1975. *Psychology in Africa.* London: International African Institute.
Wylie, R. 1967. *The Self-concept.* See Chapter One.

Index